The Major Realist Film Theorists

The Major Realist Film Theorists

A Critical Anthology

Edited by Ian Aitken

EDINBURGH
University Press

Edinburgh University Press is one of the leading university presses in the UK. We publish academic books and journals in our selected subject areas across the humanities and social sciences, combining cutting-edge scholarship with high editorial and production values to produce academic works of lasting importance. For more information visit our website: www.edinburghuniversitypress.com

Edinburgh University Press Ltd
The Tun – Holyrood Road
12 (2f) Jackson's Entry
Edinburgh EH8 8PJ

First published in hardback by Edinburgh University Press 2016

Typeset in 11/13 Ehrhardt by
Servis Filmsetting Ltd, Stockport, Cheshire,
and printed and bound in Great Britain by
CPI Group (UK) Ltd, Croydon CR0 4YY

A CIP record for this book is available from the British Library

ISBN 978 1 4744 0221 7 (hardback)
ISBN 978 1 4744 2596 4 (paperback)
ISBN 978 1 4744 0222 4 (webready PDF)
ISBN 978 1 4744 1371 8 (epub)

Contents

Introduction

Ian Aitken

I ATTITUDES TOWARDS THE MAJOR REALIST FILM THEORISTS

This book is concerned with the 'major realist film theorists'. Who may count as a 'major' realist film theorist may be open to question, and some theorists may also be considered to be more 'major' than others. Few would disagree, however, that Siegfried Kracauer and André Bazin should be counted as 'major' realist film theorists, and, though the names of John Grierson and Georg Lukács may be more contentious, it will be argued here that there are reasons for including the two under this rubric, and for studying the ideas of this group as a whole. One of those reasons, touched on briefly, concerns the shared historical locus and critical providence of these theorists. The publications of the major realist film theorists emerged from the 1910s to the 1960s, that is, from near the beginnings of film theory, as such, to the emergence of a structuralist, post-structuralist, screen theory paradigm ('structuralist' for short) which dominated film theory from the 1960s until at least the 1980s. The emergence of that paradigm created a divide between itself and what came before and, in the process, consigned the realist tradition in particular to the periphery of critical concern. As the structuralist paradigm advanced through the 1970s classical realist film theory – and also, for that matter, realist film practice – additionally became regarded not only as extraneous but also problematic because (a) the emphasis on understanding and portraying the relationship between film and the experience of perceptual reality within that theory and practice meant that the foregrounding of signifying practice in film – a prerequisite of the newly dominant paradigm – was not given priority; (b) the epochal-humanist orientation of classical realist film theory was seen to be at odds with the politics of more historically specific class, race and gender activist intervention which became a preoccupation of post-classical realist film theory; and (c) the classical-realist stance was seen to contribute in part towards the ongoing and escalating naturalisation of the status quo so that what was required was an 'anti-realist' film theory and practice which would deconstruct and undermine such naturalisation – and, while the preoccupation with postmodern film theory and practice from the early 1980s onwards led away from such political-modernist deconstruction, that preoccupation served only to sideline further the classical-realist tradition. As the authors of one illustrative publication put it, 'film theory gradually transformed itself from a meditation on the film object as the reproduction of pro-filmic phenomena into a critique of the very idea of mimetic reproduction' (Stam and Flitterman-Lewis 1992: 184).

Nevertheless, at least one of the major realist theorists, Siegfried Kracauer, became an increasing focus of critical attention from the early 1990s onwards, though most of the attention paid to Kracauer focused on the accounts of modernity found in his early Weimar writings rather than on the coverage of realism found in his 1960 book on cinematic realism, *Theory of Film*; and it has even been argued that an 'epistemological shift' can be detected between the superior 'early' Kracauer and poorer 'late' 'realist' Kracauer (Petro, in Ginsberg and Thompson 1996: 97). In contrast to Kracauer, the theories of the remaining major realist film theorists, Grierson, Bazin and Lukács, have been more neglected. It has been attested that Bazin suffered the most here and that 'Since the 1960s we have gone through a period in which Bazin bashing has become fashionable in film-theoretical discussion' (Rosen in Margulies [ed.] 2003: 42). Whether Bazin has been 'bashed' more than has Grierson or Lukács is, however, a moot point. Some recent books on Bazin have appeared which seek to counteract such bashing, including Margulies (ed.) (2003), *Rites of Realism: Essays on Corporeal Cinema*, and Andrew and Joubert-Laurencin (eds) (2011), *Opening Bazin: Post-War Film Theory and its Afterlife*; and it seems that the re-evaluation of Bazin will continue, spurred, it is to be hoped, by the essays on Bazin in this anthology. The two least tackled figures are Grierson and Lukács, and that is partly because they are connected to a Hegelian tradition of thought that is little accommodated within contemporary English-language film studies. Grierson continues to be a focus of attention on account of the role he played within the development of the documentary film in Britain and elsewhere, and, against a background of growing interest in the colonial official film, a number of reassessments of Grierson are currently underway. While, however, it has been established since at least the 1970s that Grierson's approach to the documentary film sprang from neo-Hegelian sources, there seems to be little ongoing interest in Grierson's intellectual theory of film, though this is covered in Hillier and Lovell (1972), Aitken (1989, 1990, 1998, 2001, 2006, 2007, 2013) and Ellis (1968, 1973, 2000). Of course, Grierson's reputation as someone who promoted a limited-reformist rather than radical vision of the documentary film has also contributed to this lack of interest, and even antipathy, with one critic, writing in 1983, going as far as to assert that 'the basic thing is to break open the "prison" of Griersonism' (Lovell, in Macpherson, D. (ed.), 1980: 18).

As with Grierson, so with Lukács, though the latter is arguably perceived to be more problematic than the former: Grierson may have been a 'conservative' but Lukács, some claim, was a 'Stalinist'. Lukács's theory of aesthetic realism has also been the subject of criticism, and one of the most scathing of such is that his model of literary realism dismissed some of the most vital artistic movements of the nineteenth and twentieth centuries. Lukács's disavowal of naturalism proved relatively uncontroversial given the extent to which the naturalist tradition had fallen out of favour by as early as the 1940s. His rejection of modernism, however, brought his theory of realism into disfavour against a context in which modernism was widely regarded as a progressive form of artistic intervention. Nevertheless, an analysis of Lukács's early and late writing on film reveals it to be compatible with both naturalism and modernism. For example, in the early 'Thoughts Towards an Aesthetic of the Cinema' (1913) Lukács celebrated the modernist possibilities of film; while, in the *The Specificity of the Aesthetic* (1963), he developed an impressionist-naturalist theory of film (Aitken 2012).

In addition to the charge of anti-modernist bias, a second accusation levelled against Lukács concerned his alleged association with Stalinism and Soviet totalitarianism. This accusation, summed up in Lezlek Kolakowski's assertion that Lukács helped forge 'the conceptual instruments of cultural despotism', has been reiterated by many commentators from the 1930s onwards (Kolakowski 1978: 305). In fact, however, Lukács's relationship to the Soviet dictatorship was ambivalent. When the Hungarian Revolution broke out on 23 October 1956, Lukács was made Minister of Culture. After the Soviet invasion of 4 November, however, he was deported, narrowly escaping execution, and expelled from the Communist Party. Between 1957, when he was allowed to return to Budapest at the age of seventy-two, and his death in 1971, Lukács played only a minor role in high political affairs, though he continued to agitate for political reform. Throughout the bulk of his career, therefore, Lukács championed positions to the liberal left of official party policy, and, though a committed Leninist, he was also a staunch opponent of Stalinism.

II THE WRITINGS OF THE MAJOR REALIST FILM THEORISTS

The writings on film of the major realist film theorists span a period from the 1910s to the 1960s. Probably the earliest published contribution came in 1913, and from Georg Lukács. His 'Thoughts Towards an Aesthetic of the Cinema' appeared in the German newspaper *Frankfurter Zeitung und Handelsblatt* that year as a contribution to the ongoing debate about the cinema known as the 'Kino debate'. The article, written in German, has been translated into English several times. Lukács also wrote a number of essays on film translated into Italian in the Italian Marxist film journal *Cinema Nuovo* in the 1950s and 1960s. Finally, his chapter on film in his *The Specificity of the Aesthetic* (1963) was translated into English for the first time in 2012 (Aitken). In addition to these writings on the cinema, though, it is not really possible to ignore Lukács's writings on literature when considering him as a major realist film theorist because those writings contain ideas that reappear in and/or contradict the writings on film.

John Grierson began writing on film in 1925, initially on issues related to how the Hollywood film might accommodate a social-realist dimension. Grierson's early model of 'epic cinema' was based on such a premise. When he realised that Hollywood was beyond such reform, however, Grierson turned to the documentary film. His first written piece on the documentary film, 'Notes for English Producers', appeared in 1927, and remains unpublished to this day. This is surprising given that it proved to be the founding document of the documentary film movement. 'Notes for English Producers', a memorandum written for Grierson's then employer, the Empire Marketing Board, set out the model of documentary film which was eventually realised in the shape of his 1929 film *Drifters*. Between 1929 and 1939 Grierson wrote on the cinema and documentary film, and these writings have appeared in a number of outputs, most notably *Grierson on Documentary* (F. Forsyth Hardy [ed.] 1946). The influence of philosophical idealism on Grierson appears across these writings to one extent or another. That influence also appears, however, in unpublished essays which Grierson wrote while at university. The ideas expressed in these published and unpublished writings, covering a period from 1919 to 1939, include the key works written by Grierson. After 1939, his writings become less significant at a theoretical level and what happened here is that an early concern with philosophical aesthetics was superseded by a less sophisticated discourse on propaganda, corporate public relations and instrumental 'civic education' (Aitken 1988: 41).

Grierson remained based in the United Kingdom for most of his career, with some relatively brief periods spent in Canada, and in travelling from place to place. Lukács also remained mainly in Hungary though often under conditions of restraint. The career of Siegfried Kracauer was, however, divided into two parts. The first phase of Kracauer's career was spent in Germany, and his German writings appeared between 1923 and 1930. In 1925, Kracauer published an essay entitled *The Detective Novel*, on aspects of everyday life in the modern German society surrounding him. After that, he continued to write on aspects of contemporary mass culture, and essays on this were published in 1927 as *The Mass Ornament*. Finally, in 1930, he published *The Salaried Masses*, on the growth of the white-collar employee class in Germany. The majority of this work had little to do with film. In 1933 Kracauer left Germany to escape the threat of Nazism. He then stayed in France until 1941 after which he left for the United States. In 1947, he published his first full work on film, *From Caligari to Hitler: A Psychological History of the German Film*, and then, in 1960, *Theory of Film: the Redemption of Physical Reality*. Kracauer died in 1966, and his final work, on history rather than film, was published posthumously in 1969.

In contrast to the much-travelled Grierson, Lukács and Kracauer, all of whom were strongly influenced by German classical philosophy, the final major realist film theorist, André Bazin, remained firmly at home in France, and was mainly influenced by the French intellectual tradition, though the influence of phenomenology also links him to the other three. Bazin began writing film criticism in 1943 and co-founded the film journal *Cahiers du Cinéma* in 1951, writing in this journal and elsewhere until his death in 1958 at the age of forty. Virtually all of his writings were, therefore, essays in film criticism which appeared between 1943 and 1958, and, after his death, these were republished in various anthologies, beginning with the four-volume *Qu'est-ce que le cinéma?* (1962), and followed by a two-volume selection and English translation of this in 1967–71. After this, the following appeared, compiled by a variety of editors: *Jean Renoir* (1973), *Orson Welles: A Critical View* (1978), *French Cinema of the Occupation and Resistance: The Birth of a Critical Aesthetic* (1981), *The Cinema of Cruelty: From Buñuel to Hitchcock* (1982), *Le Cinéma Français de la Liberation à la Nouvelle Vague* (1983), *Essays on Chaplin* (1985), *Bazin at Work: Major Essays from the Forties and Fifties* (1996) and *André Bazin and Italian Neorealism* (2011).

III A PROVISIONAL PHILOSOPHICAL JUSTIFICATION FOR REALISM

One of the objectives of this introduction is to establish the core conceptual framework underlying the thought of the major realist film theorists. Before attempting that, it may be helpful to set out an understanding of what might be meant by the term 'realism' more generally. There is, admittedly, no need per se to engage in such an undertaking, as it would suffice to provide an exposition on the core conceptual framework just referred to. On the other hand, we are, as the term indicates, dealing with supposedly *realist* film theory here, and, given that, there is some obligation to address, and also a challenge to confront, the issue of what that term might mean in general, as well as in relation to film.

The term 'realist' in 'realist film theory' implies an attempt on the part of the theorist to establish a link between film and 'reality'. As mentioned, however, the supposition of such a link has also been responsible for the derogation of realist film theory and the major realist film theorists because the aggregation of the two terms 'represent' and 'reality' is seen to imply both a belief in objectivism and the idea that reality is in some sense 'unitary'; and both premises are at odds with contemporary commendation – within film studies – of a stance founded on pluralism and difference. It is also argued, as mentioned, that the quest to establish such a link between film and 'reality' may play an, albeit unintended, part in the legitimation of dominant discourses concerning what is and is not warranted, true and real because a prevailing hierarchical order will always seek to tie essentialism of different sorts, including that related to film, to its own expediency. Here, the notion is that the supposed essentialist tendency within realist film theory accrues to and reinforces ongoing general processes of hierarchical naturalisation by implication. This is one reason, among others, why some recent writing on cinematic realism has tended to focus on the conventionalist characteristics of realist techniques and avoid such essentialism; and this has become something of a paradigm limit wall. For example, one writer attempts to study the 'reality effect' of film and also relates the concept of realism to notions of vital affect, strong feeling, realistic-ness, and so on: in other words, to conventionalist and culturally established relations (Pomerance 2013: 3–5). Another asserts that the aim is to:

> analyse some of the ways in which realism is experienced . . . not aim to provide a definition of what is real, but to describe and characterise some of the different processes and elements that cause viewers of audiovisual representations to have an experience of 'realism'. (Grodal in Jerslev 2002: 67)

Other examples could be given of this attempt to understand realism in terms of technique, convention and expectation. This is, of course, a perfectly valid and sensible way to approach the issue. It does not, and should not, rule out other approaches, however, and the importance and magnitude of the question of realism have therefore led to the recent appearance of work which seeks to probe the issue from a variety of angles and uncertainties, including Margulies (2003), Nagib (2011), Nagib and Mello (2009), Hallam and Marshment (2000), and Rushton (2011). The term 'probe' used here is also notable because it seems that the elusive question of realism can only be probed rather than 'faced'; can only be engaged and disengaged with in a series of critical, ongoing, cautious encounters. Thus, the various contributors to this book also approach the question of classical cinematic realism in different ways to open up the subject further; while the ambitious project of this introduction is to construct a reconsidered model of what I shall call 'phenomenalist realism', explore key concepts from continental philosophy in some depth, and also relate these to the analytical tradition in philosophy. This introduction is therefore *speculative* and explorative in character, and aims to probe the issue of realism from a number of perspectives to suggest new ways of considering classical realist film theory and encourage new pathways of research into the subject. Classical realist film theory is a form of realist film theory. The latter, however, still comprises only a small part of a substantive body of theory which addresses the major issue of realism, and, to place classical/realist film theory within that larger body, it will be helpful to outline the principal representational models that comprise it. This will require a brief excursion into the field of analytical philosophy.[1]

Realism need not imply simple objectivism. Theories of realism which imply such replication are sometimes referred to as theories of 'direct' realism because, in them, representation is seen to correspond directly to reality. Though such direct or 'naive-realist' theories of representation have a considerable historical lineage, however, they are difficult to support at a theoretical level and few contemporary theorists subscribe to them. In contrast to direct realism, 'representational realism' is premised on the conviction that, though external reality exists independently of our representations of it, it cannot be *known* independently of such representations. Though representations are our own constructions, representational realism contends that they have some sort of relationship to reality and are able *indirectly* to represent reality (Hesse, in Morick [ed.], 1980: 198). The indirect character of representation proposed by representational realism, however, also carries within it the potential for a relativist locus based on the idea that we might in fact *only* have knowledge of representational systems and have no way of knowing whether or not those systems have any link to 'reality'. Such a position implies, and may also lead to, extreme forms of 'ontological idealism' and solipsism, as is, for example, implicit in Bishop Berkeley's postulate that the world may be an 'emanation of the ego' (Russell 1965: 20). Like direct realism, such ontological idealism is also difficult to maintain, though, because it leads to the proposition that mind is the only reality, and that reality is the creation of mind, and, since Berkeley, 'most philosophy' has sought to distance itself from such a position, which is considered 'inimical to social sanity' (20). Ontological idealism is, therefore, not only contrary to realism but also precluded by most so-called 'anti-realist' philosophies, including 'conceptual idealist' ones.

Conceptual idealism is probably the most common anti-realist or non-realist philosophical position today. Conceptual idealism picks up on the palpable flaw in any realist position: that, if representation does converge with reality, such convergence cannot be easily, or at all, demonstrated; and asserts that, though 'reality' may exist in some sense, we can have little or no knowledge of it per se and only have knowledge of our concepts, consciousness and representations of it. There is, for us, no *'reality itself* (whatever *that* might be) but reality-as-we-picture-it . . . reality-as-we-think-it = our reality, is the only reality we can deal with' (Rescher 1973: 167). Conceptual idealists do not adopt the ontological idealist position that reality is the product of mind but, instead, argue that the main task of the theorist is to understand how our conceptual schemes construct meaning for us. This also implies that attempts to theorise the link between representation and reality will largely be a waste of time and effort. This conceptual idealist account of representation also implies a relational and conventionalist, rather than correspondence, model of knowledge in which it is thought better to assess a representation in terms of its relationship to other representations within a conceptual scheme than in terms of any correspondence to 'reality'. Such a theory of meaning can also become formalised around terms and relations internal to a conceptual scheme, and to the exclusion of external reference, as, for example, is the case with some semiotic and structuralist theories.

At one level, it could be argued that no fundamental distinction exists between representational realism and conceptual idealism, that the difference between the two is one of degree, that there are therefore similarities between the two and that both can be categorically separated from the twin extremes of ontological idealism and naive realism. While accepting that, however, there also remain significant differences between representational realism and conceptual idealism, and these also have a bearing on realist film theory. In terms of similarity, both representational realism and conceptual idealism stress that the world exists (both are therefore forms of ontological realism) but cannot be considered independently of any particular representation of it, and that, therefore, a completely concept-independent reality cannot be meaningfully experienced or theorised (Putnam 1987: 27). Representational realism differs from conceptual idealism, however, in stressing that correspondence between reality and representation *can* be justifiably theorised to an extent and *should* be so theorised. Realist theory, whether related to philosophy or film, is ineluctably connected to a sense of vocation to develop a model which can account for the relationship between representation and reality. Representational realists believe in the need to account for this even though no 'objective' account can ever be elaborated. This is what is meant by the phrase 'realism of intent' which will be discussed shortly in relation to the ideas of the philosopher, Hilary Putnam. Realism, like other abstract universals, is, therefore, a calling for some, and, within philosophy, one such model which has answered that call, and which will be outlined here by way of example before returning to issues related to realism and film, is Putnam's theory of 'internal realism'.

'Internal' realism is so called because, as Putnam argues, any representation of reality must be formulated *within* a particular conceptual scheme and cannot transcend such a scheme in order to face external reality even though – Putnam contends – such a reality must be presumed to exist (Putnam 1981: 52). This premise, as has already been argued, is central to any representational-realist position, and differentiates such a position from naive realism and ontological idealism. Crucially for Putnam, however, this position also means that fundamental dichotomies between inside and outside: between subjectivity and objectivity, convention and fact, reality and representation, truth and falsity, must be eradicated because what Putnam refers to as the 'cut' between inside and outside cannot be made: 'The attempt to draw this distinction, to make this cut, has been a total failure. The time has come to try the methodological hypothesis that no such act can be made.' (Putnam 1987: 27) If it is accepted that external reality exists, yet cannot be grasped directly, objectivism and subjectivism are insufficient and a middle ground between both must be established. Such a position actually has greater implications for conceptual idealism than representational realism because, while representational realism encompasses both inside and outside, conceptual idealism effectively brackets out the outside on the grounds that it is not worth considering in that, though it exists, it cannot be comprehended. This is, in Putnam's terminology, and to all extents and purposes, a 'cut' between inside and outside to the detriment of outside; and, if conceptual idealism believes in the existence of a reality outside of mind, it is a cut that should not be made. If, though, reality is brought back into the equation in some way then the conceptual-idealist stance (including its related politics) is brought into question. In place of such a cut Putnam proposes a suture of inside and outside that accommodates the middle ground of each as he adopts a model based on a continuum of the 'relatively subjective' and the 'relatively objective' (or relatively inside–relatively outside) (29).

Putnam's model of internal realism rules out ontological idealism and naive realism, and, as argued, also undermines aspects of conceptual idealism. What are still required, however, are methods and procedures for knowing something 'relatively objectively'. If the 'cut' cannot be made, what means and approaches can accomplish such approximation? As a philosopher in the analytic tradition Putnam is concerned to elaborate conceptual means to this end and so has developed a model based upon the privileged status of rational procedures – what he refers to as 'canons and principles of rationality' and 'warranted assertability' criteria – which set limits upon the remit, acceptability and array of interpretation (34). These canons, principles and criteria interact with experience to create an 'explanation space', a circumscribed area within which certain accounts of reality can be argued to be more justified than others because they are 'instrumentally efficacious, coherent, comprehensive and functionally simple' (Putnam, in Passmore 1991: 106). What we have here, therefore, is what amounts to a 'regulative conception' of realism: a 'realism of intent', rather than 'definitive truth', delimited by conceptual principles (Rescher, in Trigg 1989: 201–2).

It will be argued here that Putnam's notions of the 'relatively subjective', 'relatively objective' 'warranted assertability', 'canons and principles of rationality' and the idea, from other sources, of a 'realism of intent', go part way to establishing an adequate-enough basis for a representational-realist position; that is, they provide part of an intellectual justification for realism and rebuttal of the core premise of conceptual idealism. Realism is *necessary* because the 'cut' between inside and outside cannot be made, because the outside *exists*, and because the inside can (perhaps must) strive to become *proximate* with the outside. Realism involves a *pursuit* of this approximation and is a 'realism of intent' as a consequence. Warranted assertability criteria and canons of rationality do not, of course, have much bearing on the ideas of the major realist film theorists, most of whom seek to limit, rather than lionise, rationality. As will be argued later, however, the notions of a 'realism of intent' and desire to retrieve the 'outside' have considerable resonance with those theorists. In addition to these ideas derived from Putnam and others, there is one final area of philosophical enquiry which must be considered before turning to realist film theory, and one also which adds an additional dimension to the overall justification of realism attempted here. Conceptual guidelines may help in achieving 'convergence' between inside and outside but so might empirical experience, an area crucial to the major realist film theorists and any realist film theory.

Many philosophical realists believe that perceptual experience constitutes our most dependable, though still circumlocutory relation to a reality that exists outside our conceptual schemes. Within such experience our perceptual apparatus constructs a phenomenal world that surrounds us. Our perceptual apparatus constructs that world *in relation to something*, however, and that something can only be something outside of our conceptual schemes which is influencing how our perceptual apparatus is constructing perceptual experience for us. Unless one takes the view that our perceptual apparatus constructs appearance in relation to the internal functioning of the apparatus this has to be the case. So, there is a reputed link between perceptual experience and independent, unobservable causal factors, and, because of this, perceptual experience must be a, or even the, starting point for understanding or appreciating those factors. It is because unobservable causal factors *are* unobservable, and also because the phenomenal world is observable and is also linked to those factors, that perceptual, empirical experience has for many theorists a special status in relation to the question of reality (Devitt 1997: 108).

One formulation which also relates to this and is relevant here is that of 'empirical adequacy'. Here, for a representational scheme – for present purposes a theory about something – to possess empirical adequacy, it must engage with a substantial quantity and diversity of perceptual phenomena (Trigg 1989: xiv). Such a degree of engagement is beneficial because such phenomena are linked to external reality and because phenomenal experience generates a more extensive and nebulous quantity and diversity of connotations and relations than concepts which are fashioned and limited by their determinate conceptual nature (Hesse, in Morick 1980: 217). So, there are two issues here: the link which phenomenal representations have to external reality; and their ability to qualify theoretical supposition. These issues also really relate here to the notion of *evidence*: evidence that is used to sustain or negate a theoretical formulation; and this is because the notion of empirical adequacy is derived from the philosophy of science and is chiefly concerned with issues of theory verification and refutation. If, in place of a theory, however, a *representational system* is considered in relation to the notion of 'empirical adequacy', the following emerges. For a representational system – say, a film – to possess empirical adequacy, that system should engage with a substantial quantity and diversity of empirical phenomenal materials. The presence of a surfeit of empirical phenomenal materials in the representational system (film) will enhance and enrich the array of signification and problematics present. In addition, if the representational system is a film which contains, albeit cinematically coded, representations of perceptual experience, given that, as previously argued, there is a link between perceptual experience and independent, unobservable causal factors in reality, there will also be a link between the coded representations of perceptual experience in the film and factors existing in reality; and this also means that the *more* such coded representations of perceptual experience constitute the film, the closer and greater that link will be, at least on the basis of quantity: these representations therefore have a *mass* which bears down upon the unobservable. Such hypothetical approximation can, of course, never be verified in the commonly accepted sense of that term but works rather in the way of a guideline and as a 'realism of intent'. Of course, as an aesthetic structure, the film will contain other sorts of coded structural and conceptual components. According to the tenor of the above, however, coded representations of perceptual experience should predominate.

As will be argued later, the notions referred to above have implications for understanding the ideas of the major realist film theorists. Before turning to these, though, it will be useful to return to Putnam's model of internal realism in order to discuss an aspect of his thought which is congruent with those ideas. Putnam has argued that his model was formed partly in response to a scientific world view that had 'turned the external world' into 'mathematical formulas', therefore making our own experience of the world a 'second-class' one (Conant, in Putnam 1992: xiv). Putnam claims that he wishes to resist this and confront the hegemony of the scientific world view by raising up such experience, and, in doing so, he invokes the idea of the *Lebenswelt*, or 'life-world': 'I am concerned with bringing us back to precisely these claims which we do, after all, constantly make in our daily lives. Accepting the "manifest image", the *Lebenswelt*, the world as we actually experience it.' (xlix–l) The trajectory of Putnam's thinking thereby leads him to a conception of realism which embraces the 'manifest image' of the *Lebenswelt*: that which is phenomenally *felt*; and his notions of 'realism with a human face' and 'realism with a small r' also reflect this concern to comprehend 'ourselves-in-the-world' (xiv). The idea of turning towards everyday experience within the *Lebenswelt* and concomitantly limiting the latitude of conceptual rationalisation is, of course, central to the ideas of the major realist film theorists, particularly Lukács and Kracauer, and, it could be argued, underlies the whole of Kracauer's *Theory of Film*. Putnam's emphasis upon the notion of what he also calls 'human flourishing' also brings him in line with the humanist orientation of Kracauer, Bazin and Lukács, and there is a particular resonance, for example, between the notion of 'human flourishing' (xv) and Kracauer's idea of the 'family of man' (Kracauer 1997: 68). Nevertheless, while these aspects of Putnam's thought may correlate with the ideas of the major realist film theorists his focus on conceptual categories such as 'canons and principles of rationality' does not because film, for the realist film theorists, is an aesthetic rather than rational-cognate form of representation. There is, therefore, a need to understand how the sort of realism discussed in the previous pages might be framed in aesthetic terms.

IV   INTUITIONIST REALISM: AN AESTHETIC SUMMARY

One starting point here is the notion of empirical adequacy and the idea of phenomenally laden realism. The notion of empirical phenomenal adequacy also suggests, however, that the empirically laden aesthetic object will also be indeterminate because what is largely empirical is also necessarily largely indeterminate. Aesthetic objects, including films, may, of course, not be empirically laden, and may also vary in indeterminacy in terms of their aesthetic structures. It has been argued, however, that the process of encountering an aesthetic object – aesthetic experience – is, in general, marked by indeterminacy. So, for example, it is argued that works of art are rarely judged to make truth claims about a subject because people do not come to the work of art to find specific answers as perhaps they might to a cognitive tract such as a cookery manual, or an instructional film. The 'knowledge' which is generated during aesthetic experience is not veridical *cognisable* knowledge. Rather, the spectator is on the lookout for something that might be 'intellectually illuminating' in a broad sense rather than cognitively definite (Passmore 1991: 125).

Instead of making truth claims, works of art 'offer a subject' up for scrutiny or 'show something as' similar to that which the spectator might experience or believe (Beardsley 1981: 375). Here, the work of art shows something as *like* something in a general, rather than specific way; it 'draws attention to' a subject, or puts a subject 'up for consideration', instead of making more precise claims; and it does not thereby display truth so much as 'interesting candidates for truth' which the recipient can then consider (Passmore 1991: 125). Within this process, the role of the formal organisation and ideational content of the work of art is also regarded by the recipient as providing a broad rather than narrow perspective on the subject (138). Of course, these are generalisations, and some works of art may be more purposely directive, and received as such, than others. The point here, however, is that, in general, works of art are not generally taken to provide definite truth claims, and even the most highly composed works of art may be interpreted, or experienced, in a largely indeterminate fashion. This adds an extra dimension of indeterminacy to the already indeterminate phenomenally laden aesthetic form indicated previously, and may suggest that such a form might be more appropriate to aesthetic experience than one which is not so phenomenally abundant.

The indeterminacy referred to above is also predicated upon the concept of intuition, which is a key aspect of classical realist film theory. It has been argued that three main categorical epistemologies of knowledge can be posited: empiricist, rationalist and intuitionist (Beardsley 1981: 387). Within an empiricist epistemology, all knowledge stems from experience and can be understood only through a process of rational generalisation from perceived instances. In contrast, within a rationalist epistemology, it is held that real knowledge may be given independently of experience and may also subsist within some ideal realm separate from the world of nature, accessible through reason. Classical realist film theory, however, cannot be associated with either of these positions. For example, despite the emphasis upon the empirical which underlies such theory, that theory cannot be said to rely upon an empiricist theory of knowledge in that Lukács, Grierson, Bazin and Kracauer do not adopt the view that *all* knowledge stems from experience and can only be understood through a process of inference from experience. Similarly, none of the above theorists accept the alternative rationalist proposition that real knowledge may be appropriated independently of experience or that it may subsist within some ideal realm accessible through reason. Instead, classical realist film theory is most closely aligned with the third major categorical epistemology of knowledge, 'intuitionism'.

The first thing to be said about intuitionism as a theory of knowledge is that it is not a theory of knowledge in the typical sense understood by that phrase because it does not seek to provide a rationale for 'proving' anything and so does not involve the making of specific truth claims about anything. This effectively means that there is no actual obtained knowledge involved here, if knowledge is understood as something demarcated and delimited, something that can be *definitely known* and also something that can be clearly communicated to others. In contrast to that, an intuitionist theory of knowledge is concerned with indefinite knowledge which is also comprehended 'intuitively': with an equivocal awareness of something ambiguous but resonant 'grasped' or 'felt'. In addition to such indeterminacy, intuitive understanding cannot really be communicated in its essence because it is something experienced in the moment by the individual person who experiences the intuition. Intuitionist understanding is, therefore, related to personal revelation though, because human beings live a shared existence, it also has a collective and communicable – but, as stated, not *essentially* so – dimension. In this sense, intuition, though primarily subjective, is also secondarily intersubjective. Whether subjective or intersubjective, though, intuitive awareness cannot be anchored and set down for scrutiny because it is momentary and transient and appears and disappears in a process of transient flux and change. No painting, for example, can 'capture' an intuitive insight, though it may be the product of such insight and may act as a catalyst for spectatorial insight that may or may not be similar to the original insight. Finally, in addition to the above, intuitive understanding is also *conjectural and hypothetical* in character rather than *conclusive and summative*. It is not concerned with solutions either elementary or elaborate.

Two consequences stem from the above which have ramifications for an understanding of intuitionism in general and classical realist film theory in particular. First, and *in terms of experience*, the conjectural, hypothetical and transient character of the form of knowledge proposed within an intuitionist theory of knowledge implies that there will be no definite bracketing in or out or categorising taking place within the formation of such knowledge and this means that intuitively provoked knowledge will not be complicit with proclivities towards jurisdiction, regulation and the imposition of authority. In other words, intuitive understanding stands outside and is foreign to processes of authorisation, and is associated instead with the antithesis of such processes, that is, non-discriminatory disinterestedness. Second, and *in terms of aesthetic representation*, because intuitive understanding is related to feeling rather than intellect, to mood rather than concept, it is best, or can only be, portrayed through non-verbal non-conceptual forms of art; and this also means that such forms of art can also, in principle at least, be similarly related to notions of non-discriminatory disinterestedness. These issues of freedom, control, and the importance of non-verbal modes of representation will be returned to later as they are central to classical realist film theory. Before that, however, it will be necessary to focus further on issues of 'reality' and representation within intuitionist theories of knowledge.

Intuitionist theories of knowledge, under which rubric classical realist film theory falls, are experience oriented in the sense that the reality in question is understood as, or limited to, that which is experienced. To one extent or other, this focus on experience can also be related to, or even be directly influenced by, the phenomenological notion of the *Lebenswelt*: the surrounding ever-changing world of our everyday experience and perception. As we have seen, this notion is referred to by Putnam but other philosophers in the analytical tradition have also made reference to the notion or similar. For example, John Dewey has argued (without mentioning the term *Lebenswelt*) that human experience is marked by a fluid continuum that is essentially inchoate and unstructured. A particular experience may have definite parameters but is also extracted from the more extensive parameterless inchoate flow of overall experience (Hanfling 1994: 151). This conception of human experience as characterised by flux has a lineage within Western philosophy and emphasises becoming rather than being, process rather than conclusion, change rather than stasis; and is summed up in a phrase attributed to the Greek philosopher Heraclitus: 'nothing ever is, everything is becoming' (Russell 1965: 63). This notion of becoming was later taken up by Hegel, Nietzsche and others and went on to influence classical realist film theory.

The *Lebenswelt* is, therefore, the reality addressed within intuitionist theories of knowledge, and this also means that the reality indicated within classical realist film theory is a reality of becoming rather than being. This may suggest that intuitionist theories of knowledge do not seek understanding of a reality which may lie beyond experience. The previously discussed notion of 'empirical adequacy', however, and idea of a prospective link between perceptual experience and external reality, provides a rider to this which is important to classical realist film theory and will also be discussed in more detail shortly. The idea that the *Lebenswelt* is characterised by becoming and seamless flux also implies that, as argued, it should be represented as such in art, and this also implies that such artistic representation must partake of the fluidity and connectedness of the *Lebenswelt* at the level of representational form. This means that it is the non-verbal arts that can best portray this fluidity and con-nectedness because the verbal arts articulate such connectedness and fluidity, and, in doing so, change it into something that is not true of human experi-ence. In the verbal arts, as in science and logic, an unavoidable periodisation takes place which is at odds with and the converse of the authentic seamless-ness of human experience.

An intuitionist theory of knowledge may also define intuitive understand-ing at two different levels of consequence. First, there is the general intuition of something meaningful. This can be of almost anything in terms of what is experienced but is nevertheless always characterised by a similar type of process: an intuitive grasp of resonant meaningfulness through feeling and personal encounter. Intuition is not generated unless the object of intuition is worth intuiting. The traveller stands in front of the mountain and experiences its magnificence, or terror, and it is personal experience of aspects of the life-world such as this that generates this type of intuitive experience. If the viewer looks at a painting of a mountain the same type of experience may be generated, though that experience may also be different from ones experienced by the painter, as he or she attempted to embody those experiences in the painting (though the painted mountain may also be entirely the product of the artist's imagination and not based on his/her personal experience of a mountain).

In addition to these kinds of intuitive understandings, however, there can also be a more particular intuitive awareness of the authentic quotidian character of experience of the *Lebenswelt*, of the phenomenal world, and this can also be accompanied by insight into what a superior comportment of the individual within the *Lebenswelt* might consist of. This now takes us back to the idea of empirical adequacy and to the notion that, if our perceptual representations are linked indirectly to an external world which exists outside of our conceptual schemes, then empirical adequacy based on and in perceptual representation in aesthetic representation also links us to that world and to a kind of experience of knowing that world. Nothing *mystical* is involved here, and what is being referred to is a concrete sense of being in the world: a sense of grasping the authentic – and therefore *realistic* – character of our place within a *Lebenswelt* which is also ineluctably linked to external reality. Here, empirical adequacy in the film connects us to this deeper level of experience of insightful experience of our existential situation. This idea is also taken up by Dewey (though, of course, not in relation to film), and also related to the notion of becoming, when he asserts that:

> life goes on within an environment . . . we continually interact with our surroundings, seeking an enrichment, stability and harmony with them . . . a fulfilment that reaches to the depth of our being – one that is an adjustment of our whole being with the conditions of existence. (Dewey, in Hanfling 1994: 151)

Dewey's expressive language: 'a fulfilment that reaches to the depth of our being . . . an adjustment of our whole being with the conditions of existence' sums up the importance of this notion not only for him but also, and as will be argued shortly, for the major realist film theorists, whose underlying ideas embody similar sentiments concerning the revelation of the individual's relation to the *Lebenswelt*, the world of phenomenal experience, and, through various representational formulations of empirical adequacy (though that phrase is not used by them), to external reality. Before considering those underlying ideas, though, one important misconception must be confronted concerning intuitionist theories of knowledge, and that is that they may constitute some sort of romantic numinous repudiation of intellect. In fact, this is rarely the case, and most intuitionist theories of knowledge do not repudiate intellect per se but rather seek to position it better within the totality of human experience. Intuitionist theories of knowledge, including classical realist film theory, generally seek to argue that intellect and rationality have become too dominant within modern human experience at the expense of other important areas and must now be placed within a more appropriate perspective, one which also recognises the importance – perhaps overriding – of intuitive experience.

V THE MAJOR REALIST FILM THEORIES: INTUITIONISM AND PARTICULARITY

The preceding section of this introduction has set out an overall framework of aesthetic realism related to classical cinematic realism and premised on notions of phenomenal adequacy, the indeterminate character of aesthetic experience and the nature of aesthetic intuition. The objective will be eventually to use this framework as a basis for understanding the general and, to some extent, *collective* theoretical position of the major realist film theorists more clearly. This section of the introduction will therefore proceed to that end by first prefacing the intuitionist aspect of classical realist film theory – in order to link up with the previous account of aesthetic intuition – before going into more detail on a general categorical feature of that theory, and perhaps the one that will best enable an overarching understanding of classical cinematic realism to be reached: the focus on particularity. The many specific ideas and concepts found in the writings of these theorists will only be considered briefly, however, and in part, in the preface on intuitionism set out here, and will not be considered extensively in the larger section on particularity. This is because that would be unachievable given the space remaining here and has anyway been carried out reasonably exhaustively elsewhere (including Aitken 2001, 2006, 2007, 2012 and 2013); and because the intention here is to arrive at an understanding of the general classical cinematic realist category of particularity through relating that category to other general theoretical formulations which influenced it rather than instances which comprise it.

VI THE MAJOR REALIST FILM THEORIES AND INTUITIONISM: A BRIEF OVERVIEW

The outline of classical realist film theory carried out in the following few pages reveals that such theory is demonstrably part of the larger intuitionist paradigm indicated in previous pages. Lukács's early and late writings on film are full of intuitionist notions. For example, in his 1913 'Thoughts Towards an Aesthetic of the Cinema', he writes that:

> The world of the 'cinema' is a life without background or perspective, without distinction in terms of weight and qualities . . . a life without measure or order . . . the essence of cinema is movement as such, perpetual flux, the never-resting change of things. (Lukács, in Aitken 2012: 182–3)

Lukács's early work was strongly influenced by phenomenology, and the notion of the *Lebenswelt* underlies the 1913 essay. Similarly, in the chapter on 'Film' in the 1963 *Specificity of the Aesthetic*, Lukács makes distinctions between what he calls 'indefinite objectivity', 'definite objectivity', and 'interiority'. Art forms such as literature are able to portray interior subjective experience well because they employ conceptualisation. Visual and auditory art forms such as film, however, are able only to depict interiority *indirectly*: to *indicate*, rather than conceptualise; and this process of the indirect non-conceptual depiction of interiority is what Lukács refers to as 'indefinite objectivity'. Lukács also argues that because film is a primarily visual medium within which language plays only a secondary role it must prioritise the 'visual-auditory', or 'sensuous-immediate', rather than conceptual (Aitken 2012: 214). Also, in *The Specificity of the Aesthetic*, Lukács proposed the highly intuitionist concept of *Stimmung*, or 'atmosphere'. Here, the film sequence is conceived of as evoking a general 'atmosphere', or tone: a *Stimmung*. These atmospheric sequences succeed each other across the course of the film, ultimately cohering into final aesthetic unity of atmosphere, or *Stimmungseinheit* (103–4).

Such intuitionist concepts also suffuse the writings of the other major realist film theorists. For example, Grierson's notion of the 'real' as underlying the actual, his notion of *Zeitgeist*, and intuitive understanding of the 'absolute' are all intuitionist concepts. Grierson was influenced by the ideas of the British neo-Hegelian philosopher W. H. Bradley, who argued that forms of religious and aesthetic experience were better able to comprehend reality because such forms of experience were essentially intuitive (Bradley 1914: 175), and Grierson adopted this view when arguing that 'The artistic faculty means above all the power to see . . . the hidden harmonies of man and nature.' (Aitken 2013: 44) As with Grierson, so with Kracauer, who argued that the way to escape from a debilitating modern condition was through transcending abstraction and experiencing the world in its phenomenological richness using revelatory insight. Finally, André Bazin was influenced by the ideas of the French phenomenologist Henri Bergson. Among these ideas was that of 'self-conscious instinct' (Russell 1965: 758). Here, intuition does not operate in the way that intellect does, through dividing up experience, but, instead, comprehends experience as flux.

Many of the above ideas will be discussed in greater depth in the next section of this introduction. For the moment, though, this brief exposition serves to situate the major realist film theorists within an intuitionist paradigm. It will also be argued later, however, that it will be both misleading and not enough to subsume these theorists entirely under an intuitionist label. The intuitionist paradigm must, therefore, be qualified and modified, particularly in relation to phenomenology, and that will take place in the conclusions section of this introduction. Prior to that, the relationship of the major realist film theorists to what has been established to be a central component of any realist theory, particularity as found in empirical experience and representation, will be addressed.

VII CLASSICAL REALIST FILM THEORY AND THE ROLE OF PARTICULARITY IN EMPIRICAL EXPERIENCE AND REPRESENTATION

This section of the introduction focuses on conceptions of empirical representation which influenced the major realist film theorists. These conceptions will be considered in depth with a view in the conclusions section of this introduction to gathering them together into a reassessed model of theoretical cinematic realism.

Kant, Husserl – Kracauer

Siegfried Kracauer's belief that modernity was characterised by abstraction led him to assert that such abstraction could be reversed by close and meaningful focus on empirical perceptual experience and the aesthetic representation of such. Kracauer drew directly on the phenomenological notion of immersion within the *Lebenswelt* here. For Kracauer, close attention to immediate experience 'redeems' reality for the individual and leads to a greater understanding of the individual's existential situation within the *Lebenswelt*. In addition to the idea of the *Lebenswelt*, which has already been covered in this introduction, Kracauer's theory of cinematic realism was also influenced by three related Kantian concepts: the 'harmony of the faculties'; *Naturschöne*; and 'disinterestedness'; all of which are closely related to modes of empirical representation and experience.

The 'harmony of the faculties' refers to a harmony between the 'faculties' of the 'Understanding' and 'Imagination'. For Kant, the faculty of Imagination unites the sense impressions which human beings experience into various evolving structures and patterns while the faculty of the Understanding then applies higher-level regulative concepts and classifications to these. The 'harmony' of these faculties occurs when the Understanding seeks order and totality and also interacts with the Imagination in such a way that the latter also seeks meaningful formations and a sense of wholeness in the object of contemplation (Aitken 2007: 106). There is a dialectic at play here in which the Understanding, when seeking order and totality, stops the Imagination from becoming anarchic and engaging in what Kant refers to as 'lawless freedom', while the Imagination, regulated by an order-seeking Understanding, opens up the last to new, diverse, but still lucid possibilities (Aitken 1998: 126). Kant believed that this interactive dialectic between Imagination and Understanding underlies and shapes all cognitive activities and leads to the generation of knowledge. He also believed, however, that, within aesthetic experience, that interactive structure does not lead to the generation of definite knowledge because aesthetic experience is concerned with feeling rather than concepts. This means that the knowledge which is garnered during aesthetic experience is indefinite in character. Within aesthetic experience, in which the harmony of the faculties is generally directed at an art object, the empirical also plays a crucial role because an empirical array is inevitably present where the object of contemplation is a concrete object. Here, the empirically constituted art object provides the foundational material and parameters for the Understanding and Imagination to seek an indefinite order and meaningfulness. In a similar way, however, the contemplation of nature also provides such foundational material – though different parameters – and Kant refers to such contemplation of nature as an experience of *Naturschöne*.

Naturschöne: 'natural beauty', or the 'beauty of nature', refers to meaningful formations and a sense of wholeness found when the Imagination and Understanding contemplate nature. Here, the harmony of the faculties is achieved through the experience of nature. In *Naturschöne* the empirical abundance of the natural environment enables the Imagination freely to explore diverse possible structures, formations and movements, and also enables the Understanding to shape and regulate, and be affected by, such exploration. Here, nature helps both Imagination and Understanding seek and establish a sense of order, pattern and wholeness which is enhanced by contact with the compound and indeterminate non-human environment. A dialectic interaction between the Understanding and the Imagination occurs here in the encounter with nature. Such a dialectic is also involved in the encounter with the art object, though there is a difference between the two. In the encounter with the art object the concrete richness of the material art object provides a circumscribed empirical foundation for the interaction of the Imagination and Understanding. The empirical foundation for such an interaction provided by the encounter with nature is, however, richer and more indeterminate than any art object could establish, and circumscribed only by the viewing horizon of the spectator. There is a sense here of the experience of *Naturschöne* as providing the basis for more complex interaction between the Understanding and Imagination than can be afforded by the work of art, and this might also imply that works of art – including films – should be 'nature-like': should be largely indeterminate while leaving some space open for ordering activity.

In addition to this ability to generate a more multifaceted interaction between the Imagination and Understanding, the experience of *Naturschöne* involves a re-enchantment of human experience in which the individual returns to a vibrant nature lost under the prevailing abstractions and conditions of modernity. Here, the experience of *Naturschöne* amounts to a resonant and animated experience of a nature full of what Kracauer calls meaningful 'correspondences'; (Kracauer: 68) and also returns lost nature to the individual, creating a unity of experience linking humankind to nature. Here, the gap opened up within modernity between nature and the typical and degraded experience of nature is sealed, and a sense of return to a more authentic and meaningful experience is established. It is, therefore, encounter with the empirical landscape that provides a foundation for the materialisation of a qualitatively enhanced synthesis of empirical experience, reason and intuition to emerge, and for a sense of re-enchantment and unity of experience to occur. And, this also suggests that works of art, including films, should accord with the form of interaction between the Imagination and Understanding which occurs within the harmony of the faculties.

Finally, it is unsurprising that Kracauer, a student of Kant, should turn to the notion of 'disinterestedness', a notion, though, that has also 'probably been the single most important concept in the last three centuries of aesthetic theory' (Collinson in Hanfling [ed.], 1994: 134). Disinterestedness refers to the notion that aesthetic judgement, and the object of contemplation at which that judgement is directed, should stand outside instrumental purpose and need. In the *Critique of Judgement*, Kant argued that the 'judgement of taste': the judgement that something is aesthetically valuable, is not related to any interest on the part of the perceiver but only to the free experience of the object of judgement: 'The judgement of taste is simply contemplative, i.e. it is a judgement which is indifferent to the existence of an object, and only decides how its character stands with the feeling of pleasure and displeasure.' (135–6) Disinterested aesthetic experience is what Kant calls 'free liking', and 'pleasurable liking'. Kant thinks that such 'liking' may also be the 'one and only disinterested and free delight' because it lies outside of interest (136). The idea of 'contemplation' here also means something like an act of deep and long consideration, observation or admiration, and can involve both thoughtfulness and simply 'looking at' something. The only 'interest' involved here is a 'looking-for-pleasure' in order to experience pleasure. Kant argues, however, that this is so deeply embedded in our cognitive existential make-up that it does not count as an 'interest' in the customary sense of the term as something related to 'self-interest' or personal advantage.

Disinterested aesthetic experience is not only free because it is free from such interest, however, but also in that it is not constrained by the parameters of conceptual reason. Kant argues that the disinterested judgement of taste cannot lead to definite knowledge because it is based on feeling. Because it is based on feeling, and is unrelated to conceptual knowledge, the judgement of taste is indefinite in character. It is the product of an interaction between the Imagination and the Understanding which generates indefinite meaning grasped intuitively through feeling. So, we have an experience which is indefinite, is afforded through feeling, and cannot be rendered via language. Here, the Imagination and Understanding interact to generate indefinite but harmonious feelings – the latter because harmony is intrinsically pleasurable. Freedom is involved here but so, also, is order, and both 'lawless freedom' and domineering regulation are avoided (137). In addition to being 'nature-like' and according with the harmony of the faculties, therefore, the art object (including the film) should be free from interest, and not linked to purpose or intent; and all of this is additionally further indicated by a notion that Kant relates to the notion of disinterestedness: that of 'purposiveness without purpose'.

What Kant means here is that, in the encounter with nature or with a work of art, patterns and arrangements are perceived and there therefore seem to be 'purposes' evident in the sense of the patterns and arrangements being as they are through some cause or organisation. No definite purpose or meaning can be discerned, however. This indefinite purposiveness, when perceived in a landscape or work of art, is particularly important because it makes the Imagination and Understanding interact *equivalently*, and therefore causes both to engage in an activity which is law-like and free. Here, a meaningful sense of union is established with the art object or nature premised on the notion of purposiveness without purpose. These Kantian notions will be returned to later when an attempt is made to link them to a general model of cinematic realism underlying classical cinematic realism. Before that, however, the relationship of Lukács to the German philosophical tradition will be considered.

German tradition – Lukács

Unlike Kracauer, there are fewer specific theoretical influences from other theorists relating to the empirical that can be identified per se in the writings on film of Georg Lukács. Lukács was influenced by the German philosophical tradition in general, and by Kant and Hegel in particular, with the second of those two having the greater influence. Lukács's writings on film often combine these and other influences in various ways, however, and change them in the process to the extent that few clear paths of influence can be traced. One consequence of this is that, unlike in the review of influences on Kracauer just undertaken, in which general philosophical conceptions were explored, it will be necessary here first to place a more directed emphasis on Lukács's writings on film before considering such conceptions.

A key empirical notion which arises in Lukács's film writings is that of *Geradesosein* which Lukács develops from Hegel, Engels and other sources. *Geradesosein*, or the 'just-being-so' of things, refers to the ability of film to capture an important aspect of human experience. Here, whatever we experience and whatever attitude we adopt towards such experience, we also experience that which we encounter as materials which are perceived by us as existing in-and-for-themselves. Because the encounter with the just-being-so of things is an authentic aspect of human perceptual encounter Lukács argues that, in addition to other aspects of filmic representation, the medium should also attempt to portray this encounter. It is also because of this imperative that Lukács maintains that the relatively autonomous image must be retained as 'an essential element of . . . film art' (Lukács 1981, II: 473).

A further way of understanding *Geradesosein*, and also connecting the notion to broader conceptions, is to refer to Hegel, although Hegel does not use that term himself. In the *Phenomenology of Spirit* Hegel refers to the empirical particularity as the 'this' (*Dieser*): the immediate object of sense perception, or what Hegel also calls 'sense-certainty' (Desmond 1986: 21). Hegel, however, does not regard the 'this' as an unmediated particularity but as a mediated 'concrete universal'. The idea of the concrete universal is a complex one, has been widely interpreted by various scholars, and cannot be considered in depth here. Put succinctly for present purposes the notion suggests that every particularity is associated with a range of universals and cannot be separated from these. For example, when one views a tree one does not simply view the tree as a single entity but as one which is inseparably linked to a range of universals which 'inhere' to the entity; universals such as 'woodenness', 'natural', 'greenness', 'shape', and so on. These universals inhere to our perception of the particular tree and are inseparable from that perception so that we cannot see the tree as a bare 'this'. This is, epigrammatically, what Hegel means by the phrase concrete universal.

In the *Aesthetic*, Lukács takes on board this conception of the concrete universal, but only to a certain extent. For example, in a chapter entitled 'Besonderheit as an Aesthetic Category', he sets out an account of inherence in which he asserts that relations and determinations are inherent to any particular manifestation of singularity as no one thing can be entirely separated from the determinations and relations associated with it (Lukács 1981, II: 232). Lukács, however, does not go on from this to adopt the abstract idealism implicated by the idea of the concrete universal. Hegel's argument led him and later interpreters to the position that universals not only inhere to a singularity but actually constitute it, so that all that really exists for us is an interactive network of universals, and no foundational 'substance-of-the-object' can be identified (Putnam 1992a: 46–8). As a Marxist-realist, however, Lukács was unable to accept such a relational model of meaning, and he insisted instead on a correspondence model in which properties and relations inhere to a definite *object modality*, though, and as will be argued, a modality that is still not a singular 'this' but rather a 'micro-totality'. This emphasis on the identity-ness of the object – and in this case person – is clear from Lukács's reference to Engels's iconic 1885 'Letter to Minna Kautsky' in which, according to Lukács, Engels insists that, in the work of true realist literature, 'everyone is a type, but also simultaneously a single individual, a *Dieser*, as old Hegel would have expressed himself' (Lukács 1981, II: 232). Lukács uses this assertion that a singularity is also a multiplicity to argue that inherence must be interpreted as referring to a situation in which relations and determinations do not overwhelm or make up the identity-ness of the singularity (Parkinson in Parkinson [ed.], 1970: 136). The question then arises, however, as to what that 'identity-ness' consists of, and how it and the ideas of *Geradesosein* and inherence relate to film.

For Lukács, in terms of *Geradesosein*, the 'object' is first of all understood as that which is both perceived by, and also impresses itself on, the senses. By the experience of *Geradesosein*, the experience of the 'this', therefore, Lukács refers to an encounter with an object in our experienced life-world in which the object looms up out of its various relations, contexts and connotations to be encountered as an entity per se apparent within our perceptual field. Here, the object–entity consists, firstly, of basic perceptual properties. A desk, for example, will consist, at a basic level, of shape, colour, size, and so on. There is no 'essence' to the desk: no *one* substance that is 'desk'. There are, however, a number of cohering basic properties and relations between those properties which constitutes them as an object–entity. What, therefore, Lukács means by *Geradesosein* is a situation in which a cohesion of basic properties emerges out of the flux of the life-world to constitute a composite object, and one which can also then be scrutinised in further detail, both at this basic primary level, and at the level of secondary properties which, to return to the example of the tree, would include those such as texture, colour gradation and pattern.

The experience of *Geradesosein* then seems to be based on contemplation of the coherence of these basic and secondary attributes to constitute an 'object' which exists as object within our experience of the *Lebenswelt*. Though the 'object' as singularity does not exist *per se*, it does exist meaningfully *as such* for us. The idea of the object consisting of basic and secondary properties and relations with no essence also leads Lukács to define particularity (*Einzelheit*) as a 'micro-complex'. As Lukács puts it, each particular possesses its own spheres of meaning: its own mini-grouping of properties and relations (*Besonderheit*): 'the *Einzelheit* has its own *Besonderheit* inherent to itself'. Lukács also argues, however, that these micro-complexes inherent to the particular are latent until activated by particular acts of cognition and intuition: they are, as Lukács colourfully puts it, in a state of 'undeveloped in itself imprisoned form' (*unentfalteten, in sich eingesperrten Form*) – they are metaphorically 'speechless' (*Stummheit*) (Lukács 1981, II: 232).

A distinction also has to be made here between artificial and natural objects within the *Lebenswelt* in relation to *Geradesosein*. Artificial objects will be more suffused with connotation, relation and properties, uses, expectations and purposes than natural objects. When we see a tree, for example, and focus on that tree, its basic and then secondary properties emerge more clearly and vividly than when we view a desk because the tree cannot be subsumed under use–value to the extent to which the desk can. Lukács refers to this experience of nature-based *Geradesosein* in the *Aesthetic* when discussing the ability of film to portray the natural world. Here, he argues that, in film, 'a visible, sensuous and evident world emerges *sui generis*' (Aitken 2012: 190). In the earlier 'Thoughts Towards an Aesthetic of the Cinema', he also expresses the idea more strongly when asserting that, in film, 'The livingness of nature here acquires artistic form for the first time' (184). Here, 'livingness' (*Lebendigkeit*) refers to the nature-based experience of *Geradesosein*.

There were many reasons why Lukács wished to hold on to the idea of particularity in the *Aesthetic*. In addition to the Marxist-realist stance on object–identity just mentioned, he was also influenced by Hegel's contention that, while, in ancient times, abstract thought had been necessary in order to lift up humanity from immersion in concrete immediacy, in the modern world such abstraction had gone too far and there was now a need to bring knowledge back to the 'concrete wealth of the world thereby to regain a fullness lacking to merely abstract thought' (Desmond 1986: 20). He was also influenced by the Hegelian notion that true thinking meant bringing abstract thought to bear on the material realities of the world. In his 1957 work *On Besonderheit as an Aesthetic Category* (*Besonderheit*), which was later abridged to form a chapter in the *Aesthetic*, Lukács asserted that *Besonderheit* was a 'prolegomena' to the later *Aesthetic*, in the Kantian sense of that word. In the *Prolegomena to any Future Metaphysics*, Kant had argued that Hume had 'first interrupted my dogmatic slumbers and gave my speculations in the field of speculative philosophy a new direction' (Kadarkay 1991: 445). That new direction was towards the study of empirical reality, and represented a shift away from a scrutiny of abstract philosophical generalisation towards an understanding of the particular and specific. As with Kant, in both *Besonderheit*, and the later *Aesthetic*, Lukács is concerned with identifying the *specificity* of the aesthetic. *Besonderheit* is a little-known work. Nevertheless, it succeeded in arousing the wrath of the Communist establishment when it appeared because its focus on what Lukács called the 'dialectics of the particular' was read as a metaphor for a need both to understand the specificity of Hungarian Communism and reject more general communist models imposed from outside. In *Besonderheit*, therefore, Lukács is calling directly for a philosophical shift from a study of axioms to a consideration of particularity, and, indirectly, for a political shift from the Soviet model to a specifically 'Hungarian road to socialism' (445). As with Kracauer, these notions are returned to later when an attempt is made to link them to a general model of cinematic realism underlying classical cinematic realism. Before that, however, the influence of the French tradition on Bazin will be considered.

Bergson – Bazin

Turning to Bazin, it is possible, as with Kracauer, to return to an exploration of some general philosophical conceptions first, and, in particular, Henri Bergson's conceptions of 'duration' and intuition. Bergson considered the experience of temporality to be an essential aspect of the human condition and the most important kind of such experience to be that of 'duration'. In his *Time and Free Will: An Essay on the Immediate Data of Consciousness* (1889) Bergson argued that the experience of duration, or *durée*, is important because it is 'the form which our conscious states assume when our ego lets itself *live*, when it refrains from separating its present state from its former states' (Russell 1965: 759). In the experience of *durée*, past and present are fused into a totality so that we experience a 'succession without distinction' which, in fact, corresponds to the authentic experience of temporality (759). Duration is, therefore, real and true temporality for us, and our experience of this real and true temporality is of a duration characterised by unceasing evolution without beginning or end within which change occurs constantly. Here, a 'qualitative multiplicity' of states which are heterogeneous and interpenetrating and which succeed each other without distinction are experienced (Bergson 2010: 165–8). Bergson also argued, however, that, within the modern world, the authentic character of our experience of duration had become replaced by an intellectual conception of time characterised by succession *with* distinction, and, therefore, by *immobility* rather than fluidity, *analysis* not synthesis. The 'artificial' time of science and reason ('*temps*') distorts authentic experience of *durée* because categorising analytical concepts are unable to comprehend fully the fluid, boundary-less character of our experience of a temporality which can only be grasped through a means that conforms to that character. In addition to this stance on the inauthentic nature of *temps*, Bergson also came to believe that the intellect in general and per se was unable to comprehend fully the authentic character of our experience of temporality because the intellect is only one part of our overall experience of life and therefore unable to look beyond itself in order to achieve such comprehension. Despite such intrinsic inability, though, the unremitting incursion of the intellect into all areas of experience within modernity has the effect of making 'the total activity of life shrink to the form of a certain human activity which is [in fact] only a partial . . . manifestation of life' (Pearson 2007: xv).

As a consequence of all this, Bergson came to the conclusion that the authentic character of duration could be grasped only through intuition. In departure from most standard accounts of intuition, however, Bergson also made a distinction between intuition and feeling. For Bergson, intuition is a method of contemplating duration *within* the experience of duration. Intuition here is a type of psychological activity, just as feeling and conceptual thought are, but one which takes on the structure of duration as fluid continuum. This is not so much 'feeling' as a particular mode of psychological awareness, one akin to meditation, though one, like feeling and unlike reason, accessible only through immediate experience. Bergson also argued that this kind of intuition provides us with metaphysical knowledge concerning the fundamental nature of temporal experience, just as intellect provides us with more practical knowledge regarding that experience. Like the major realist film theorists, Bergson does not seek to dispense with intellect here but to add something to it so that an enhanced knowledge of human experience is achieved. In this respect Bergson argued that the mind 'overflows' intellect and that this overflow area is better accessed through the kind of psychological awareness afforded through intuition (Pearson xviii). The relationship here to the phenomenological idea of immersion within the *Lebenswelt* is clear, as Bergson talks about placing oneself *within* duration and experiencing duration as pure mobility and being (Bergson 2007: 216).

Bergson was a major influence on French philosophy during the 1930s and 1940s and also influenced Bazin's conception of cinematic realism, even though Bazin may have had little direct acquaintance with Bergson's writings themselves and probably became aware of them through the interpretations of others. In his essay 'The Ontology of the Photographic Image', Bazin focused on the ability of the photograph to wrench the image out of the flow of temporality and preserve it (Bazin 1967: 15). Elsewhere, he referred to the 'autonomy of the [artistic] pictorial microcosm, which is forever crystallised outside time' (Bazin 2001: 3). The ability of photography to crystallise moments of duration was important to Bazin but he also argued that film was able to go beyond such momentary preservation because the medium possessed the ability to conserve a continuous span of time. Bazin refers to this process whereby a 'span' of duration is captured as 'change mummified', a process of embalmment in which 'The image of things is likewise the image of their duration' (Bazin 1967: 15). This led Bazin away from a preoccupation with the individual film shot, which cuts reality up into fragments, to the idea of 'framing the fleeting crystallisation of a reality' within a film sequence which is structured as a continuum and is meant to be grasped intuitively as a totality (Andréw 1990: 21).

In his essay 'The Picasso Mystery', a review of the 1956 documentary film of the same name by Henri-Georges Clouzot, Bazin referred directly to the notion of duration. In this essay Bazin argued that the 'great novelty of Clouzot's film resides . . . in its revelation of the temporality of painting', and that the 'phenomenon of unpredictability [in the film] in turn implies another that I shall examine next: that of pictorial duration' (Bazin 2001: 2). Bazin argued that, in showing the development of a painting by Picasso, Clouzot's film reveals that 'duration may be an integral part of the work itself, an additional dimension, which is foolishly ignored once a painting is completed' (3). Because the process of artistic creation took place over time, was temporal, it was also 'cinematic' (4). Bazin also links duration to freedom here, as the activity of painting is shown to be freely motivated and the act of painting makes this freedom visible, revealing that 'this freedom lies in duration' (5). Again the link between freedom and duration here also connects Bazin to Bergson. Bazin also fastens on the term 'metamorphosis' to describe the evolution of Picasso's painting, where previous states are not subordinate: 'the intermediate stages are not subordinate and inferior realities . . . they are already the work itself' (3). Bazin also makes a similar point to this elsewhere, when discussing Luchino Visconti's 1948 film *La Terra trema*, when he argues that, in this film, 'Things happen . . . each at its appointed hour, one after the other, but each carries an equal weight (Bazin 1971: 59). Here, the 'cinematic', freedom, temporal duration and a kind of egalitarianism of the substance are associated with one another, again returning us to Bergsonian notions.

One other aspect of Bazin's thought relevant here, which is also partly influenced by the Bergsonian tradition, is his notion of the 'dialectic of the abstract and concrete'. Following his assertion that film is able to portray spans of duration, Bazin went on to contend that film should remain close to perceptual experience at the level of film form and, within this, Bazin conceived of a special role for empirical representation in what he referred to as the 'dialectic of the abstract and concrete'. Here, concrete instances in film link up to abstract universals. When discussing Carl Theodor Dreyer's 1928 film *La Passion de Jeanne d'Arc/The Passion of Joan of Arc*, Bazin argued that abstract conceptions arise from a scrutiny of empirical characteristics in the film. Bazin argued that the 'pores' and 'movements of wrinkles' that make up this 'documentary of faces' the film portrays form a richly textured empirical fabric which constitutes the film's 'secondary details', and that this establishes the 'concrete' basis of the 'dialectic of concrete and abstract' (Bazin 1967: 109), a dialectic in which the 'abstract' dimension relates to the invocation of Joan's suffering and her torturers' brutality (110). For Bazin, the function of these 'secondary details' within the 'dialectic of concrete and abstract' is to reign in the influence of 'primary' detail – that is, theme, concept and idea. In discussing Robert Bresson's *Les dames du Bois de Boulogne* (1945), Bazin also argued that such secondary details not only reign in, but are also 'indifferent to the action' because they retain a degree of relative autonomy that transcends their functional role within the film (110). Here, 'indifference' takes us back to the Kantian 'disinterestedness' which influenced Kracauer so much, and to the idea that aesthetic judgement, and the object at which such judgement is directed, should stand outside of instrumental purpose to constitute an autonomous realm of freedom and self-realisation. This notion of 'secondary detail' and relative autonomy also appears to correspond to the Lukácsian idea of *Geradesosein*.

It is not clear where Bazin derives the notion of the dialectic of concrete and abstract from. As a phrase, its origins can be found in Hegel, where the dialectic of concrete and abstract stands for the movement of knowledge from the abstract to the concrete. Bazin's notion of secondary detail appears to partake of this to some, but not full, extent, and his notion that universals inhere to the particular is also reminiscent of the Hegelian notion of the concrete totality. The idea of the secondary detail also takes us back to Bazin's discussion of *The Picasso Mystery* in which he asserts that various sections of the film have equal weight and do not lose their essential substance as the film evolves. Here, the presence of the secondary detail contributes to this. There is no evidence, however, that Bazin derived his ideas on the role of the empirical from Hegel, and it is more likely that he was influenced by Bergsonian thought and by an appropriation of Marxist and Hegelian ideas which reached him through the Christian existentialist groups he associated with at the time (Andrew 1990: 27) (there is no fundamental difference between the Hegelian and Marxist notions of the dialectic of the abstract and concrete, as both assume the concrete to be a diverse unity to which universals inhere [Ilyenkov 2008: 32]). In terms of the influence of Bergsonian thought, the phrase 'dialectic of the concrete and abstract' can be related to Bergson's notion of the 'double form of consciousness' (Bergson 2007: 115). Here, Bergson refers to a 'reciprocal interpenetration' between 'intelligence' and 'intuition' in which the intelligence will 'apply itself to matter' while intuition then supplements intelligence in following 'the stream of life' (115). This dialectic between intelligence and intuition, and also the idea that the engagement of the intelligence with matter creates 'the push that has made it [intelligence] rise to the point it has reached', in intuition, which 'transcends intelligence' even though it is also dependent on the latter, can be related to the Bazinian dialectic of the concrete and abstract even though Bazin does not refer directly to the Bergsonian 'double form of consciousness' (115). As with Kracauer and Lukács, these influences on Bazin will be returned to later when an attempt is made to link them to a general model of cinematic realism underlying classical cinematic realism. Before that, however, the influence of the Hegelian tradition on John Grierson will be considered.

Bradley – Grierson

The aspects of Grierson's thought which are most relevant here are derived from philosophical idealism, and, in particular, from the ideas of the British neo-Hegelian philosopher W. H. Bradley. As we have seen, Bergson defined the experience of duration as experience of a 'qualitative multiplicity'. Bergson asserted, however, that such multiplicity also constituted a totality: the intuited experience of temporality *as a totality*. Here, 'life', consisting of many things, is also one thing: life; and the many occur within the parameters of the one – the totality of experienced being. This conception is, in many respects, derived from the Hegelian understanding of totality in which all elements within the totality are superseded yet do not disappear and remain within the evolving system (see also the previous discussion of Bazin and *The Picasso Mystery*) which Hegel refers to as the 'Absolute'. Change takes place here but that which changes also remains present to a degree or in some form. Hegel referred to this process whereby one state replaces another yet the initial state does not entirely disappear but remains in a changed configuration within the evolving system as 'sublation', and the notion is a key aspect of the Hegelian dialectic.

As has been argued, Bergson's totality, which he also referred to as the 'Absolute', was 'being': the world of experience which could be glimpsed as a totality through intuition, and, according to Bergson, 'the Absolute is revealed very near us . . . it is psychological and not mathematical or logical essence' (Bergson 2007: 191). In other words, the immediate experience of duration is also experience of the Absolute because the structure of duration partakes of the structure of the Absolute. In a similar way, Bradley also conceived of reality as a totality and referred to this using the Hegelian term the 'Absolute'. Like Bergson, so for Bradley, the Absolute is 'a seamless whole . . . in which all contradictions and antinomies are overcome' (Bradley 1914: 188); and, also like Bergson, Bradley's Absolute was the world of experience. Again like Bergson, this totality, in which all psychological states persist within one overall system of appearances, could not be comprehended conceptually because conceptual thought compartmentalised and broke up what was, in fact, a unified totality. According to Bradley, the procedures of scientific and rational understanding develop by connecting isolated phenomena within increasingly comprehensive explanatory schemes. Bradley argued, however, that such 'relational thought' was unable to grasp the ultimate reality of the Absolute because it was unable to encompass all the terms and relations which constitute reality and because relational thought was itself only a part of the Absolute (Passmore 1957: 66). The Absolute could be comprehended intuitively, however, through aesthetic or religious experience (Bradley 1914: 174). All of this is very close to Bergson, though Bradley did not make the distinction between feeling and intuition that Bergson had.

The presence of these ideas in the writings – particularly the early writings – of John Grierson has been covered extensively elsewhere, and so only a few examples will be given here. The distinction between rational understanding and generalised intuition is, for example, summed up in the distinction Grierson posited between the 'actual' and the 'real' which he made when referring to his 1929 film *Drifters*. Grierson argued that:

> The popular success of the film depends, I believe, on bringing the weight of the impersonal background (of the sea and the wind, of the gulls, the underwater and the boats) and giving it all the mystery, movement and size we know how to ... The fishing detail and the human detail should fit into this background and should not be allowed to take charge. (Aitken [1990] 2013: 107) In documentary we deal with the actual, and in that sense with the real. But the really real, if I may use that phrase, is something deeper than that. The only reality that counts in the end is the interpretation that is profound (109). [The camera] ... stirs the mind to most necessary wonder, it does it itself by picking out from the chaos of daily fact and daily happening, moments of size and strength and beauty, giving promise of that higher articulation in which the chaos of daily event is beauty itself. (110)

Grierson is concerned with intuitive experience here, and also with symbolic generalisation. In his early writings, he also referred to the Absolute, arguing that 'it . . . [the Absolute] . . . is yet different in kind from thought, and finally unattainable in thought' (44); and that 'the Absolute is not a logical harmony . . . it is supra-relational, beyond space and time' (44). Finally, following the intuitionist tenor of both Bergson and Bradley, Grierson asserts that 'philosophical enquiry is lower than the imaginative power of the poet and the prophet to reach God at the first leap' (44). Many other such examples could be given. All relate Grierson's early thought to the philosophical idealist education he received when young, and situate Grierson within the neo-Hegelian, neo-Kantian and phenomenological paradigms that influenced the other major realist film theorists.

CONCLUSIONS

Classical realist film theory: an intellectual reconstruction

This part of the introduction attempts to draw on the theoretical formulations just considered in order to develop a coherent theoretical model relating to both film and spectator which underlies and influences the ideas of the major realist film theorists. Below, these formulations are set out on the left, while a number of categories central to the concerns of classical cinematic realism are set out on the right. These are the categories of totality, the concrete, inde-terminacy, intuition, temporality and freedom. The objective is to see what emerges when these formulations and categories are placed in conjunction, what underlying intellectual matrix can be reconstructed from such conjunc-tion, and how such a matrix can be further developed into the coherent theo-retical model referred to:

Kant and Husserl (Kracauer)

• *Lebenswelt*	Immediate experience
• Harmony of the faculties	Totality
• *Naturschöne*	Indeterminate concrete
• Disinterestedness	Freedom
• Purposiveness without purpose	Order and freedom
• Film as 'nature-like'	Indeterminacy

Hegel (Lukács)

• *Geradesosein*	Concrete
• Concrete universal and micro-complex	Indeterminate totality
• Inherence	Indeterminate totality
• Sublation	Indeterminate totality
• *Lebendigkeit*	Indeterminate concrete

Bergson (Bazin)

• Duration	Indeterminate temporality
• Intuition	Intuitionism
• Double form of consciousness	Totality
• Dialectic of concrete and abstract	Indeterminate totality

Bradley (Grierson)
- Absolute   Totality
- Non-relational intuition   Intuitionist totality

Following the same approach as above, earlier sections of this introduction provide the following:
- Realism of intent   Experience and external reality
- Empirical adequacy   Concrete
- Representational realism   Experience and external reality
- Realism as a regulative conception   Experience and external reality
- The cut between inside and outside   Experience and external reality
- Intuitionist realism   Intuitionist concrete totality
- Set up interesting candidates for truth   Intuitionism
- Becoming instead of being   Indeterminate temporality
- Intuition of character of the *Lebenswelt*   Concrete intuitionism
- Indefinite objectivity   Intuitive indeterminacy
- *Stimmung*   Concrete indeterminacy
- Succession without distinction   Indeterminate temporality

What is clear from this is that there is little direct connection between classical realist film theory and philosophical representational realism, and, while representational realism is preoccupied with the relationship between experience and external reality, classical realist film theory is primarily concerned with experience only. Of all the major realist film theorists, the only one to attempt to theorise the relationship between representation and external reality is Lukács. This, however, still forms only a small part of *The Specificity of the Aesthetic*, which is primarily concerned with the relationship between aesthetic representation and experience. What this also makes apparent is the familiar gap between the analytical and continental traditions, a gap that stretches back in time to the bifurcation between philosophical idealism, with its emphasis on appearance, minds and ideas; and empiricism, with its emphasis on empirical verifiability. Bridging that gap may prove difficult, though such a bridge has been attempted here in relation to the notion that empirical adequacy and phenomenal plenitude 'bear down upon' unobservable external reality.

Turning to the intellectual matrix which underpins classical realist film theory, it appears that the most common trope to be found is that of indeterminate totality emerging through encounter with the empirical. And, though totality is clearly a common trope, it is indeterminacy that is the primary one. In contrast, the concrete per se is less so. Immediate experience also comes through less strongly, as does intuition, perhaps unsurprisingly, as classical realist film theory is not intuitionist per se, and attempts to link intuition and intellect together into an indeterminate totality accessed through the concrete, though with intuition playing the greater role. This raises the question as to what to *call* 'classical realist film theory'. The term 'classical' is incongruous, while, given the above, the phrase 'intuitionist realist film theory' no longer appears appropriate. Given the emphasis on experience here, perhaps 'experiential–realist film theory', or, better, 'phenomenalist–realist film theory'?

Phenomenalist–realist film theory and the consequences for film

This conclusions section will now end with a brief assessment of the consequences which the intellectual matrix outlined here has for both film and film spectator. The sort of film form and style predicated upon the thought of the major realist film theorists has been covered extensively elsewhere, and so will only be set out here in outline. Film, for example, should be 'nature-like' in terms of empirical density and indeterminacy, yet still contain some – limited – areas in which conceptualisation is employed. Empirical materials in the film will also provide the basis for the imagination to generate meanings which are ordered by the understanding. Such ordering can be constructed into the film as part of the film-making process but should be intangible enough to allow the spectator to employ her/his imagination and understanding in order to generate meaning. There should also be an inbuilt tendency within the film to seek harmony and wholeness at some level because this is related to totality but this, in turn, would not rule out the presence of contradiction at other levels. Film should also be mainly free from interest, not linked to purpose or intent, yet partake of the form of purposiveness, so that the understanding and imagination of the spectator interact in seeking an order which is explored but never definitely sought or discovered. Film is an essentially non-verbal medium which generates feeling that is intuited. This means that feelings, rather than ideas, should predominate. In terms of the *Lebenswelt*, the film should 'flow' and intersect with things in an organic-like manner, emphasising becoming, rather than being. The concern with appearance, experience and phenomena here also implies that film will be perceptually realistic in terms of the overall structure of the image but also fluid and impressionistic and, therefore, also modernist. One of Kracauer's favourite films, *Regen* (Joris Ivens, 1929), provides a good example here which also establishes that phenomenalist–realism need not be set against modernism. *Regen* is characterised by symphonic form, cutting on movement, an indeterminate, flowing interaction between rain and the city that the film portrays (Amsterdam), the use of special effects techniques, modernist form, montage editing, and an abundance of close-ups which create graphic design effects.

Such a style also encompasses types of symbolic and 'magic' realism, epitomised by the idea of the 'dialectic of the concrete and abstract' and the 'concrete universal'. Examples here might be the so-called 'sensibilist' strand of West German and German cinema, including the films of Wim Wenders and Werner Herzog. Herzog's *Aguire, The Wrath of God* (1972) provides an example with its focus on the visuality and detail of the image and scene and less focus on plot and script. Herzog's film is also characterised by loose narrative structures, improvised and minimal dialogue and an emphasis on the immediacy of experience. There is also an attempt to emphasise the physicality of nature and perception with location shooting focusing on the surrounding natural environment. Other strategies found include the pronounced use of music to evoke atmosphere, suspension of narrative, and presence of surreal imagery which denies explanation via cause and effect. There is also a generally contemplative attitude and fluidity of camerawork and imagery which accord with a phenomenalist–realist approach. Herzog's film is selected at random here, and other, similar films are discussed elsewhere in this anthology.

Phenomenalist–realist film theory and the consequences for the film spectator

The form of spectatorship involved in watching a film which embodies the central tropes of phenomenalist–realist film theory has been indicated through quotes taken from Dewey and Kracauer earlier in this introduction, and involves an immersion within the materiality of the audio-image. Encounter with the vibrant concrete heightens the sensory experience of the spectator and induces a phenomenological experience. But, beyond such heightening, is there additional inherent value in such an experience? To address this question it will be necessary to turn once more to Husserl and, specifically, to the conception of the *Lebenswelt* found in late works such as *The Crisis of European Sciences* (1936). Of course, there are other dimensions to Husserl's thought, and different conceptions of the *Lebenswelt* found in his work (Christensen, in Luft and Overgaard 2012: 211). It is, however, the late conception of the *Lebenswelt* that will be considered here.

That conception entails conceiving of the 'world' as an existential phenomenal field of appearances which the observer experiences at any one moment. Husserl refers to this as the 'horizon' of phenomenal being within which the conscious human being persists. According to Husserl, the conscious being is always conscious *of* something and that something is, at the most fundamental level, the horizon constituted by the phenomenal field and things perceived as occurring within that field (Stewart and Mickunas 1990: 45). The ultimate or most primal human experience is, therefore, this consciousness of the phenomenal field and that within it. To use the well-known phenomenological construct: 'Consciousness is always consciousness of . . .' where the ellipsis stands for something occurring within the phenomenal horizon. This formulation also, therefore, links consciousness to the world to form a phenomenological realism because, without this phenomenal world, consciousness would not be possible, would be only of a void – nothingness rather than being. The 'world is not only the correlate of consciousness but that without which there would be no consciousness'. There is, therefore, *no division* between the subject and the world, and both are the 'givens of concrete experience which can only be separated by a process of abstraction' (64–5). Husserlian phenomenology does not deny the existence of a reality external to the world of appearance but merely leaves the question aside in order to focus on the world of appearance, and, here:

> To make the world appear as phenomenon is to understand that the being of the world is no longer its existence or its reality, but its meaning, and that this meaning of the world resides in the fact that it is a *cogitum* . . . [an object/target of consciousness] . . . intended by the *cogito* . . . [literally, 'the thinker', but here the 'conscious being'] . . . [as something that a particular consciousness has become conscious of]. (10)

The *Lebenswelt*, the phenomenal horizon of the perceiving consciousness is, therefore, a basic 'given':

> a realm of self-evidences. That which is self-evidently given is, in per-ception, experienced as 'the thing itself', in immediate presence, or in memory remembered as the thing itself. There is a need to bring to recognition the primal validity of these self-evidences . . . the ultimately accomplishing life, the life in which the self-evident givenness of the life-world forever has, has attained, and attains anew, its prescientific ontic meaning [ontic – that which relates to being] . . . the path leads back here, to the primal self-evidence in which the life-world is ever pregiven. (Moran and Mooney 2006: 167)

To focus attention reflectively on this ultimate human reality of being con-scious of something within the phenomenal field is to grasp that ultimate reality meaningfully instead of overlooking it through adherence to scientific abstraction or distracted purpose (Stewart and Mickunas 1990: 23), and what is involved here is a kind of *philosophical* attention to the 'primal validity of these self-evidences' in which the world is 'ever pregiven' (Moran and Mooney 2006: 167). What Husserl refers to as the 'natural concept of the world', or 'natural attitude' to the world, always exists as the basic characteristic of the life-world, and can be returned to (Christensen, in Luft and Overgaard 2012: 211). In fact, in Husserl's late work the 'natural attitude' becomes synonymous with the *Lebenswelt*: a world in which we actually exist, and which we can reflect on (Sobchack 1992: 35) – a notion that is also commonly found in the writings of Kracauer.

It may, therefore be, that, at the heart of the phenomenalist–realist film theory emanating from the major realist film theorists there is a hope that each film image or scene may function as a lens which establishes a horizon of phenomena that encourages the spectator to then focus on and return to the 'primal validity' of the 'self-evidences' in which the world is 'ever pregiven'. That pregivenness also encompasses the fundamental unity of consciousness and the 'world', and this also entails a source of utopian fulfilment which film might facilitate. Husserl asks that this ultimate human reality be brought to recognition, and it is not surprising that the major realist film theorists believed that film, as a primarily visual-auditory medium, would be able to bring such, or similar, recognition about. The shift which occurred from Husserlian to existentialist phenomenology from the late nineteenth to mid-twentieth centuries also brings an additional level to this. The idea that consciousness is intentional – always consciousness of something, and directed towards something by the *cogito* – was taken further within existentialism to emphasise the free intentionality of being-in-the-world (Stewart and Mickunas: 1990: 64). This shift from the notion of consciousness *facing* the *Lebenswelt* to the idea of it *being-in-the-world/Lebenswelt* as embodied consciousness, also shifts the focus in the sort of film being considered here from the phenomenal field to figures moving within that field: to characters being *in* the world and acting against a surrounding context which they influence and which influences them. Here, the film would become more person oriented, rather than world oriented. This also points to a difference of accent within the major realist film theorists, with Kracauer emphasising the portrayal of the *Lebenswelt*, and Bazin and Lukács that of embodied consciousness and being-in-the-world. This is not a fundamental difference, however, only one of emphasis, and not one that affects the overall phenomenalist–realist paradigm constituted by the theories of the major realist film theorists.

That paradigm is also principally theorised at a humanist level and relates to the spectator's response to the manifest image of the *Lebenswelt*. This is a universal spectator, though also a modern spectator: one shaped by the various forces of modernity. What is left out here are, therefore, social, gender and other mediations. It is undeniably the case that this is the approach adopted by the major realist film theorists. Any film based on a phenomenalist–realist – and particularly an existentialist phenomenalist–realist approach – would, however, contain characters and stories constructed in terms of social position, race, gender, age, ethnicity, psychological make-up, and so on. A phenomenalist–realist film could not rule out such a make-up, one which would, however, be bracketed by the phenomenal horizon and 'being-in' that horizon.

Finally, it should be clear that, while this introduction has attempted to cover a good deal, it has not been able to cover all that matters sufficiently.

Two principle areas, in particular, stand out as in need of further attention. The first is the relationship between realist film theory and the analytical tradition of philosophy. The second relates to the use of some of the underlying conceptual formulations considered here in reassessment of the *particular* ideas of the major realist film theorists: aspects of *Theory of Film*, for example, viewed in detail through the lens of the Kantian notion of disinterestedness, or the Hegelian notion of the concrete universal. These areas of further enquiry will require a future monograph.

NOTE

1. I have already covered some of what follows in the next few pages in previous publications. It will be necessary to go over this ground again, however, to connect it more clearly to the subsequent sections of this introduction.

REFERENCES

Aitken, Ian (1998), *The Documentary Film Movement: An Anthology*, Edinburgh: Edinburgh University Press.
— (summer 1998), 'Kracauer and Surrealism', *Screen*, 39: 2, pp. 124–40.
— (2001), *European Film Theory and Cinema: A Critical Introduction*, Edinburgh: Edinburgh University Press.
— (2006), *Realist Film Theory and Cinema: The Nineteenth-Century Lukácsian and Intuitionist Realist Traditions*, Manchester: Manchester University Press.
— (2007), 'Physical Reality: The Role of the Empirical in the Film Theory of Siegfried Kracauer, John Grierson, André Bazin and Georg Lukács', *Studies in Documentary Film*, 1: 2, pp. 105–21.
— (2012), *Lukácsian Film Theory and Cinema: A Study of Georg Lukács' Writings on Film, 1913–71*, Manchester: Manchester University Press.
— [1990] (2013), *Film and Reform: John Grierson and the Documentary Film Movement*, London: Routledge.
Andrew, Dudley (1976), *The Major Film Theories: An Introduction*, Oxford: Oxford University Press.
— (1990), *André Bazin*, New York and Oxford: Columbia University Press.
Andrew, Dudley and Joubert-Laurencin, Herve (2011) (eds), *Opening Bazin: Post-War Film Theory and its Afterlife*, Oxford and New York: Oxford University Press.
Bazin, André (1958–62) *Qu'est-ce que le cinéma?*, volumes une–quatre, Paris: Éditions du Cerf.
— (1967), *What is Cinema?*, Volume I, Berkeley, CA and Los Angeles, CA: University of California Press.
— (1972), *What Is Cinema?*, Volume II, Berkeley, CA and Los Angeles, CA: University of California Press.
— 'Le mystère Picasso', *Qu'est-ce que le cinéma?*, volume deux, pp. 133–42.
Beardsley, Monroe, C. (1981), *Aesthetics: Problems in the Philosophy of Criticism*, Indianapolis, IN: Hackett Publishing Company Inc.

Bergson, Henri [1889] (1971), *Time and Free Will: An Essay on the Immediate Data of Consciousness*, London: G. Allen & Unwin.

— [1907] (2007), *Creative Evolution*, London: Palgrave Macmillan.

— [1946] (2010), *The Creative Mind: An Introduction to Metaphysics*, New York: Dover Publications Inc.

Bradley, F. H. (1914), *Essays on Truth and Reality*, London: Clarendon Press.

Cardullo, Bert (summer 2001), 'A Bergsonian Film: The Picasso Mystery by André Bazin', *Journal of Aesthetic Education*, 35: 2, pp. 1–9.

— (2011) (ed.) *André Bazin and Italian Neorealism*, London: Continuum.

Collinson, Diane (1994), 'Aesthetic Experience', in Hanfling, Oswald (ed.), *Philosophical Aesthetics: An Introduction*, Oxford: Blackwell, pp. 111–78.

Christensen, Carleton B. (2012), 'The World', in Luft, Sebastian and Overgaard, Søren (eds), *The Routledge Companion to Phenomenology*, London and New York: Routledge, pp. 211–21.

Conant, James (1992), 'Introduction' in Putnam, Hilary, *Realism with a Human Face*, Cambridge, MA and London: Harvard University Press, pp. xv–lxxiv.

Desmond, William (1986), *Art and the Absolute: A Study of Hegel's Aesthetics*, New York: State University of New York Press.

Devitt, Michael (1997), *Realism and Truth*, Princeton, NJ: Princeton University Press.

Ellis, Jack, C. (2000), *John Grierson: Life, Contributions, Influence*, Carbondale, IL: Southern Illinois University Press.

Engels, Friedrich [1885] (1977), 'Letter to Minna Kautsky', in Craig, David (ed.), *Marxists on Literature: An Anthology*, Harmondsworth: Penguin Books, pp. 267–8.

Ginsberg, Terri, and Thompson, Kirsten Moana (1996) (eds), *Perspectives on German Cinema*, New York: G. K. Hall & Co.

Hallam, Julia, with Marshment, Margaret (2000), *Realism and Popular Culture*, Manchester: Manchester University Press.

Hanfling, Oswald (1994), *Philosophical Aesthetics: An Introduction*, Oxford: Blackwell.

Hesse, Mary (1980), 'The New Empiricism', in Morick, Harold (ed.), *Challenges to Empiricism*, London: Methuen, pp. 208–29.

Hillier, J. and Lovell, A. (1972), *Studies in Documentary*, London: Secker and Warburg.

Husserl, Edmund [1936] (1970), *The Crisis of European Sciences and Transcendental Phenomenology: An Introduction to Phenomenological Philosophy*, trans. David Carr, Evanston, IL: Northwestern University Press.

— [1936] (2002), 'The Way into Phenomenological Transcendental Philosophy by Inquiring back from the Pregiven Life-World', in Moran, Dermot and Mooney, Timothy (eds), *The Phenomenology Reader*, London and New York: Routledge, pp. 151–74.

Ilyenkov, E. V. (2008), *The Dialectics of the Abstract and Concrete in Marx's Capital*, Delhi: Aakar Books.

Kadarkay, Arpad (1991), *Georg Lukács: Life, Thought and Politics*, Cambridge, MA: Basil Blackwell Inc.

Kolakowski, Leszek (1978), *Main Currents of Marxism*, Volume Three: *The Breakdown*, Oxford: Clarendon Press.

Kracauer, Siegfried [1946] (1974), *From Caligari to Hitler: A Psychological History of the German Film*, Princeton, NJ: Princeton University Press.

— [1968] (1995), *History: The Last Things before the Last*, Princeton, NJ: Markus Wiener Publishers.

— [1927] (1995a), *The Mass Ornament, Weimar Essays*, Cambridge, MA and London: Harvard University Press.

— [1960] (1997), *Theory of Film: The Redemption of Physical Reality*, Princeton, NJ: Princeton University Press.

— [1930] (1998), *The Salaried Masses: Duty and Distraction in Weimar Germany*, London and New York: Verso.

Lovell, Alan (1980), in Macpherson, D. (ed.), *British Cinema: Traditions of Independence*, London: British Film Institute, p. 18.

Lukács, Georg (10 September 1913), 'Thoughts Towards an Aesthetic of the Cinema', Frankfurt: *Frankfurter Zeitung und Handelsblatt*.

— (1981), *The Specificity of the Aesthetic*, Berlin and Weimar: Aufbau-Verlag.

— (1982), *The Ontology of Social Being*, Volume One: *Hegel*, London: Merlin Press.

Macpherson, D. (ed.) (1980), *British Cinema: Traditions of Independence*, London: British Film Institute.

Margulies, Ivone (ed.) (2003), *Rites of Realism: Essays on Corporeal Cinema*, Durham, NC and London: Duke University Press.

Moran, Dermot and Mooney, Timothy (eds) (2002), *The Phenomenology Reader*, London and New York: Routledge.

Morick, Harold (ed.) (1980), *Challenges to Empiricism*, London: Methuen.

Nagib, Lúcia (2011), *World Cinema and the Ethics of Realism*, London: Continuum.

Nagib, Lúcia and Mello, Cecillia (eds) (2009), *Realism and the Audiovisual Media*, London: Palgrave Macmillan.

Parkinson, G. R. H (1970) (ed.), *Georg Lukács: The Man, His Work and His Ideas*, New York: Random House.

Parkinson, G. R. H (1970), 'Lukács on the Central Category of Aesthetics', in Parkinson (ed.), pp. 109–46.

Passmore, John (1967), *A Hundred Years of Philosophy*, Harmondsworth: Penguin Books.

— (1985), *Recent Philosophers: A Supplement to A Hundred Years of Philosophy*, London: Duckworth.

— (1991), *Recent Philosophers*, London: Duckworth.

Pearson, Keith, Ansell (2007), 'Introduction', in Bergson, Henri, *Creative Evolution*, Basingstoke: Palgrave Macmillan.

Petro, Patrice, 'Kracauer's Epistemological Shift', in Ginsberg, Terri, and Thompson, Kirsten Moana (1996) (eds), *Perspectives on German Cinema*, New York: G. K. Hall & Co.

Putnam, Hilary (1981), *Reason, Truth and History*, Cambridge: Cambridge University Press.

— (1987), *The Many Faces of Realism*, New York: Open Court.

— (1992), *Realism with a Human Face*, Cambridge, MA and London: Harvard University Press.

Rescher, N. (1973), *Conceptual Idealism*, Oxford: Blackwell.

Rosen, Philip (2003), 'History of Image, Image of History: Subject and Ontology in Bazin', in Margulies (ed.), pp. 42–79.

Russell, Bertrand (1965), *A History of Western Philosophy*, London: George Allen & Unwin.

Sobchack, Vivian (1992), *The Address of the Eye: A Phenomenology of Film Experience*, Princeton, NJ: Princeton University Press.

Stam, R. and Flitterman-Lewis, Sandy (1992), *New Vocabularies in Film Semiotics: Structuralism, Post-structuralism and Beyond*, London and New York: Routledge.

Stewart, David and Mickunas, Algis (1974), *Exploring Phenomenology: A Guide to the Field and its Literature*, Columbus, OH: Ohio University Press.

Trigg, Roger (1989), *Reality at Risk: A Defence of Realism in Philosophy and the Sciences*, New York and London: Harvester Wheatsheaf.

CHAPTER I

Displaced Vision: The Politics of Realism in Kracauer and Kluge[1]

Tara Forrest

The motive for realism is never the confirmation of reality but protest.
(Alexander Kluge)

In the *Poetikvorlesungen* (Poetics Lectures) he delivered in Frankfurt in 2012, Alexander Kluge argued that the Frankfurt School tradition of Critical Theory 'works with an antagonistic conception of realism' (Kluge 2013). Kluge himself, who is best known outside Germany as a founding member of the New German Cinema, is a contemporary heir to that tradition. As a young lawyer, he served as the legal counsel for the Institute for Social Research which fostered the work of scholars associated with the Frankfurt School including Theodor W. Adorno, Max Horkheimer, Walter Benjamin and Siegfried Kracauer. Kluge's experimental film, television and literary productions bear the traces of his intimate involvement with both Adorno and Benjamin's work. On the question of realism – and cinematic realism in particular – a connection can also be drawn between Kluge's writings on film and those of Kracauer. While little has been written on the important affinities between their conceptions of the task of cinematic realism, it is clear that both Kracauer's and Kluge's writings in this field are concerned with the role that a realist film practice can play in displacing the spectator's vision and, in the process, prompting them to engage with their environment from a rejuvenated perspective. Focusing on Kracauer's *Theory of Film: The Redemption of Physical Reality* (Kracauer [1960] 1997) and on Kluge's writings on the political promise of an 'antagonistic' realist aesthetic, this chapter will explore the role that a realist film practice could play in facilitating a mode of perception and experience that challenges the viewer's previously held conceptions about the material world.

THE PHOTOGRAPHIC GAZE OF THE CAMERA

Both Kracauer and Kluge draw a distinction between two different types of reality. The first, which Kracauer describes as 'conventional' (Kracauer 1997: 48) is characterised by a sense of abstraction insofar as it is an image of reality which is shaped not by reality itself but by values and desires of a particular ideological bent. Ideology, Kracauer states, functions as a veil which 'delimit[s] our horizon' (296) because it conceals from our gaze the multiple possibilities inherent within reality itself. This reality (which is variously described in *Theory of Film* as 'nature', 'physical reality', 'material reality', 'physical existence' and 'actuality') is the 'reality' of the book's subtitle. Its contours are neither defined nor predetermined by ideology. Rather it is a reality which is rich in possibility because it is 'unstaged', 'indeterminate' and 'open-ended' (60, 68, 71).

The basic premise of *Theory of Film* is that the photographic media (and film in particular) are uniquely placed to 'record and reveal physical reality' (28). In the preface to the book, Kracauer argues that his analysis of the possibilities of the medium is based on 'the assumption that film is essentially an extension of photography and therefore shares with the medium a marked affinity for the visible world around us' (xlix). For Kracauer, this affinity is born out of what he describes as the camera's 'inherent realistic tendency' (5); that is, its capacity – in the role of an 'indiscriminating mirror' (15) – to both sidestep the abstraction of ideology and extend our vision beyond the realm of subjective intention. In doing so, he argues that the camera 'renders visible what we did not, or perhaps even could not see before its advent' (300).

A key figure for Kracauer's thinking in this regard is Marcel Proust whose analysis of the alienating effects of photography in *In Search of Lost Time* had an important impact on Kracauer's understanding of the camera's capacity to transcend human vision. The passage to which Kracauer refers most frequently appears in Volume 3 of the book and revolves around the narrator Marcel's chance encounter with his grandmother who – 'absorbed in thoughts in her drawing room' – is unaware that her grandson has arrived home (Proust 1996: 155). Upon entering the room, Marcel – not having anticipated his grandmother's presence – is transformed into a 'spectator of [his] own absence' whose alienated view of the scene is akin to that of a 'stranger', a 'witness', or a 'photographer' (155–6). As the narrator makes clear:

The process that mechanically occurred in my eyes when I saw my grandmother was indeed a photograph. We never see the people who are dear to us save in the animated system, the perpetual motion of our incessant love for them, which before allowing the images that their faces present to reach us, seizes them in its vortex, flings them back upon the idea we have always had of them, makes them adhere to it, coincide with it. [. . .] I, for whom my grandmother was still myself, I who had never seen her save in my soul, always at the same place in the past through the transparent sheets of contiguous, overlapping memories, suddenly in our drawing room which formed part of a new world, that of time, saw, sitting on the sofa, beneath the lamp, red-faced, heavy and common, sick, lost in thought, following the lines of a book with eyes that seemed hardly sane, a dejected old woman whom I did not know. (cited in Kracauer 1997: 14)

As Kracauer's analysis of this passage makes clear, this experience of aliena-tion (and, by extension, photographic alienation more generally) is produc-tive because it allows the narrator to view the scene as it 'really is, not as he imagines [or remembers it] to be' (109). Reality, in this sense, is shaped neither by memory nor by ideology. Rather, the 'photographic' gaze of the camera produces an image independent of 'ego-involved frames of refer-ence' (Kracauer 1996: 84). As Kracauer makes clear, what is significant about these images is the degree to which they bypass ingrained habits of thinking by engaging the spectator on a sensorial rather than an intellectual level: 'We literally redeem this world from its dormant state [. . .] by endeavouring to experience it through the camera' (300). While Kracauer is not suggesting that all films function in this manner, in *Theory of Film* he provides an overview of the history of the medium that explores how and with what effects the radical promise of realist cinema has been undermined by film-makers who have shaped reality for ideological and/or strictly narrative ends.

THE 'SUGGESTIVE INDETERMINACY' OF REALIST FILM

In *Theory of Film* Kracauer argues that the history of the medium is marked by a split between 'formative' and 'realist' tendencies which can be traced back to the beginnings of cinema and, more specifically, to the divergent conceptions of the possibilities of the medium embodied in the films of Georges Méliès and the Lumière brothers. For Kracauer, the films of the Lumières are '[d]etached records' (31) that, as per Proust's delineation of Marcel's unexpected encoun-ter with his grandmother, alienate the viewer from habitual modes of engaging with the world around them. In contrast, Kracauer argues that Méliès's films revolve around the creation of illusion and fantasy because they are based upon 'imagined events' and 'fairy-tale plots' that bear little resemblance to reality (32).

This distinction – between film-makers who seek to 'exhibit and penetrate reality for its own sake' (69) and those who employ the camera in aid of the construction of a fictional story – is not limited to a discussion of early cinema. Rather it forms the basis of Kracauer's analysis of the realist/cinematic and formative/theatrical camps into which he divides the history of the medium. As he makes clear, the shortcomings of the latter can be illuminated, in part, by Proust's analysis of the affinity between the reductive nature of everyday perception and the limitations of classical tragedy. As Marcel reflects in a passage via which Proust extrapolates on this connection: 'our eye, charged with thought, neglects, as would a classical tragedy, every image that does not contribute to the action of the play and retains only those that may help to make its purpose intelligible' (Proust cited in Kracauer 1997: 216). In *Theory of Film*, Kracauer argues that formative/theatrical film functions in a similar manner because it generates a distorted image of reality that is built around 'a whole with a purpose' (221). As such, it is divorced from the 'suggestive indeterminacy' of 'camera reality' and thus runs counter to the promise and capacities of the medium (71).

In contrast, films that fall into the 'realist/cinematic' camp capture 'aspects of physical reality with a view to making us experience them' (40). It is, Kracauer writes, 'the experience of things in their concreteness' (296) which serves as a remedy for ideological abstraction. Unlike the tightly organised structure of formative/theatrical films, the realist film practice for which he argues is 'permeable' (254) to environmental phenomena such as 'buildings', 'trees', 'undulating waves', 'passers-by', 'moving clouds' and 'inanimate objects'(27 and 120) that are not subservient to the telling of a story. He claims, for example, that the magnified images revealed by close-ups, in particular, play an important role in disclosing 'hidden aspects of the world about us' (49): '[T]hey cast their spell over the spectator, impressing upon him the magic of a leaf or the energies which lie dormant in a piece of cloth' (280). While cinematic films will not 'exhaust themselves in depicting these phenomena' (271), the film practice Kracauer privileges allows the material world to speak to the viewer on its own terms. Paraphrasing Walter Benjamin, Kracauer argues that the significance of such images lies in the extent to which they 'blow up our environment in a double sense: they enlarge it literally; and in doing so, they blast the prison of conventional reality, opening up expanses which we have explored at best in dreams before' (48).[2]

As Kracauer is keen to point out, however, this radical capacity is thwarted by the emphasis placed by the theatrical film on the development of dialogue and character. What troubles him, in particular, about this emphasis is the degree to which '[i]t opens up the region of discursive reasoning, enabling the medium to impart the turns and twists of sophisticated thought, all those rational or poetic communications which [because they] do not depend on pictorialisation to be grasped and appreciated' are not only 'alien to' but also fail to engage the capacities of the medium (104 and 223). Referring again to

In Search of Lost Time, Kracauer argues that the 'patterns of meaning' generated by dialogue, in particular, 'are much in the nature of the loving memories which Proust's narrator retains of his grandmother [. . .] Evoked through language, these patterns assume a reality of their own, a self-sufficient mental reality which, once established in the film, interferes with the photographic reality to which the camera aspires.' (104)

In *Theory of Film*, a more productive relationship between image and sound is illustrated via a memory which Kracauer recounts of attending a cinema in which the screening of silent films was regularly accompanied by a drunken pianist who 'was so completely immersed in himself that he did not waste a single glance on the screen' (137). 'Sometimes', Kracauer writes,

> he improvised freely, as if prompted by a desire to express the vague memories and ever-changing moods which the alcohol stirred in him; on other occasions he was in such a stupor that he played a few popular melodies over and over again, mechanically adorning them with glittering runs and quavers. So it was by no means uncommon that gay tunes would sound when, in a film I watched, the indignant Count turned his adulterous wife out of the house, and that a funeral march would accompany their ultimate reconciliation. (137)

What appeals to Kracauer about the experience of disjunction generated by this lack of affinity between the musical accompaniment and the image on screen is the degree to which it shrouds the film in a veil of 'indeterminacy' – a realist quality ordinarily stamped out by the formativist aspirations of much narrative-oriented cinema. In contrast to the 'utilitarian' structure of the formative/theatrical film, the realist film practice for which Kracauer argues would be organised around the inclusion of images 'not yet stripped of their multiple meanings, shots still able to release their psychological correspondences' (69). The director, he states, must 'alienate these elements – shots, or combinations of shots, of environmental phenomena – from any preconceived meaning, so that each of them may exert its own independent impact' (Kracauer 1996: 87). For Kracauer, what is significant about this 'suggestive indeterminacy' (Kracauer 1997: 71) is the degree to which it prompts the viewers to form their own connections and associations with the 'unstaged reality' presented on screen (60). Such shots, he writes, 'function as an ignition spark' that 'touch[es] off chain reactions in the moviegoer – a flight of associations which no longer revolve around their original source but arise from his agitated inner environment' (165). For Kracauer,

> [t]he salient point here is that these discoveries [. . .] mean an increased demand on the spectator's physiological make-up. The unknown shapes

he encounters involve not so much his power of reasoning as his visceral faculties. Arousing his innate curiosity, they lure him into dimensions where sense impressions are all-important. (158–9)

ANTAGONISTIC REALISM – KLUGE

This emphasis on the relationship between the generation of indeterminacy and a sensorially charged mode of engagement is also central to Alexander Kluge's analysis of the role that a realist film practice might play in facilitating a mode of perception and experience that encourages viewers to engage with their environment from a rejuvenated perspective. The films for which Kluge argues are described as 'antagonistic' because they are pitted against the pervasive idea that the reality in which we live – as both experienced by people on an everyday basis and represented by the mainstream media – accurately reflects the wealth of possibilities inherent within existing circumstances. Within this schema, the edict commonly espoused by politicians – that, when reflecting on politics, policy and the possibilities of the future, one must, in fact, be *realistic* – is indebted to a conception of realism committed to the maintenance of the status quo. 'Public opinion', Kluge argues, 'is very strongly determined by people who [. . .] furnish themselves in reality as if in a tank or a knigh's armour' (Phillip 2000: 10). As this statement makes clear, this hegemonic conception of realism (of what it means to *be realistic*) is, for Kluge, extremely limiting, not only because it functions to protect the interests of those who employ it as both shield and weapon but also because it disregards the 'subjunctive' realities that 'exist side by side with reality' that are born out of the feelings and wishes of people who actually 'want something completely different' (Laudenbach 2012). For Kluge, these subjunctive realities are significant because, as alternative visions of what could be, they play an important role in animating thought, discussion and debate about how and with what effects the so-called reality in which we live could be transformed into something very different.

As Kluge makes clear, it is this capacity for interrogating reality – for actively imagining alternatives to the status quo – that constitutes a truly realistic approach, an approach that is fuelled by a dissatisfaction with, and a desire to protest against, the prevailing conditions. 'If', he writes, 'I levy a protest against the reality principle, against that which this reality does to me, I am realistic' (Kluge 1999a: 229). It is thus not the reality principle but 'the realism of the human brain with its reshaping reaction to reality' that is 'the fundamental condition of realism' (Kluge 2012: 190). This condition has, however, been undermined by the emphasis placed on the importance of being 'realistic', of channelling one's energies and confining one's hopes to activities and goals that are recognised by, and sit comfortably within, the paradigm supporting and maintaining the status quo. In a similar vein to Kracauer, Kluge argues that reality (in this restrictive sense) is not a 'natural state' which exists autonomously outside the subject (Kluge 1999a: 229). On the contrary, he claims that it is manifested in a mode of thinking which has been imposed on the subject via ideology, an ideology so pervasive that it has overridden the instinctive capacity – inherent in our feelings – for distinguishing not only between right and wrong but also between that which works for or against our own interests.[3] Extending the metaphors described above, the reality principle functions, in this context, as a tank or suit of armour that inhibits feeling because it seals off the subject and anaesthetises it from the capacity to make connections and draw distinctions that are grounded in the experiences of the subject.

THE 'ANTI-REALISM OF FEELINGS'

The realist film practice for which Kluge argues is driven by a desire to motivate feelings, to break through the ideological straitjacket imposed by the reality principle in an attempt to facilitate possibilities for cultural and political change. As Kluge makes clear, the guiding assumption of the reality principle – that, when making plans and forming decisions, one must *be realistic* – is bolstered by a system of reasoning completely divorced from the knowledge of the senses. 'The whole culture industry', he states, 'is busy persuading people to divide their senses and their consciousness'; to not 'interest themselves in the elementary basis of their awareness, in their way of observing, in their sensuality' (Dawson 1977: 37). Kracauer, too, states something very similar when he notes that, however 'conscious' we may be of the world around us, 'we have not yet experienced it emotionally'. 'There is', he argues, 'a gap between our consciousness and our senses which demands to be filled' (Kracauer 1996: 91).

For Kluge, the instinctive function of feelings – that can distinguish intuitively between something which is fair and unjust, between that which is disturbing and pleasing – has the potential to protest against a form of reality that generates fear, unhappiness and suffering. Kluge describes this elementary, albeit undervalued, capacity as the 'anti-realism of feelings' (Laudenbach and Kluge 2009). It can, he argues, be stimulated by the experimental form of realist cinema, the significance of which, as Kracauer makes clear, lies in its capacity 'to open up new, hitherto unsuspected dimensions of reality' (Kracauer 1997: 8). For Kluge, the method governing the construction of realist film is based on a conception of 'realism that takes the imagination and wishes of human beings just as seriously as the world of facts' (Kluge 1999b: 59). A 'materialist' film practice, he argues, does not seek to impose its ideas on the viewers but rather encourages them to draw on their own experience and imagination in order to participate autonomously in the meaning-making process. As Kluge points out: 'We call this position materialist because it thinks from the bottom up, from the spectator and the cinema in his mind, to the cinema on screen' (Dawson 1977: 33–4). Meaning, in this context, is not conveyed directly by, nor contained autonomously within, the film itself. Rather, it is generated by a process of exchange between the viewers and the film that is initiated but not foreclosed by the director. Such a film practice seeks neither to explain nor to generate understanding. 'Understanding a film is', Kluge writes, 'conceptual imperialism which colonises its objects. If I have understood everything then something has been emptied out. We must make films that thoroughly oppose such imperialism of consciousness' (Kluge 2012b: 38).

According to Kluge, both Hollywood cinema and conventional documentary film are incongruous with this materialist/realist model. What troubles him about the former is the 'strict separation' that exists between films that are organised around generating entertainment and the experiences of viewers watching them (Liebman 1988: 27). 'Excite the viewer, but there can't be any consequences' is, he notes, one of the 'guiding principle[s] of the entertainment industry in Hollywood' (Kluge, cited in Kluge, Alexandra 1977: 96).[4] Instead of taking the audience seriously as 'co-producers' who participate in the meaning-making process, Kluge argues that the narrative-driven structure of Hollywood cinema encourages the 'audience to give up their own experience and follow the more organised experience of the film' (Dawson 1977: 34). Instead of relying on, and/or cultivating, the viewer's capacity to draw distinctions, their refined form channels the viewer's feelings in specific directions, leaving the audience with scant opportunity to reflect on, and/or think autonomously about, the issues and ideas at hand.

If Kluge is also wary of conventional documentary film, it is because he has little faith in one of its defining tenets: that is, that the camera is able to provide the viewer with a truthful re-presentation of reality. In stark contrast to Kracauer's delineation of the alienated image of reality facilitated by the so-called objective eye of the camera, Kluge (following Bertolt Brecht) argues that documentary realism is incapable of capturing reality because the camera 'can only photograph something that's present' (Dawson 1977: 35):

On the subject of realism, Brecht says: Of what use is an exterior view of the AEG if I cannot see what is going on inside the building in terms of relationships, wage labour, capital, international investments – a photograph of the AEG says nothing about the AEG itself. Thus, as Brecht says, most of the real conditions have slipped into the functional. This is the heart of the problem of realism. If I conceive of realism as the knowledge of relationships [*eine Kenntnis von Zusammenhänge*], then I must provide a trope for what cannot be shown in the film, for what the camera cannot record. (Kluge 2012b: 46)

These 'relationships' or '*Zusammenhänge*' (which can also be described as 'interconnections') refer not only, as per Brecht's example, to the alienated labour conditions and financial affiliations rendered invisible by the camera's so-called 'objective' re-presentation of reality but also to the viewer's capacity to draw distinctions and form connections that are grounded in the experience of the subject. As Kluge makes clear, '[m]ere documentation forecloses *Zusammenhang*' (that is, the context and/or capacity for interconnection). '[O]bjectivity', he adds, 'does not exist without emotions, actions and desires, that is, without the eyes and the senses of the people involved' (Kaes 2012: 105).

For Kracauer, too, the image of reality generated by a realist film practice is productive insofar as it facilitates an active, sensorially charged mode of engagement. In contrast, however, to Kluge's critique of the so-called 'objective' eye of the camera, Kracauer argues that the rejuvenated mode of perception cultivated by realist film is facilitated by the camera's status as an 'indiscriminating mirror' (Kracauer 1997: 15), that is, its capacity to capture an image of the world that exists beyond the realm of subjective intention. Kluge's approach, on the other hand, is very different in the sense that he relies not on the so-called objective eye of the camera but on montage to stimulate the senses and, in the process, both to complicate and undermine the reality effect generated by the refined, organised and conventional structure of much narrative and documentary cinema. In contrast to the harmonious structure he associates with Hollywood film, the experimental form of Kluge's work generates contrast, ambiguity and tension that isn't easily resolved. The key device employed by Kluge, in this regard, is the mixed form according to which his films are constructed; an experimental aesthetic that consists of both documentary and fictional material that is either shot specifically for the film in question or gleaned from various sources including newsreels, books, paintings, photographs, drawings and early cinema. In contrast to the divide Kracauer draws between the work of Méliès and Lumière, Kluge dissolves the traditional distinction between documentary and fictional film. By mixing black-and-white and colour footage, and by editing it together with intertitles, quotes, photographs, diagrams and pictures, Kluge generates a series of contrasts and connections that disrupt the 'unequivocal picture of reality' produced by both documentary and fictional film (Deuber-Mankowsky and Schiesser 2012: 355). For Kluge, this mixed aesthetic generates a more realistic representation of reality because the complex nature of the world it depicts challenges the idea that the reality in which we live is somehow immutable or set in stone.

In a similar vein to Kracauer's delineation of the sensorially engaged specta-torial relationship facilitated by realist film, Kluge's montage practice does not seek to channel or close down meaning but to stimulate the viewer's capacity to draw their own connections, associations and ideas. 'We do not', he states, 'fashion the associations of the viewers, that is what Hollywood does, we do not channel them at all, but we stimulate them, so that something independent comes into being, something which without these incentives, would not have been actualised' (Kluge in Lewandowski 1980: 36). This independent 'third image' (which is manifested not in the film itself but rather in the head of the spectator watching it)[5] is not an obvious association generated by two images that have been edited together to produce a connection conceived in advance by the director. 'We are not', Kluge states:

> the god over the materials. We do not provide a red thread to lead them through the film the way that straightforward narratives do. [. . .] It requires another way of being involved. It's as if you are walking down the street and are looking in the windows. You don't know which is the most important; you are required to think and make distinctions. (Kluge in Liebman 1988: 55)

For Kracauer, too, it is the 'suggestive indeterminacy' (Kracauer 1997: 71) generated by the realist film practice for which he argues that is responsible for facilitating this active, sensorially driven mode of engagement. 'Film renders visible what we did not, or perhaps even could not, see before its advent. It effectively assists us in discovering the material world with its psychophysi-cal correspondences' (300). In a similar vein to Kluge's delineation of the active, creative mode of spectatorship facilitated by realist cinema, these cor-respondences are predetermined neither by the form nor the content of the film. '[T]he spectator', Kracauer writes, 'cannot hope to apprehend, however incompletely, the being of any object that draws him into its orbit unless he meanders, dreamingly, through the maze of its multiple meanings and psy-chological correspondences.' (165) As per Kluge's description of the viewer as someone who wanders through the streets gazing at windows, Kracauer argues that the mode of engagement cultivated by realist film is marked by 'a veritable stream of consciousness whose contents [. . .] still bear the imprint of the bodily sensations from which they issue' (166).

Both Kracauer and Kluge argue that this embodied form of consciousness opens up a window via which the spectator can experience a displaced vision of reality. The aim, Kracauer states, is not 'to cast an anchor in ideological certainties' but to support us to 'find [. . .] something we did not look for, something tremendously important in its own right – the world that is ours' (296). For Kracauer and Kluge, this world is neither fixed nor predetermined in its structure. If the realist film practices they describe are radical, then it is because they facilitate an active, creative mode of engagement. This mode of engagement is itself realistic not because it confirms the status quo but because it recognises alternative possibilities inherent within existing circumstances. As Kluge makes clear: '*The motive for realism is never the confirmation of reality but protest.*' (Kluge, 2012d: 192)

NOTES

1. Thanks to Ian Aitken for his productive feedback on an earlier draft of this chapter.
2. The phrase in question appears in Walter Benjamin's essay 'The Work of Art in the Age of Mechanical Reproduction' (Benjamin 1992: 229).
3. See, for example (Kluge 2012c).
4. Alexandra Kluge is the sister of Alexander Kluge.
5. This idea of the film in the spectator's head is regularly discussed by Kluge. See, for example (Reitz, Kluge and Reinke 1988: 87) and (Kluge 1999: 227).

REFERENCES

Adorno, T. W. (1991), 'The Curious Realist: On Siegfried Kracauer', *New German Critique*, 54, Autumn, pp. 159–77.

Benjamin, W. (1992), 'The Work of Art in the Age of Mechanical Reproduction' in H. Arendt (ed.), *Illuminations*, London: Fontane Press, pp. 211–44.

Dawson, J. (1977), '"But Why are the Questions so Abstract?" An Interview with Alexander Kluge', in J. Dawson (ed.), *Alexander Kluge and the Occasional Work of a Female Slave*, New York: Zoetrope, pp. 26–42.

Deuber-Mankowsky, A. and Schiesser, G. (2012), 'In the Real Time of Feelings: Interview with Alexander Kluge', in T. Forrest (ed.), *Alexander Kluge: Raw Materials for the Imagination*, Amsterdam: Amsterdam University Press, pp. 352–62.

Kaes, A. (2012), 'In Search of Germany: Alexander Kluge's *The Patriot*', in T. Forrest (ed.), pp. 95–126.

Kluge, A. (1999a), 'Interview von Ulrich Gregor (1976)', in C. Schulte (ed.), *In Gefahr und größter Not bringt der Mittelweg den Tod: Texte zu Kino, Film, Politik*, Berlin: Vorwerk 8, pp. 224–44.

— (1999b), 'Ein Hauptansatz des Ulmer Instituts (1980)', in C. Schulte (ed.), *In Gefahr und größter Not bringt der Mittelweg den Tod: Texte zu Kino, Film, Politik*, Berlin: Vorwerk 8, pp. 57–9.

— (2012a), 'The Sharpest Ideology: That Reality Appeals to its Realistic Character', in T. Forrest (ed.), pp. 191–6.

— (2012b), 'On Film and the Public Sphere', trans. Thomas Y. Levin and Miriam B. Hansen, in T. Forrest (ed.), pp. 33–49.

— (2012c), '"Feelings Can Move Mountains . . .". An Interview with Alexander Kluge on the Film *The Power of Feelings*', in T. Forrest (ed.), pp. 241–6.

— (2012d), 'The Sharpest Ideology: That Reality Appeals to its Realistic Character', in T. Forrest (ed.), pp. 191–6.

— (2013), *Theorie der Erzählung: Frankfurter Poetikvorlesungen*, Berlin: Suhrkamp.

Kluge, Alexandra and Steinborn, B. (1977), 'Film ist das natürliche Tauschverhältnis der Arbeit . . .', *Filmfaust* 1: 6.

Kracauer, S. (undated manuscript), 'Entwurf über das Verhältnis direktor visueller Erfahrung und der durch Photographie vermittelten'.

— (1996), 'Tentative Outline of a Book on Film Aesthetics [1949]', in Volker Breidecker (ed.), *Siegfried Kracauer – Erwin Panofsky Briefwechsel, 1941–1966*, Berlin: Akademie Verlag, pp. 83–92.

— [1960] (1997), *Theory of Film: The Redemption of Physical Reality*, Princeton, NJ: Princeton University Press.

Laudenbach, P. and Kluge, A. (2009), '"Träume sind die Nahrung auf dem Weg zum Ziel"', *brand eins: Wirtschafismagazin* 8.

— (2012), '"Wir sind Glückssucher"', *Der Tagesspiegel*, 13 February 2012: http://www.tagesspiegel.de/kultur/wir-sind-glueckssucher/6201290.html (last accessed 10 April 2015).

Liebman, S. (1988), 'On New German Cinema, Art, Enlightenment, and the Public Sphere: An Interview with Alexander Kluge', *October*, 46, pp. 23–59.

Phillip, C. (2000), 'Vertrauenswürdige Irrtümer: Ein Gespräch mit Alexander Kluge', *Kolik*, 13, pp. 3–15.

Proust, M. (1996) *In Search of Lost Time*, Volume 3, London: Vintage.

Reitz, E., Kluge, A. and Reinke, W. (1988) 'Word and Film', *October*, 46, pp. 83–95.

CHAPTER 2

The Rhetoric of Madness in Realist Film Theory

Temenuga Trifonova

Dissociative identity disorder is distinguished by distinct personality states and amnesia while depersonalisation/de-realisation disorder is characterised by a feeling of unreality and estrangement from the self, body and surroundings. Early symptoms of autism include the inability to distinguish the animate from the inanimate and excessive focus on non-relevant parts of objects. Distractedness and the inability to focus are symptoms of attention deficit disorder. Melancholy's clinical features include disturbances in affect (blunted emotional response), psychomotor disturbance expressed as retardation (slowed thought, movement, and speech), and cognitive impairment (reduced concentration and working conscious memory). The 'negative symptoms' of schizophrenia include flat affect, avolition and alogia, while delusions, hallucinations, and suspiciousness/paranoia are considered 'positive symptoms'. Apathy can be an early symptom of depression or schizophrenia.

What does this have to do with film theory? Hugo Münsterberg, author of the first work of film theory, *The Photoplay: A Psychological Study*, considered the following features – reminiscent of the symptomatic language of dissociative identity disorder – essential to cinema: decentralisation (the ability to assume alternate points of view), mobility (the ability to invert the past and the present, the real and the virtual), and de-realisation and disembodiment (characteristic of film reception). Both Jean Epstein's revelationist aesthetic and Béla Balázs's anthropomorphic film theory are informed by animistic beliefs, translating into the realm of the aesthetic the symptoms of various types of disorders (for example, autism) characterised by the inability to distinguish the living from the non-living. In *Theory of Film*, Kracauer posited affective states commonly perceived as symptomatic of mental disturbance – detachment from reality, ennui, melancholy, distraction, and disinterestedness/apathy – as necessary to film's redemption of physical reality. Indeed, many of the privileged concepts in classical film theory could be seen as aestheticised symptoms of a range of mental illnesses, such as affective flattening (cf. de-dramatisation and dead time in neorealist theory), avolition (cf. the weakening of character and narrative motivation in realist film and theory), fragmentation (cf. the privileging of episodic over unified dramatic narratives), dissociative fugue (cf. Kracauer's notion of distraction; the privileging of defamiliarisation as a way of re-establishing a more intimate connection to reality; or the temporal deregulation of the 'time–image') and spatial dislocation (cf. Kracauer's notion of the solidarity of spaces foregrounding the interconnectedness of things). Thus, one of the distinguishing characteristics of classical film theory is its promotion of non-cognitive forms of expression – often couched in the rhetoric of madness and mental illness – as a resistance to the rationalising forces of modernity.

The mental rather than mimetic realism of early film theory, which construes cinema as obeying the laws of the mind, rather than those of the physical world, can be traced back to Münsterberg's *The Photoplay*, an examination of 'the means by which the moving pictures impress us and appeal to us. Not the physical means and the technical devices . . . but the mental means' (1970: 17). Anticipating Epstein's and Balázs's idea of cinematic time and space as belonging to a mental/spiritual dimension, rather than representing properties of the material world, Münsterberg argues that the impression of depth and movement in cinema is 'produced by the spectator's mind and not excited from without. [. . .] Depth and movement . . . are present and yet they are not in the things. We invest the impressions with them.' (27, 30) Cinema's specificity lies in successfully mimicking the mind's independence from the temporal and spatial limitations of the material world by reproducing the basic mental functions through which we make sense of it: attention (the close-up) and memory (the flashback). Film reproduces our mental functions in the absence of the essential material conditions for perception and projects them back to us as if they existed outside us, disembodied: in the photoplay, '[t]he massive outer world has lost its weight, it has been freed from space, time, and causality and it has been clothed in the forms of our own consciousness' (41, 95).[1]

Similarly, Epstein and Balázs locate film's specificity in its derealisation of material reality through the manipulation of time and space. While some have read the notion of *photogénie* as evidence of Epstein's sensorial film theory, *photogénie* is actually indicative of Epstein's belief in film as a technology for *deranging* reason and the senses. Already in *La Lyrosophie* (1922) his description of filmic illusion, indebted to medieval Jewish mysticism, emphasises film's collapse of the distinction between personal subjective experience and the reality of the external world, an experience one could also describe as psychotic:

The word, the exterior sign of representation and the interior sign of the things, is identical with the representation and the thing. Thus there are no longer representations of things, but things-representations. [T]he Kabbalist . . . does not differentiate between two categories of phenomena: objective and subjective. All are located for him on a unified plane of consideration, a subjective plane – that is to say, that of feeling. (Epstein, in Keller and Paul 2012: 284)

Epstein consistently privileges film techniques – the close-up, slow motion, superimposition, and experimental sound – that derange the 'seemingly fundamental and solid classifications of the extra-cinematographic universe' (312) by detaching objects from their spatio-temporal context, producing effects similar to a delusion or hallucination. Cinema mimics the architectural principle of the dream through its indeterminacy and illogical continuity, which bind shots together affectively rather than logically, just as in a dream representations are joined together because of their figurative rather than literal value: 'It is out of our faithfulness to mental realism – perhaps the more real of the two – that film so widely dares to transpose the signification of forms, to substitute people for things and vice versa, to use the part for the whole.' (356) Ironically, cinema's derangement of the senses brings it in line with modern scientific discoveries about the instability or porousness of matter and with the theory of relativity. Contrasting cinema's visual thought with language's rational thought, Epstein praises cinema for reinvigorating:

the delirium of interpretation, freeing it from the syllogistic yoke, so as to reach or remind people to use their poetic faculty. Since no philosophy, no science, no discourse, no judgment, no understanding, no narrative, no memory, no sensation exists that is not essentially paranoid; since interpretation is the universal mode of knowledge; since paranoia typifies the function of the mind and the senses, the true genius that cinema makes manifest is its own authentic capacity for surrealization. (372)

Cinema's inherent paranoia refers to the inexhaustibility of cinematic interpretation, which, in turn, reflects the infinite nature of the unconscious.

Throughout his writings, Epstein associates the unconscious with the inarticulate and thus with the inanimate, and it is this association that underlies *photogénie*, as becomes clear in his discussion of the close-up. The close-up allegedly reveals the mobility constitutive of the material world; this mobility, however, is interesting to Epstein only insofar as it 'translates in minute detail the mobility of a soul' (339). He criticises avant-garde film for misusing the close-up in a mechanical way, failing to tap into cinema's true nature as 'the photography of delusions of the heart' (304). Objects to which we attach a sentimental value provide the clearest example of *photogénie*: 'We are incapable of seeing them as objects. What we see in them, through them, are the memories and emotions, the plans and regrets that we have attached to those things.' (304) *Photogénie*, then, refers to our blindness to things in their sheer materiality: 'Close-up of the telephone . . . you no longer see a mere telephone. You read: ruin, failure, misery, prison, suicide.' (305) Epstein's close-up fulfils a function similar to that in Münsterberg's theory: it does not 'reveal' the material world but only its significance for us, making visible to us the mental functions (perception, memory and imagination) through which we attribute meaning to things.

Ironically, while photography and film were instrumental in the transition from physiognomic to psychological theories of madness at the *fin de siècle*, Epstein and Balázs revive the obsolete concept of physiognomy to describe cinema's 'redemption' of material reality. Epstein's numerous descriptions of the face in close-up are poetic yet striking in their scientific attention to the subtle movements of facial muscles. While critics have explored the links between Balázs's physiognomy and eighteenth-century aesthetics, no one has yet noted the continuities between Epstein's *photogénie* and eighteenth- and nineteenth-century physiognomy, specifically the shift from early physiognomy's conception of the mobility and ephemerality of facial expressions as indicative of insanity, to late physiognomy's challenge of the association of the mobile face with insanity. In the earliest treatise on the subject, *Physiognomy, or the Corresponding Analogy between the Conformation of the Features and the Ruling Passions of the Soul*, Lavater describes physiognomy as 'reading the handwriting of nature upon the human countenance' (1775:3). He argues that the repetitious, well-regulated contraction of facial muscles produces normal facial expressions which become deformed when an element of disproportionate change and randomness is introduced into the muscles' habitual work. Here the normal is associated with the habitual/recognisable and the abnormal with the accidental/unpredictable; the immobile face signals normality, the mobile face abnormality. Similarly, in *The Physiognomy of Mental Diseases* (1843), Sir Alexander Morrison endorses physiognomy as the most reliable method for classifying the insane, positing the *habitual* contractions of facial muscles, resulting in a recognisable expression, as 'proof' of sanity.

The desire to understand how mental states become manifest in a person's visual appearance was the motivating force behind the work of G. B. Duchenne de Boulogne; contrary to Lavater and Morrison, however, Duchenne 'sought to understand the face in motion, describing facial expressions as a mobile muscular phenomenon' (Gunning 2004: 149). It is Duchenne's legacy that informs Epstein's reflections on the close-up. In *The Mechanism of Human Facial Expression* (1862) Duchenne rejected the crude association of particular mental states with corresponding facial expressions, proposing instead to decompose general facial expressions into the set of facial muscles that produces them. He discovered that a single contraction of a facial muscle does not cause all other muscles to contract; accordingly, he classified the isolated or combined contractions of the face as expressive on their own, expressive only in a complementary way, or partly expressive. Challenging early physiognomy's assumption of a correspondence between the visible (body) and the invisible (mind), Duchenne described mental deformity as a kind of illegibility: the deformed mind could not be 'read' through the body. Even as he held on to the idea that physical deformity (the contraction of the facial muscles in non-habituated ways) points to mental deformity, Duchenne emphasised much more the illegibility (the non-habituated being 'illegible') of the visible (physical deformity) which translated into an illegibility of the invisible (mental deformity). He underscored the fragmentary/illegible nature of the body (hence his interest in the contraction of isolated facial muscles) and, by implication, the fragmentary/illegible nature of the mind. By distancing himself from earlier physiognomic theories, and using photography to capture the ephemeral and the instantaneous, Duchenne was already beginning to understand the face *cinematically* (149).

Epstein's descriptions of the close-up echo Duchenne's accounts of his experiments through the method of localised 'electrization':

> Muscular preambles ripple beneath the skin. Shadows shift, tremble, hesitate. Something is being decided. A breeze of emotion underlines the mouth with clouds. The orography of the face vacillates. Seismic shocks begin. Capillary wrinkles try to split the fault. A wave carried them away. Crescendo. A muscle bridles. The lip is laced with tics like a theater curtain. Everything is movement, imbalance, crisis. (Epstein in Abel 1993: 235–6)

Epstein's *photogénie* conforms to Duchenne's notion of the face as a mobile phenomenon and, more generally, to a modern view of human expression as syntactic rather than semiotic. It cannot really be otherwise given that the physiognomy/soul of things refers to their place in our subconscious which, as Wall-Romana points out, consists mostly of 'sensorial impressions and affective comportments' (2013: 20) and should thus be distinguished from the too narratively based Freudian unconscious.

Katie Kirtland traces Epstein's 'lyrosophical mode' – in which objects are invested 'with an intensified sense of life via their position in an atemporal nexus of the viewer's subconscious emotional associations' (Epstein, quoted in Keller and Paul 2012: 281) – back to his appropriation of experimental psychologist Edouard Abramowski's *Le Subconscient normal* (1914) wherein Abramowski posits a connection between chronic intellectual fatigue and a hyperactive subconscious, concluding that the subconscious is the seat of the aesthetic and that 'the aesthetic element is found in the generic sentiment of the forgotten' (quoted in Kirtland 108). Art is an instance of paramnesia, 'the appearance in consciousness of either the forgotten, or perceptions that had never been elaborated in the first place' (108). The link between paramnesia and *photogénie* is only one instance of Epstein's implicit association of *photogénie* with various types of psychological and physiological disturbances. The cinematic techniques he champions as most 'photogenic' can be seen as aestheticised versions of two opposite types of mental disorders: depersonalisation and psychosis.

Epstein praises the camera's inhuman analytical properties: it is 'an eye without prejudices, without morals, exempt from influences' (Epstein, in Keller and Paul 2012: 292). He compares it to the experience of descending a spiral staircase lined with mirrors:

> Each of these mirrors presented me with a perverse view of myself, an inaccurate image of the hopes I had. These spectating mirrors forced me to see myself with their indifference, their truth. I seemed to be in a huge retina lacking a conscience, with no moral sense, and seven stories [*sic*] high. (291)

Cinema's view of the world transposes into the realm of the aesthetic the symptoms of depersonalisation disorder: flat affect and alienation from the self. Cinema's depersonalising power is reflected in its equivalent treatment of the animate and the inanimate, that is, in Epstein's animism, part of the aesthetic of isolation characterised by the perceptual decomposition of objects, an extreme focus on minute details, and an inability (refusal) to perceive an object in its totality:

> One of the greatest powers of cinema is its animism. On screen nature is never inanimate. Objects take on airs. Trees gesticulate. [. . .] A hand is separated from a man, lives on its own, suffers and rejoices alone. And the finger is separated from the hand. (290)

Epstein's animism is complemented by a fascination with various disturbances of our sensory-motor apparatus, as evidenced by his obsession with deformed, truncated, or stilled movements.

The aesthetisisation of various symptoms of depersonalisation and sensorimotor disorders, disclosing cinema's non-humanity, is only one side of Epstein's discourse; the other – represented by the aesthetic of proximity – foregrounds precisely those powers of cinema that make it human: its affective, rather than depersonalising, powers. Insofar as the aesthetic of proximity construes the boundaries separating the self from the external world as porous, it translates into the aesthetic realm the symptoms of psychosis, a condition marked by the failure to distinguish subjective mental states from objective reality. Within the psychotic structure of Epstein's aesthetic of proximity, the ontological distinctions between screen and reality which circumscribe the realm of 'normal experience' collapse: 'Between the spectacle and the spectator, no barrier. One doesn't look at life, one penetrates it.' (272) Similarly, Epstein's 'natural movies', in which he works on the 'exchange of substances and properties' (water, clouds, wind),[2] celebrate the (psychotic) dissolution of ego boundaries and of the boundaries between physical objects.

Balázs's theory, like Epstein's, is undergirded by what appear to be aestheticised symptoms of various mental disturbances. Like Epstein, Balázs attributes to cinema the structure of paranoia, for 'while words can be meaningless, there is no such thing as a meaningless image' (Balázs 2010: 57). Paradoxically, the image is defined both by its dearth of meaning (determinate, logical meaning) and by its excess of meaning (indeterminate, surface meaning): 'Words cannot be understood when they are incomprehensible. [. . .] But a sight may be clear and comprehensible even though unfathomable.' (59) The paranoid structure of cinema's visual thought is evident in the microphysiognomy of the close-up which derives its power from a mistrust of everything conscious and intentional. Cinema promotes a paranoid delusional stance towards reality insofar as it feeds our mistrust of the surface appearances and consciously expressed ideas that cover up 'true' meaning which is to be found in the nuances of the close-up rather than in the long shot, in the micro-drama of the moment rather than in large-scale narrative shifts. Objectivity in cinema exists 'as no more than an impression that certain shots may consciously create', for 'whatever is not really deformed is imperceptible' (115). On the level of sound, too, cinema does not aim to reproduce the sounds of the external world but to derealise the world, to transform 'outward perceptions [into] internal mental associations [. . .] [a]coustic impressions, acoustic emotions, acoustic thoughts' (199). Thanks to the camera's mobility, cinema dismantles the distinction between the self and the external world so that the spectator no longer feels a boundary between real space and the virtual space of the screen, an experience not that dissimilar from an hallucination.

Like Epstein, Balázs identifies the close-up as the essence of cinema. Since he gives the close-up as an example of cinema's new language of gestures, claiming that 'whatever is expressed in his face and his movements arises from a stratum of the soul that can never be brought to the light of day by words' (9), what matters to him is not the scale of the close-up but its silent expressiveness which it shares with the wordless language of gestures. Balázs's belief that all objects in cinema assume a 'physiognomy', that is, that they are inherently symbolic and, on the other hand, that their meaning dwells on the surface, immediately perceived rather than demanding interpretation, appears contradictory until we acknowledge that this symbolism is not produced by the film-maker but by the spectator. The intended symbolism of a shot is irrelevant: what matters is the spectator's apperception of the represented object which is automatically perceived as already coloured by the spectator's subconscious. In cinema, as in dreams, we never see objects for what they are and immediately see them as coloured by our memory, wishes, and fantasies. To say that all objects are necessarily symbolic is simply to acknowledge that physiognomy describes the structure of human perception. Echoing Münsterberg's description of cinema as 'clothing the material world in the forms of our own consciousness' (Münsterberg 1970: 153) Balázs views the material world as 'merely an extension of my inner world rather than an autonomous, self-sufficient realm' (Balázs 2010: 49). The physiognomy of inanimate things refers not to their material existence but to the inarticulate feelings and thoughts they provoke in us.

Whereas inarticulate thoughts and feelings are generally recognised as possible signs of a mental disturbance in Balázs's theory, the close-up's inarticulateness makes it especially suitable to 'photograph the unconscious': 'microphysiognomy is the direct making visible of micropsychology' (103–4). While a verbal description takes time and fails to capture the ephemerality of feelings, the close-up nullifies all sense of time, displaying the most varied emotions simultaneously. The close-up's expressiveness is independent of any spatial and temporal context, positioning the viewer as similarly disembodied, unable to position himself/herself in time or space: the close-up 'locates the filmic image not within the linear time of narrative and epic but in the temporality of affect and the dream' (Carter, in Balázs: xxix). Like Duchenne, Balázs detaches expression (which transcends time and space) from its medium (the face as a series of muscles existing in space and time):

> Physiognomy has a relation to space comparable to that existing between melody and time. The facial muscles that make expression possible may be close to each other in space. But it is their relation to one another that creates expression. These relations have no extension and no direction in space. No more than do feelings and thoughts, ideas and associations. All these are image-like and yet non-spatial. (Balázs 2010: 101)

Like Balázs and Epstein, Kracauer's mistrust of a rationalised culture of words finds expression in an aesthetic of fragmentation or atomisation that aestheticises various forms of mental disturbance. Recently, critics have begun to challenge the previously accepted division between Kracauer's pre- and post-exile writings, a presumed epistemological shift from the early Kracauer, the phenomenological[3] observer of the ephemeral and the everyday, and the late Kracauer, 'the sociological reductionist' and 'unredeemed humanist' (Petro quoted in Aitken 2006: 2). In their 'Introduction' to *Siegfried Kracauer's*

American Writings: Essays on Film and Popular Culture, Johannes von Moltke and Kristy Rawson maintain that 'the émigré Kracauer remained true to Kracauer the Weimar critic in his enduring attention to detail, to the forms and materials of culture,' pointing specifically to Kracauer's emphasis on inanimate objects as revealing the continuity between Kracauer's American writings and his feuilletons on material culture for the *Frankfurter Zeitung* (2012: 23). Though Kracauer never articulated a physiognomic theory of film, like Balázs and Epstein, many of his observations on inanimate objects, particularly in his articles on Hollywood's 'terror films', Jean Vigo, and silent film comedy, reveal significant continuities with Epstein and Balázs, although Kracauer puts a 'malicious' spin on physiognomic theory by suggesting that cinema redeems the inanimate world mainly by acknowledging its maliciousness towards us.

'Hollywood's Terror Films: Do They Reflect an American State of Mind?' (1946) begins as a critique of 'terror films', which, rather than dealing with social abuses, as the gangster films of the Depression era had done, explore psychological aberrations, taking for granted the 'sickness of the American psyche' (Kracauer 2012: 44) without ever attempting to motivate the introduction of sadistic violence and terror, and intentionally blurring the distinction between normal and abnormal mental states. What redeems these films, however, is their explicit attention to the physical environment. Their heightened attention to the material world is not accidental because:

> ... people emotionally out of joint inhabit a realm ruled by bodily sensations and material stimulants, a realm in which dumb objects loom monstrously high and become signal posts or stumbling blocks, enemies or allies. This obtrusiveness of inanimate objects is infallible evidence of an inherent concern with mental disintegration. (45)

Kracauer links mental instability or abnormality with a heightened interest in bodily sensations and in the inanimate world: distorted mental states heighten both our corporeal self-awareness (Epstein's 'coneaesthesis') and the 'physiognomy of things' (Balázs), that is, our perception of things as extensions of our mental states.

In 'Jean Vigo' (1947) Kracauer praises Vigo's camera for not discriminating 'between human beings and objects, animate and inanimate nature. As if led by the meandering camera, he exhibits the material components of mental processes.' (48) Vigo's originality consists in treating objects not only as 'silent accomplices of our thoughts and feelings' (49) but in exploring situations in which objects influence dramatically our thoughts and feelings rather than merely accompanying them. While, in the article on 'terror films', Kracauer associated abnormal mental states with a heightened attention to the inanimate world, here he draws a similar connection between the unconscious and the material world: 'And since increasing intellectual awareness tends to reduce the power of objects over the mind, [Vigo] logically chooses people who are deeply rooted in the material world as leading characters.' (49) The unconscious connects the animate with the inanimate: inanimate objects embody our unconscious in a way reminiscent of Epstein's *photogénie* and Balázs's physiognomy.

It is in 'Silent Film Comedy' (1951) that Kracauer's view of the inanimate world on film comes fully into focus. Silent film comedy is essential to his theory of film inasmuch as its exposure of the powerlessness of human beings, reduced to automatons, and its heightened attention to inanimate objects, especially to their 'malice towards anything human' (214), prefigures 'the aesthetics of alienation' Kracauer would develop more fully in *Theory of Film* (1960). Kracauer describes the relationship between humans and inanimate objects as a power struggle in which humans are repeatedly defeated: 'Instead of making us independent of the whims of matter [the progressive gadgets of modernity] were the shock troops of unconquered nature and inflicted upon us defeat after defeat,' (214) from which the only rescue was 'a matter of sheer chance rather than personal accomplishment' (215). We can trace Kracauer's idea of film's affinity for 'the fortuitous' and 'the random' in *Theory of Film* back to his acknowledgement of the material world's maliciousness towards us in this essay. Echoing Balázs's association of 'visible man' with silent cinema, Kracauer points to the introduction of sound as marking the end of 'genuine cinema'. Sound and speech shifted cinema from the 'the depths of material life which words do not penetrate' to 'the dimension of discursive reasoning in which everything was, somehow, labeled and digested verbally' (216–17). Thus, 'the depths of material life' refers not only to the inanimate realm but also to the subconscious inasmuch as it shares the inarticulateness and irrationality of the material world.

The material world as 'the pranks of objects and the sallies of nature' (216) represents only one side of Kracauer's idea of material reality on screen. Throughout his writings, he alternates between describing the relationship between cinema and reality in terms of 'malicious physiognomy' and describing cinema as a 'barren' inventory of the material world. Departing from Balázs's notion of the inherently symbolic nature of objects, he underscores photography's inherent meaninglessness by contrasting it with memory: 'Photography grasps what is given as a spatial (or temporal) continuum; memory images retain what is given only insofar as it has significance [the latter not being reducible to spatial and temporal terms].' (Kracauer 1995: 50) Photography as a technology is predicated on the 'evacuation of meaning from the objects' (53) because its likeness 'does not immediately divulge how it reveals itself to cognition' (52). The shudder that photographs – especially old photographs – provoke in us results precisely from this quality: photographs eternalise 'not the knowledge [truth content, semiotic value] of the original but [only] the spatial configuration of a moment' (56).

It is, however, precisely in photography's, and film's, evacuation of meaning from objects – whose psychological equivalent is a condition known as 'flat affect', one of the 'negative symptoms' of schizophrenia – that Kracauer locates its redemptive potential. Film's 'barren' inventory of nature, its 'warehousing of nature':

> promotes the confrontation of consciousness with nature. [. . .] But if the remnants of nature are not oriented toward the memory image, then the order they assume through the image is necessarily provisional. [. . .] The capacity to stir up the elements of nature is one of the possibilities of film. (62)

The evacuation of meaning from material reality is linked to another cinematic feature translating 'flat affect' into aesthetic terms – the episodic narrative, an embodiment of cinema's 'affinity for endlessness' which it shares with the modern novel. In the novel and in film, both products of modernity's groundlessness, the eternity of epic time has been replaced by a 'chronological [fallen] time without beginning and end' (Kracauer 1997: 233) which arranges events in a never-ending, affectively flat series of 'one after another' with no hope for transcendence/meaning/value.

Theory of Film locates cinema's redemptive potential in its derangement of perception, memory, time, space and causality. The theory of redemption depends on Kracauer's own redemption of certain negative aspects of modernity and psychological abnormalities into positive aesthetic qualities which he posits as 'the basic affinities of film': film's affinities for the indeterminate, the unstaged, the infinite, the fortuitous, and the transient disguise negative effects of mass culture – fragmentation, distraction, groundlessness, relativism, and solitude – and mental disturbances (affective flattening, avolition, dissociative fugues). Echoing Balázs's celebration of micro-physiognomy's challenge to rationalising interpretation, Kracauer insists that we can reconnect with reality not by trying to revive an impossible sense of wholeness but by fragmenting it even more, breaking it down into unfamiliar configurations (for example, through composition and editing). He redeems distraction and fragmentation – symptomatic of various mental disorders – as a desirable aesthetic quality signifying autonomy and indeterminacy. He posits the failure to construct a coherent view of the world – to narrativise the world instead of merely doing an inventory of it – not as a regression of our perceptual and cognitive stance towards reality but as a way in which to reconnect with reality. Conversely, he condemns the inability to atomise the world, to break down all connections between things, to see everything as disembedded from its habitual network of relations to other things, for reducing the world to a symbol or a metaphor, a mere mental representation. Rather than viewing the derangement of our habitual experience of time in terms of past, present and future, as a sign of mental or cognitive aberration – the inability to position oneself temporally, to distinguish the past from the present and the future, which also determines our ability to distinguish causes from effects, and to attribute motivation to certain acts – he points to it as a way of overcoming our alienation from reality. Kracauer reinterprets positively the degradation of values, beliefs and norms, suggesting that it is precisely the insignificance of events and their relative value that makes them cinematic. Thus, in a truly cinematic film, major plot events are replaced by multiple, indeterminate incidents with no clear causal relation between them. Rather than seeing randomness and arbitrariness as revealing the absurdity of existence under the conditions of modernity, Kracauer emphasises their democratising potential. He redeems distraction as episodicity (praising it for challenging the totalitarianism of plot), moral and existential relativism or groundlessness as ambiguity and indeterminacy, solitude and alienation – fragmentation on a social level – as states of aesthetic disinterestedness, and melancholy as a more ethical way of relating to reality.

Though Epstein, Balázs, and Kracauer are considered representative of an intuitionist (Aitken) or revelationist (Turvey) tradition of realism, their belief in cinema's potential to reveal the material world is, in fact, rooted in a theory of cinema as transcending the limitations of the material world, affirming the mind's triumph over matter: their theories, which combine an aesthetic of isolation with an aesthetic of alienation, articulate a mental, rather than corporeal, realism. The aesthetic of isolation refers to cinema's ability to focus our attention on things we overlook in everyday life by separating objects from spatial and temporal context, and transposing them into another, spiritual dimension. The aesthetic of alienation concerns cinema's 'tendency to the unorganized and diffuse' (Kracauer 2012: 211) which proceeds from its automatic transcription of the visual excess of the material world without any special attention to the human/the animate. Epstein, Balázs and Kracauer locate cinema's redemptive potential both in its aesthetic of alienation, predicated on diffused attention or inattention, and in its aesthetic of isolation which functions through the excessive focusing of attention (via the framing and scaling of shots). They celebrate cinema for its de-realising and depersonalising power, for denying the material world an autonomous existence – inasmuch as cinema's images are free from the temporal and spatial limitations of the material world – and, at the same time, for denying the human subject autonomy, inasmuch as the human on screen is just another material phenomenon among many, rather than an independent entity organising the world by attributing value to it.

NOTES

1. Langdale hints at the disturbing implications of Münsterberg's theory of film as perfectly mimicking the operations of the mind: 'Münsterberg's viewer may . . . be justifiably described as an automaton responding thoughtlessly to the powerful stimulus of the motion picture' (22).
2. See Brenez 2012: 227–43.
3. On the relationship between realism and phenomenology, see Allan Casebier's *Film and Phenomenology*.

REFERENCES

Aitken, Ian (2006), *Realist Film Theory and Cinema: The Nineteenth-Century Lukacsian and Intuitionist Realist Traditions*, Manchester: Manchester University Press.

Balázs, Béla (2010), *Early Film Theory:* Visible Man *and* The Spirit of Film, in Carter, Erika and Livingstone, Rodney (eds), New York: Berghahn Books.

Brenez, Nicole (2012), 'Ultra-Modern: Jean Epstein, or Cinema "Serving the Forces of Transgression and Revolt"', in Keller, Sarah and Paul, Jason N. (eds), *Jean Epstein: Critical Essays and New Translations*, Amsterdam: Amsterdam University Press, pp. 227–43.

Carter, Erica, 'Introduction', in Carter and Livingstone, pp. xv–xlvi.

Casebier, Allan (1991), *Film and Phenomenology: Toward a Realist Theory of Cinematic Representation*, Cambridge, MA: Cambridge University Press.

Cortade, Ludovic, 'The Microscope of Time: Slow Motion in Jean Epstein's Writings', in Keller and Paul, pp. 161–76.

Duchenne de Boulogne, G. B. (2006), *The Mechanism of Human Expression*, Cambridge: Cambridge University Press.

Epstein, Jean, 'Esprit de cinéma', in Keller and Paul, pp. 330–81.

Epstein, Jean, 'La Lyrosophie', in Keller and Paul, pp. 281–6.

Epstein, Jean, 'La Poesie d'aujourd'hui, un nouvel etat d'intelligence', in Keller and Paul, pp. 271–6.

Epstein, Jean, 'Le Cinéma du diable', in Keller and Paul, pp. 317–27.

Epstein, Jean, 'Le Cinématographe vu de l'Etna', in Keller and Paul, pp. 287–311.

Epstein, Jean, 'L'intelligence d'une machine', in Keller and Paul, pp. 311–16.

Epstein, Jean (2012), 'Magnification', in Abel, Richard (ed.), *French Film Theory and Criticism: A History/Anthology, 1907–1939*, Volume 1: 1907–1929, Princeton, NJ: Princeton University Press, pp. 235–41.

Gunning, Tom (2004), 'In Your Face: Physiognomy, Photography and the Gnostic Mission of Early Film', in Micale, Mark, S. (ed.), *The Mind of Modernism: Medicine, Psychology and the Cultural Arts in Europe and America, 1880–1940*, Palo Alto, CA: Stanford University Press, pp. 141–70.

Kirtland, Katie, 'The Cinema of the Kaleidoscope', in Keller and Paul, pp. 93–115.

Kracauer, Siegfried (1995), 'Photography', in *The Mass Ornament: Weimar Essays*, Levin, Thomas (ed.), Cambridge, MA: Harvard University Press, pp. 47–65.

Kracauer, Siegfried (1997), *Theory of Film: The Redemption of Physical Reality*, Princeton, NJ: Princeton University Press.

Kracauer, Siegfried (2012), 'Hollywood's Terror Films: Do They Reflect an American State of Mind?', in von Moltke, Johannes, and Rawson, Kristy (eds), *Siegfried Kracauer's American*

Writings: Essays on Film and Popular Culture, Berkeley, CA: University of California Press, pp. 41–7.

Kracauer, Siegfried, 'Jean Vigo', in von Moltke and Rawson, pp. 47–50.

Kracauer, Siegfried, 'The Photographic Approach', in von Moltke and Rawson, pp. 204–13.

Kracauer, Siegfried, 'Silent Film Comedy', in von Moltke and Rawson, pp. 213–17.

Langdale, Alan (2012), 'S(t)imulaiton of Mind: The Film Theory of Hugo Münsterberg', in Langdale, Alan (ed.), *Hugo Münsterberg on Film*, London: Routledge, pp. 1–41.

Lavater, J. C (1775), *Physiognomy, or the Corresponding Analogy between the Conformation of the Features and the Ruling Passions of the Soul*, London: T. Tegg, Welcome Library Rare Books Collection.

Liebman, Stuart, 'Novelty and Poiesis in the Early Writings of Jean Epstein', in Keller and Paul, pp. 73–91.

Lundemo, Trond, 'A Temporal Perspective: Jean Epstein's Writings on Technology and Subjectivity', in Keller and Paul, pp. 207–25.

Moore, Rachel, 'A Different Nature', in Keller and Paul, pp. 177–94.

Morrison, Alexander (1843), *The Physiognomy of Mental Diseases*, London: Longman, Welcome Library Rare Books Collection.

Münsterberg, Hugo (1970), *The Photoplay: A Psychological Study*, New York: Dover Publications, Inc.

Turvey, Malcolm (2008), *Doubting Vision: Film and the Revelationist Tradition*, Oxford: Oxford University Press.

Wall-Romana, Christophe, 'Epstein's Photogenie as Corporeal Vision: Inner Sensation, Queer Embodiment, and Ethics', in Keller and Paul, pp. 51–71.

Wall-Romana, Christophe (2013), *Jean Epstein: Corporeal Cinema and Film Philosophy*, Manchester: Manchester University Press.

CHAPTER 3

Phenomenology, Theology and 'Physical Reality': The Film Theory Realism of Siegfried Kracauer

Tyson Wils

Siegfried Kracauer's realist film theory incorporates a number of concepts and philosophical approaches. Among the key conceptual formulations is Jewish messianism and among the key philosophical approaches is phenomenology. Kracauer first started to apply such concepts and approaches to cinema during the period in which he lived as an author, journalist and critic in Weimar Germany during the 1920s and 1930s. It is, however, the last book he published during his lifetime, *Theory of Film: The Redemption of Physical Reality* (1960), that fulfils his desire to establish a theory of cinematic realism, one which he started working on in the 1940s in parallel with his ongoing interests in phenomenology, Jewish messianism, and other associated areas of thought. Why did Kracauer wish to establish a theory of film realism? It would be possible to trace his motivation in this regard to what Thomas Elsaesser (1987) has suggested was Kracauer's career-long interest in trying to come to terms with the aesthetic form internal to cinema as a medium and to the spectator's immanent experience of this internal form, an interest that kept Kracauer responsive 'to the feel and texture of [visual] experience' (69). It could be added that such interest was also linked to what Theodore Adorno (1991) has described as the particular kind of 'experiential stance' (169) that Kracauer adopted during his career, a stance reflective of his 'materially orientated mode of thought' (167) as well as a specific 'relationship to the world of objects' (177) that, Adorno claims, Kracauer formed in childhood.

Elsaesser (2014) has elsewhere noted that *Theory of Film* is, in part, also a response to new wave European cinema of the 1940s and 1950s and, in particular, the various forms of realism explored in that cinema. This includes everything from the techniques employed in Italian neorealism, to the unstaged and fortuitous qualities contained in the austerely precise works of film-makers such as Robert Bresson, to the indeterminate reality and multi-perspectivism displayed in films such as Akira Kurosawa's *Rashomon* (1950).

From Kracauer's point of view, these various forms of realism give expression to different aspects of contemporary reality. As will be explained later in the chapter, such reality is characterised, for Kracauer, by, among other things, the disintegration of patterns of thought and perception into manifold parts and features, and a new focus on interpreting experience on the basis of the contingent relations people have with the world rather than on fixed classifications of meaning.

In *Theory of Film*, Kracauer asserts that cinema is a medium that affects viewers physically, sensuously seizing them before they are 'in a position to respond intellectually' (158). In other words, it engages their material, physiological being before they have a chance to respond with their powers of reasoning. Such a material being is not purely physical for Kracauer, at least not in the sense that physical means something unrelated to and independent of mental phenomena, and he argues that the material, physiological being of the spectator which is immediately stimulated by cinema also involves various degrees of cognitive and psychological activity. Broadly speaking, the cognitive here refers to the innate organising principles of the mind that structure human perception and that make possible for the human observer the appearance of objects in space and in time. The psychological not only involves moods, emotions and scattered fragments of thought but also what Kracauer describes as unconscious dispositions (165) and deep layers of psychosomatic memory (297–8). Kracauer believes that these various aspects of mental activity are distinct from pure intellectual thinking and abstraction. The main reason he thinks this is the case is because the immediate cognitive and psychological activity stimulated by cinema develops out of, and continues to interrelate with, the world of sense-impressions and the materiality of the spectator's being. In contrast, he suggests that the powers of reason are always at one remove from the physical universe. In the context of film spectatorship, this means that reason is not immediately interrelated with, or bound by, the spectator's body or the presence of his or her material being.

Kracauer is not saying that spectators never have intellectual responses to that which they see and hear on screen. Rather, he believes that there is a number of different ways in which cinema can affect the spectator's material, physiological being before such responses develop. He argues that mimetic, behavioural experiences constitute one branch of such filmic stimulation. In cinema, he suggests, the natural world is recorded 'for its own sake' so there is a 'reality character' (158) to the images that the spectator watches. Kracauer argues that the constant flow of motion on screen, for instance, stimulates 'kinaesthetic responses' (158), that is, bodily reflexes and impulses in viewers. The physical affects of cinema, however, do not only pertain to this 'reality character' (158) of the screen image. For Kracauer, cinema also reveals aspects of material phenomena that spectators do not normally perceive or that they routinely overlook in their everyday lives. His argument here broadly concerns changes in the historical and ideological make-up of modern life. A key belief of Kracauer's is that, in the age of capitalism, modern science, technology and mass communication have had a negative impact upon peoples' experiences of the surrounding world. He suggests, for example, that abstraction and utilitarianism are some of the key characteristics of modern science and technology, including communication technology (292–3). He also argues that these characteristics have conditioned peoples' perceptions and attitudes towards external phenomena. For Kracauer, the result is a modern mentality that 'cares about means and functions rather than ends and modes of being' (292) and that obstructs peoples' abilities to enter into a prolonged, aesthetic consideration of exterior life. Kracauer argues that people are led by science and technology to 'eliminate the qualities of things' and to set those things 'in the perspective of conventional views and purposes, which point beyond their self-contained being' (300). Unable to enter into direct, concrete intercourse with the objects, things and entities of their environment, Kracauer suggests that people become disenchanted with the world around them.

As Ian Aitken (2001) has suggested, cinema can redeem for Kracauer 'a primal and underlying mode of communication' which offers 'the possibility of a return to sensory contact, and, consequently, to a more valid form of human experience' (16). Aitken argues that the reason Kracauer feels this way is because he sees the potential for images in cinema to peel away the veil of abstraction that covers the world. This is a veil which Kracauer believes strips peoples' encounters with 'physical reality' of the precious, intrinsic qualities that belong to such reality. In other words, a veil that directs peoples' perception and experience of 'physical reality' towards the instrumental purposes and goals that characterise the techniques and procedures of modern science, technology and mass communication (these are points which will be further elaborated on in the context of Kracauer's engagement with theology at the end of this chapter). For Kracauer, film can, in Aitken's words, 'redirect the spectator's attention to the texture of life which has been lost beneath the abstract discourses which regulate experience' (170). This redirection of the spectator's attention involves, as Gertrud Koch (2000) has pointed out, 'the primacy of the visual over the conceptual, of contemplation over mediation' (109) where '"seeing" is understood as "experiencing"' (111).

To appreciate fully Kracauer's argument that cinema can denaturalise spectators' normal experience of the world in order to refamiliarise them with content they have lost, it is necessary to understand, first, the relationship between cinema and what Kracauer refers to as 'physical reality' and, second, the use that Kracauer makes of a concept of history which metaphorically draws on the theology of Jewish messianism. Let us begin with the first point. In the context of discussing what he calls the 'basic properties' of

photography and cinema, Kracauer argues in *Theory of Film* that, at a fundamental level, both media are 'equipped to record and reveal physical reality'
(28). Therefore, he concludes, they are also drawn towards such reality. The
reason Kracauer gives for his conclusion is the following: both photography
and cinema have 'inherent affinities' with different aspects of the external,
phenomenal world. In other words, both media have a natural, built-in capacity for showing various dimensions and realities of physical existence. He
accepts that this gravitation towards 'physical reality' is not identical in each
medium because, in cinema, for example, the image moves. Moreover, he also
notes that the two media have different 'technical properties'. The technique
of shot editing, which involves the different ways visual units can be assembled, is a major feature that distinguishes cinema not only from photography
but also from all other art forms (29). Nonetheless, in an important respect,
Kracauer does see cinema as an extension of a basic aesthetic principle which
can be found in photography.

What does Kracauer mean by 'physical reality'? He defines physical reality as
'the transitory world we live in [. . .] Physical reality will also be called "material
reality", or "physical existence", or "actuality", or loosely just "nature. Another
fitting term might be "camera-reality"'(28). Finally, he adds to all this the term
'life' itself (28). Miriam Hansen (1993) has suggested Kracauer presents a confusing definition of 'physical reality' in *Theory of Film*. As can be seen from this
list of qualities, it is an all-encompassing definition embracing what is physical,
material, actual and natural as well as what belongs to life itself and to the reality
that the camera records. Hansen has analysed Kracauer's notebooks from the
1940s and 1950s which he wrote during the long preliminary stages of planning
for *Theory of Film*. Her examination is indispensable for understanding what
Kracauer means by 'physical reality'. Rather than see such reality simply in
terms of the notion that there is a physical and/or perceptual accord between
recorded images and the outside world, she says that such reality needs to be
understood in terms of ideology, history and time, the relations between subject
and other, and audience experiences of alienation and estrangement in film.
Moreover, 'physical reality' in cinema not only pertains to on–screen representations and subject matter but also to audience reception and, in particular, to
the effects that screen images can have on spectators (451).

Hansen argues that these aspects of 'physical reality' discussed in Kracauer's
notebooks are either absent from the final book or buried in it by being thinly
diffused throughout various sections. She also recognises, however, that, in an
important respect, the final book, with its signs and traces of the unpublished
planned material, additionally has an affinity with Kracauer's earliest writings:

> The link between the unpublished material from the forties and early
> fifties and Kracauer's earliest writings on film suggests that even in

the book in 1960 he approaches the cinema from the problematic of the subject, as both a practical critique of bourgeois fictions of self-identity and a discourse for articulating the historical state of human self-alienation. This perspective complicates the habitual charge against *Theory of Film* that its advocacy of 'realism' is naively grounded in film's referential relation to the material world as object. (444)

In other words, Kracauer's approach to cinema realism does not simply rest on the understanding that images have a substantial bond with pro-filmic material. Rather, for Kracauer, cinema realism has as much, if not more, to do with the ruptures film can cause to, in Hansen's words, 'bourgeois fictions of self-identity' (444). It also has to do with the role Kracauer believes film plays in reflecting and transforming 'the historical state of human self-alienation' (444). These points will be further elaborated on later in this chapter. For now it can be said that' in *Theory of Film*, Kracauer's concern is to make the case for the redemptive function which he believes cinema can have. This function involves refamiliarising spectators with 'physical reality', a process that entails exposing aspects of the external world which, he suggests, are otherwise covered up by the prevailing abstractness, utilitarianism and disenchantment inaugurated by science, technology and mass communication in the age of capitalism.

Other writers, such as Koch (2000) and Aitken (2006), concur with Hansen on the points concerning the realist aesthetics in *Theory of Film*: namely, that they are not based on naive, referential empiricism. Aitken, for example, argues that, while Kracauer's realism has empirical dimensions to it, it also has rational ones (223). By rational dimensions, Aitken means dimensions of reason that originate out of the innate, mental world of the individual. In accordance with Kracauer's phenomenological understanding, such dimensions are orientated towards the external world even if they do not stem from perceived experience. In other words, Kracauer's belief is that there are rational dimensions of the mind that can be related to the physical, sensuous world. In saying this, Kracauer is not suggesting that cinematic images correspond directly to the real. Rather, as Aitken argues, Kracauer's realism has to do with addressing the different kinds of convergences or correspondences that can occur between the human mind and independent, external reality. Such convergences always entail forms of mental representation. Nonetheless, such representation can 'also have some sort of substantive and authentic relationship to reality' (202).

Writers, such as Aitken and Hansen, however, also offer in key respects different perspectives on what Kracauer means by 'physical reality'. Aitken, for instance, situates *Theory of Film* in respect of the influence of, among other things, Immanuel Kant's (1724–1804) critical philosophy, particularly that aspect of it pertaining to 'the harmony of faculties', and also to Edmund Husserl's phenomenology, specifically in terms of his notion of the *Lebenswelt* (life-world). Kracauer first encountered Husserl's work in the early 1920s though, according to Theodore Adorno (1991), Kracauer's first major engagement with phenomenology was with the German sociologist and philosopher Max Scheler. Adorno suggests that Kracauer used, in particular, Scheler's 1922 book *Sociology as Science* which connected a 'material-sociological interest with epistemological reflections' to a 'phenomenological method' (163), as a critical sounding board. Thomas Elsaesser (1987) has also said that, from early on in his career, Kracauer was indebted to the 'phenomenological sociology' (71) of German intellectual Georg Simmel. Though Kracauer drew on various forms of phenomenological thinking, Aitken is right to suggest Husserl is critical to Kracauer's work in *Theory of Film*, even if Husserl's influence is covert rather than explicit. Among other reasons in support of Aitken's contention is the fact that Kracauer mentions Husserl in his posthumously published book, *History: The Last Things Before the Last* (*History*) (1969), which, as Hansen (1997) has said, 'builds on and spells out key philosophical implications of the film theory book' (x). One such implied philosophy is Husserlian phenomenology. In the context of arguing that there is an analogical relationship between history and photographic media, Kracauer says in *History* that when a historian is truly willing to investigate historical reality he/she resembles the film-maker who allows his or her camera to come into its own and record and penetrate 'physical reality'. What such an historian and film-maker share, says Kracauer, is a concern with exploring the 'common, inter-subjective world' of everyday experience, the *Lebenswelt* (46). This world is what the individual intuitively, perceptually and mentally experiences as immediate, pre-given, and presently actual. Put another way, the *Lebenswelt* is, as Aitken (2006) puts it, the 'actually concrete surrounding world which is encountered by the individual as his or her most tangible mode of being' (161).

Aitken (2007) also sees Kracauer's work as an example of intuitionist realist film theory, and argues that the French film critic and theorist André Bazin (1918–1958) is also representative of this film theory, along with the Scottish film-maker, film critic, and essayist John Grierson (1898–1972) and the Hungarian Marxist scholar and literary critic Georg Lukács (1885–1971). While Aitken identifies some of the differences between writers such as Kracauer and Bazin, he also suggests that, fundamentally, all the intuitionist realist film theorists believe that knowledge of the world should be reached through a synthesis of abstract and concrete modes of apprehending reality. This synthesis, Aitken suggests, is founded upon the subject's intuitive grasp of perceptual and empirical experience. He further claims that this perceptual and empirical experience is combined with the subject's higher mental faculties of reason and understanding. From an 'intuitionist realist film theory' perspective, the key point is not only that the higher mental faculties emerge out of perceptual and empirical experience but that the former also remain conditioned by the latter.

In her analysis of the Kracauer notebooks, as well as in other essays on Kracauer's work, Hansen does not mention philosophers like Husserl or theorists such as Bazin. Moreover, she argues that the radical, political-phenomenological perspective of Kracauer's early Weimar writings and his notebooks is ultimately repressed in *Theory of Film*. As already mentioned, while she concedes that, in this later book, there are traces of his earlier work it still occludes the:

> impulses that had motivated his politicophilosophical investment in film throughout: a materialist view of history, a critique of the bourgeois subject on the basis of film's affinity with a world alienated from intention, with human physiology and contingency, nothingness and death. (1993: 445)

By 'a materialist view of history' Hansen is referring to the historical methodology that she claims was employed by Kracauer in his Weimar essays, as well as in the notebooks for *Theory of Film*. Hansen (1993) argues that adopting a materialist approach to history allowed Kracauer to analyse cinema as a medium equipped to 'grasp the material world in all its elements' (448). By these 'elements' she does not only mean what, as earlier noted, Kracauer calls 'the reality character' of the screen image – the representation of the referent. She is also not simply referring to Aitken's (2001) suggestion that Kracauer is concerned with using cinema to return the spectator 'to sensory contact' (16) and 'the texture of life' (170) in the face of what he understands to be the prevailing abstraction and utilitarianism that characterises contemporary society. Rather, by 'elements', she also means a 'physical reality' on screen that confronts the spectator with his or her other (452). In other words, with a material world that is outside and independent of what Kracauer classifies as belonging to the human sphere. By this sphere it is meant that which has been historically and socially constituted by modern, bourgeois society.

Hansen argues that, among other things, this sphere includes the social construction of a form of unified subjecthood – the sovereign individual. She asserts that Kracauer particularly attributes this construction to art and cultural practices that he views as affirming aesthetic principles to do with the ideals of classic drama (450–1). Hansen suggests that, for Kracauer, these principles have led to the creation in the spectator of a homocentric perspective, a perspective that involves, among other things, apprehending the work of art at a distance and as a purposefully integrated and meaningful self-contained work with laws of its own. In other words, as an aesthetic totality that is built around the self-enclosed organic development of individual parts into a significant whole. For Kracauer, this totality affirms the spectator as subject with, in Hansen's words, 'unity of vision and continuity of consciousness' (459) or, as put earlier, 'bourgeois fictions of self-identity' (444).

Hansen (1993) says that, in his Weimar essays and his notebooks for *Theory of Film*, Kracauer places more radical emphasis on the affinity he believes cinema has with different dimensions and realities of the material world, with, for example, the movements and actions of inanimate things and the contingencies and shocks of non-human phenomena (448–50). She says that, on the basis of this affinity, he argues that the medium is able to push the boundaries of human consciousness. This involves not only forcing the spectator to encounter visual and corporeal phenomena that do not usually enter their experience but also immediately seizing the material and physiological layers of their being. What interests Kracauer in his earlier writings, contends Hansen, is cinema's penchant for gravitating 'toward phenomena that elude intentionality and interpretation' (448) and for visually and aurally presenting the non-human, material world as existing equally alongside, and sometimes even mixing in with, what is human. This reveals how the material world interferes with, and sometimes even displaces, human form. Hansen says that Kracauer argues that these aspects of the cinematic experience can demolish the spectator's sense of having a coherent, subjective self-identity which is disembodied: that is to say, a self-identity that feels as though it is distanced and separate from immediate sensation and other qualities belonging to physical experience. Moreover, these aspects can make spectators become receptive and attentive to non-human phenomena and also make them enter into inter-relations with a world antithetical to their historically and socially constituted sense of being human (465–6). This is the sense in which, from the spectator's perspective, cinema has an affinity with a world of nothingness and death. Understood in this context, cinema's contact with 'physical reality' involves bringing the spectator's consciousness into the orbit of material contingency.

Why this experience of otherness and of a world on screen which can fracture modern constructions of subjectivity is so important to Kracauer has not only to do with showing 'the material world in all its elements' (Hansen 1993: 448) – which includes showing, in the sense of making actual through stimulation, the spectator's material, physiological being – but also with revealing the *actual state of things*. This is the second point which needs to be understood in order to appreciate fully that Kracauer's argument is that cinema can denaturalise spectators' normal experience of the world in order to refamiliarise them with content they have lost. This second point has to do with the figurative use that Kracauer makes of Jewish messsianism in order to undertake a particular kind of historical analysis. Jewish messianism is a complex field of thought that persists throughout Kracauer's writings in a variety of tropes and motifs and in combination with other disciplines which he draws on, such as Marxism and psychoanalysis. It is also a field of thought that informs his materialist approach to history. Suffice it to note here that one key assertion which stems from this field is that modern life is characterised by social upheaval, by the increased withdrawal of absolute notions of truth and reality, and, as Hansen (1991) puts it, by disintegration 'into a chaotic multiplicity of phenomena' (50). Such a state of affairs can be described as apocalyptic because it represents a new historical reality. In this reality, the world of appearances – the external, surface world – has been atomised into a world of particularities. In this latter world, different objects and entities are no longer held together with grand metaphysical truths or certainties. In other words, in the new historical reality, human consciousness has been unhinged from the singular force of concepts such as nature, god and reason: that is to say, unhinged from the role that such concepts have played, at different historical stages, in ordering social relations and governing relationships between the human and non-human. The world has fallen, as it were. Another key claim which comes from Jewish messianism, at least in respect of the way Kracauer metaphorically uses it to analyse history, is that industrial-capitalist production, including the influence of capitalist modes of production on culture, is a major cause of these characteristics of modern society: 'Capitalist rationalisation and the concomitant alienation of human life, labour and interpersonal relations' (Hansen 1991: 50) mean that 'the subject is "thrown into the cold infinity of empty space and time"' (Kracauer quoted in Hansen 1991: 50). That is to say, thrown into a modern world which lacks the power of totalising meanings and that, as a result, has disintegrated into disorder.

Hansen (1993) says that, while Kracauer views this situation as traumatic, he also believes that mediums such as photography and cinema are well positioned to record, discover and comment on 'the material world in all its fragments and elements' (448) and confront the spectator with 'the actual state of disorder and crisis' (457). The main reason that this is the case is because media such as photography are, in part, symptomatic of industrial, technological and scientific production under the conditions of capitalism. They are, therefore, media that are intimately connected to one of the major causes of change in modern life. Yet, at the same time, because such media have an inherent affinity for revealing contingency and redeeming materiality, they are also able to embody and express the actual state of social reality. In other words, such media are uniquely placed to discover the truth of modern life and, in the process, provide an inventory of the radical break in history that modernity represents. As Hansen puts it: 'the motif of discovery is linked to the recording and inventory function of film, the messianic motif of gathering and carrying along (*mitnehmen*) the material world' in all its different parts and aspects (448).

While Hansen believes that these radical, phenomenological aspects of Kracauer's earlier writings are ultimately buried in *Theory of Film*, Aitken (2006) argues, to the contrary, that some of these aspects are still evident in respect of his realist aesthetics. In this regard, Aitken particularly stresses the Husserlian notion of *Lebenswelt* as a key to understanding Kracauer's assertion that 'physical reality' can be redeemed through cinema. As already discussed, what Kracauer means by the subject's material, physiological being has to do with cognitive and psychological activity that remains deeply entwined with sensuous properties of perception and experience. This is a phenomenological account of spectatorship that can be contextualised in terms of Husserl's thought. Unlike Hansen, Aitken also does not see Kracauer as essentially burying all the radical, political elements of this phenomenology. Rather, he argues that

> phenomenology and realism can be discerned within both Kracauer's early and late writings, as part of a sustained critique of mainstream cinema as a force for both the reinforcement of abstraction and dominant ideology, and the liberation of the subject. (3)

What Aitken is saying here is that Kracauer is aware that cinema can perform all kinds of functions, including the ideological function of presenting the world as unified rather than as chaotic. For instance, in terms of the role that media such as cinema have representing, even materialising, particular historical processes and experiences, films can distort or repress the reality of modern social existence. What Aitken is also saying, however, is that, in *Theory of Film*, Kracauer explores the question of how cinema can emancipate spectators.

As already pointed out, Aitken says that, in *Theory of Film*, Kracauer focuses on how films can liberate spectators with regard to modern experiences of instrumentalisation. As noted earlier, Kracauer feels that media such as photography and film have the potential to peel away the veil of abstraction that covers the world. If this act of disclosure is contextualised in terms of the figurative use that Kracauer makes of Jewish messianism, it can be said that what underpins the assertion that media such as cinema are able to release spectators from the disenchantment of instrumental reason is that, while photography and film are intimately connected to industrial modes of production and technical modes of invention under the conditions of capitalism – precisely those activities which are a cause of modern alienation – such intimacy also provides them with the opportunity to transform the negative affects of modern capitalism. The ability to transform experiences of disenchantment is, of course, dependent on cinema's penchant for engaging the material, physiological being of spectators, just as the value of historicising society by drawing on Jewish messsianism is tied, for Kracauer, to understanding how different contents of the material world can be restored and expressed through photography and film so that 'the sparks encrusted in even the most fallen matter can be released' (Hansen 1991: 54). As such, the act of stripping away the veil can be read not only in terms of redeeming, in Aitken's (2001) words, 'primal and underlying mode(s) of communication' (16) but also collecting and gathering the fragmented experiences of modern life into a perceptible form that reveals the actual state of social existence. Indeed, it is this last sense that gives full meaning to Aitken's phrase that film, for Kracauer, can 'redirect the spectator's attention to the *texture of life*' (170) (emphasis added). Film realism, in this sense, is about how cinema can stage and bring together different elements of the material world in a manner that preserves and makes actual what otherwise often remains invisible.

In the context of realism, more evidence of the continuity between Kracauer's Weimar writings and works such as *Theory of Film* can be found when looking at Kracauer's philosophical–theological essay, *The Detective Novel* (*Der Detektiv-Roman*). The work was finished in 1925 but only a part of it was published during Kracauer's lifetime: namely, the chapter 'The Hotel Lobby' which came out in a collection of essays called *The Mass Ornament*, first published in 1963. Gertrud Koch has said that 'the treatise as a whole brings together almost all themes of significance to Kracauer in his early work. This is also true of the discernible emphasis on the religious and theological spheres in his thought' (16). In terms of *Theory of Film*, what is particularly important about *The Detective Novel* is its argument that the narrative and aesthetic techniques employed within a given medium, such as the literary genre of detective fiction, can show that, within the existing world of appearances, the immanent, everyday world of life, transcendence can occur. In *The Detective Novel* such transcendence is directly and indirectly talked about in terms derived from traditional Jewish and biblical traditions (Mack 1999; Koch 2000), such as *halacha* (law), messiansim, revelation, and the divine and the profane. Moreover, in *The Detective Novel*, the focus is on how characters are constructed and how spaces are depicted, in a way that reveals the cohabitation of higher and lower spheres of existence. It is particularly the essay's assertion that a language of the real emerges in and through the flux and fluidity of everyday existence that resonates with aspects of *Theory of Film*, specifically those sections that focus on, in Aitken's words, 'the texture of life' or, as Hansen has put it, talking about Kracauer's Weimar writings and his notebooks for *Theory of Film*, but in a language that clearly still relates to the final film theory book, the different elements, dimensions and realties which make up the world that human beings inhabit.

In *The Detective Novel* it is also suggested that such a language of the real exists outside the instrumental use of pure logic, rational investigation based on a priori principles, empirical observation and other activities that

Kracauer associates with the work of the detective figure. Michael Mack says such a figure represents intellectual abstraction and 'rational reduction' which 'empties life of all its qualities' (410) and, hence, the detective stands in for the quantification and mechanisation of existence that, Kracauer argues, occurs with science under the conditions of capitalism. Koch suggests that the detective figure is ambiguous. She says that, because of his access to powers of reason which allow him to know what mysteries are behind everything, even if such knowledge serves, as Mack suggests, his 'intellectual experiments' rather than caring for or redeeming the people and objects he deals with (409), it can be argued that the detective figure occupies a space that has a connection to a suprarational sphere and, hence, an affinity with that which lies beyond disenchantment. However the detective figure is read, the point for now is that the language of the real which can emerge in and through the world of particularity and contingency is a language that opens up the reader (the reader of detective fiction as well as the reader of those things that belong to the cultural sphere more broadly) to that which exists beyond the levelling processes of reason and abstraction. Moreover, such a language destablises fixed approaches to identifying and defining reality and, instead, invites interpretations of experience that are enmeshed in the disorder and flow of existence.

The notion that the language of the real exists beyond such activities as the instrumental use of pure logic and rational investigation based on a priori principles relates to what, as discussed earlier, Kracauer says in *Theory of Film* about cinema's relationship to changes in the historical and ideological make-up of modern life. Film, he argues, is able to redeem modes of experience and communication lost to the dominant modern mentality which 'cares about means and functions rather than ends and modes of being' (292) and which leads people to 'eliminate the qualities of things' that they encounter in the world (300). Moreover, the idea that the language of the real invites interpretations of experience which are engaged with the chaos and fluidity of existence, connects with what in *Theory of Film* Kracauer calls the state of 'dreaming toward the object'. In such a state, he says, the spectator finds that they 'drift toward and into the objects' (165) on screen. Such a dreaming state is predicated on, first, the stimulation of the spectator's material, physiological being which, as explained earlier, involves cognitive and psychological activity that is interrelated with, or bound by, the spectator's body or the presence of their material being, and, second, on a loss of the spectator's sense of having a coherent, subjective self-identity that is disembodied. If these conditions are met, it is possible, suggests Kracauer, for spectators to become immersed in images and in 'the being of any object that draws him [or her] into its orbit' (165). In a 'trance-like' (166) state, spectators can find that the objects on screen ignite for them 'multiple meanings and psychological correspondences' (165). Such meanings and correspondences involve moods, feelings, nascent thoughts, buried memories and other embodied psychological states that are immediately and sensuously connected to the objects on screen. Such objects can include inanimate things and non-human entities. Kracauer goes so far as to suggest that: 'In experiencing an object, we not only broaden our knowledge of its diverse qualities but in a manner of speaking incorporate it into us so that we grasp its being and its dynamics from within – a sort of blood transfusion, as it were.' (297)

To be sure, it should be said that in *Theory of Film* it is the camera and the screen which take centre stage as the means through which the language of the real can emerge, rather than the narrative and aesthetic techniques of a literary genre. Nonetheless, it can be argued that there is an overall claim in *Theory of Film* which is similar to one of the key claims in *The Detective Novel*. In the latter work, it is by passing through the profane world of the finite and the contingent, including the base world of appearances, that proximity with that which lies beyond the procedures of enclosed ratiocination, which pre-structures experience on the basis of categories and instrumental ends, can be found. In *Theory of Film*, collecting and gathering material elements of the world into a perceptible form on screen and also, in the process, bringing the spectator back to the primacy of their physiological being and to encounters with the different aspects of the external world often ignored or overlooked, mean drawing the spectator into a reality that exists beyond the activities that Kracauer associates with the detective figure who stands in for the abstraction and disenchantment of capitalism more broadly. In this sense, the establishment of 'physical reality' on screen involves affecting a spectator in a manner that facilitates his or her consciousness entering an alternative sphere of experience. For such reasons it can be said that religious metaphysics still informs Kracauer's position on realism in *Theory of Film* even if such metaphysics is not explicitly referred to or discussed.

REFERENCES

Adorno, Theodore [1964] (1991), 'The Curious Realist: On Siegfried Kracauer', *New German Critique*, 54, pp. 159–77.

Aitken, Ian (2001), *European Film Theory: A Critical Introduction*, Edinburgh: Edinburgh University Press.

— (2006), *Realist Film Theory and Cinema: The Nineteenth-Century Lukácsian and Intuitionist Realist Traditions*, Manchester: Manchester University Press.

— (2007), 'Physical Reality: The Role of the Empirical in the Film Theory of Siegfried Kracauer, John Grierson, André Bazin and Georg Lukács', *Studies in Documentary Film*, 1: 2, pp. 105–21.

Elsaesser, Thomas (1987), 'Cinema – The Irresponsible Signifier or "The Gamble with History": Film Theory or Cinema Theory', *New German Critique*, 40, pp. 65–89.

— (2014), 'Siegfried Kracauer's Affinities', *European Journal of Media Studies*, 5, http://www.necsus-ejms.org/siegfried-kracauers-affinities/ (last accessed 5 May 2015).

Hansen, Miriam (1991), 'Decentric Perspectives: Kracauer's Early Writings on Film and Mass Culture', *New German Critique*, 54, pp. 47–76.

— (1993), '"With Skin and Hair": Kracauer's Theory of Film', *Critical Enquiry*, 19: 3, pp. 437–69.

— (1997), 'Introduction', in *Theory of Film: The Redemption of Physical Reality*, Princeton, NJ: Princeton University Press.

Koch, Gertrud (2000), *Siegfried Kracauer: An Introduction*, trans. Jeremy Gains, Princeton, NJ: Princeton University Press.

Kracauer, Siegfried [1960] (1997), *Theory of Film: The Redemption of Physical Reality*, Princeton, NJ: Princeton University Press.

— (1969), *History: The Last Things Before the Last*, New York: Oxford University Press.

Mack, Michael (1999), 'Literature and Theory: Siegfried Kracauer's Law, Walter Benjamin's Allegory and G. K. Chesterton's "The Innocence of Father Brown"', *Orbis Litterarum*, 54, pp. 399–423.

CHAPTER 4

'Montage, My Fine Care': Realism, Surrealism and Postmodernism after Bazin

Ramona Fotiade

Over the past fifty years, André Bazin's conception of cinematic realism has withstood wave upon wave of theoretical reappraisal and ideological reappropriation or reframing, only to resurface once again at the centre of debates following the advent of digital cinema and the transition to the new modes of production and consumption associated with DVD and 3D technology. It is perhaps time Bazin's contribution to postmodern theories of the image was considered both in terms of its legacy, as reflected in Barthes's and Deleuze's reconceptualisations of the photographic and cinematic language, and in relation to its contemporary, decisive role in shaping the aesthetics and filming practice of the French new wave. Few will doubt that the reception of Bazin's work in the 1980s, though eclipsed by the rise of anti-realist theories, owed much to the legitimacy which film art had gained as a result of his careful philosophical and critical staging of the confrontation between Hollywood, classic French cinema and Italian neorealism during the 1940s and 1950s. Whether, in this context, the new wave can be said to have fulfilled the aspirations of Bazin's film aesthetics, and may have even facilitated, in some cases, their rehabilitation in the postmodern (and 'post-realist') age, needs to be set against the often obscured, yet crucial interaction between Bazinian cinematic realism and avant-garde movements, such as surrealism. Given the unique place that the *Cahiers du cinéma* founder occupies at the crossroads between different schools and generations of film-makers, no accurate account of the postmodern relevance of Bazin's reflections on the ontology of the photographic image or the evolution of film language can ignore the critic's exchanges with at least two prominent representatives of French experimental cinema: Jean-Luc Godard and Luis Buñuel. The extent to which, in both cases, Bazin's insistence on Jean Renoir opens up, rather than precludes, the possibility of dialogue and provides a paradoxical middle ground where the new wave picks up and reaffirms the surrealist disavowal of impressionist cinema, brings out the

contemporary resonance of the fundamental issues which any in-depth exploration of the realism of cinematic images is bound to raise. Should one oppose
the inherent, 'natural' realism of cinematic images (as indexical replicas of real
objects in the world) and the 'artifice' of montage? Should film-makers discard
the depiction of immaterial, invisible phenomena of the mind for the sake of
cinematic realism? What is the ontological and temporal status of the 'realist'
images of objects and beings in the world? These questions have continued
to haunt theorists and practitioners of photography and film (from Metz to
Barthes and Deleuze, from Godard to Fellini and Lynch) long after Bazin's
untimely death in 1958.

Though the aspiring film-maker on whom Bazin's personality and conception of cinema left a lasting impression during the formative years of the new
wave was Truffaut, as opposed to Godard, who professed a certain independence of thought in his articles at the time, one can say that *À bout de souffle*,
hailed as the manifesto of the new movement on its release in 1960, paid homage
to the father of cinematic realism in ways that were no less overt to discerning
viewers than the dedication which prefaced Truffaut's debut feature, *Les quatre
cents coups / The Four Hundred Blows*, the previous year at the Cannes festival.
It is not simply a question of recalling yet again Godard's provocative use of
the documentary style of filming which Bazin had tied in with Italian neorealism and with the absence of montage and rule of the unity of space (exemplified with reference to Flaherty as well as Lamorisse, for the French tradition).
Alongside the emphasis on outdoor and location shooting, with a hand-held
camera and a reduced crew, which combined with the occasional extract from
newsreel footage (such as President Eisenhower's visit to Paris in 1959) to give a
distinct historical realism to the characters and events in Godard's film, Godard
also engaged with Bazin's auteurist reappraisal of American cinema and the
critic's endorsement of Renoir's directorial style as the pinnacle of French
realism through a range of subtle, yet salient, metadiegetic cues. Not only are
the two protagonists in *À bout de souffle*, Patricia (Jean Seberg) and Michel
(Jean-Paul Belmondo) representative of opposed sets of cultural conventions in
narrative terms but the very presence of the actors on the screen (in particular,
Seberg's, whose star status in France owed much to the leading role she played
in Otto Preminger's adaptation of Françoise Sagan's novel, *Bonjour Tristesse* –
1958) offered Godard the springboard for an intricate web of cross references,
indicative in themselves of the directorial choices and statements that made up
the ingrained manifesto of the new wave. When, after the premiere of *À bout de
souffle*, Godard argued that his film was 'really a documentary on Jean Seberg
and Jean-Paul Belmondo' (Godard 1990: 166), he referred not only to Raoul
Coutard's filming technique (as that of an experienced war photographer and
newsreel cameraman), but also to the confrontation between opposing styles of
acting and cinematic traditions.

The allusion to Jean Renoir's *mise en scène* in the hotel sequence (when Patricia seeks Michel's approval as she compares herself to the girl in a poster reproduction of a painting by Renoir's father, the impressionist painter Pierre-August Renoir), occurs in the middle of a long sequence of references to American film noir and other classic Hollywood genre films (in particular, westerns and thrillers), punctuated by the cameo appearance of Jean-Pierre Melville, author of popular French gangster films in the 1950s (*Bob le flambeur*, 1955 and *Deux hommes à Manhattan*, 1958). A range of iconic Hollywood productions of the period are similarly brought to the audience's attention in *À bout de souffle* as Belmondo's character impersonates Humphrey Bogart in *The Harder They Fall* (1956), repeatedly using his trademark lip-wiping gesture (which Patricia replicates in the final shot of the film) as he walks past a poster advertising Robert Aldrich's *Ten Seconds to Hell* (1959), and is seen coming out of a cinema where Budd Boetticher's *Westbound* (1959) was playing. Jean Seberg's character, in turn, slips in and out of a cinema where Otto Preminger's *Whirlpool* is playing in order to elude the police surveillance that she is subject to. Indeed, Godard could just as well have said that his film was a documentary about the generation of young cinephiles coming of age during Bazin's editorship of *Cahiers du cinéma* ; *À bout de souffle* is replete with references to the new wave obsession with American cinema, and boasts an in-depth knowledge of Hollywood cinematic codes and directorial styles. At the same time, Godard's debut feature implicitly points to the emerging confrontation between the established production system and the post-war national schools of film-making gathered under the banner of Italian neorealism.

If Godard engages with Bazin's aesthetic conception and rejection of montage (not only through the provocative use of jump cuts but also through the less conspicuous lack of editing in the hotel sequence, for which he seems to privilege the long take), he does so from the standpoint of a film critic turned film director who is fully aware of the position his generation occupies in the history of cinema, and, moreover, wants to make his audience aware that the 'Young Turks' are about to change 'the rules of the game': 'We were the first cinéastes to know that Griffith exists. Even Carné, Delluc, or René Clair, when they made their first films, had no true critical or historical background.' (Godard 1972k: 172) Thanks to Godard, and his uninhibited use of filmic quotations and stylistic fireworks, film suddenly seemed to skip the stage of a fumbling technique in search of an aesthetic, and acquired the status of self-reflexive art, capable of commenting on its own making, the evolution of its language and the controversial issue of cinematic realism as related to *mise en scène* and montage.

Godard's critical response to the articles which Bazin published in *Cahiers du cinéma* on montage in the 1950s (in particular, 'The Evolution of Cinematographic Language' and '*Montage interdit*'),[1] can be said to underlie all his film reviews and essays from the time, although this comes through most forcefully in three of his early writings. The first, published in the *Gazette du cinéma* (3/1950), bears the misleading title 'Towards a Political Cinema', because it advocates no definite political stance but seems rather to extol the expressive virtues of montage and the ability of the cinematic image to transcend time through the repetition of a fleeting instant which achieves the symbolic value of eternity:

> The village fleeing before the invader, the arrival of the Germans, shown in a single shot with fantastic virtuosity, the death of the young people, intensified in effect by repeating the same camera movement five times. These moments are brief, but their very swiftness is a sign of eternity [*suggère l'éternel*]. (Milne 1972: 16–17)[2]

Soviet productions as well as notorious examples of Nazi propaganda films are mentioned in the course of a typically ambivalent argument, which fore-shadows Godard's taste for provocation, his political films made after *À bout de souffle* (*Le petit soldat* – 1961 and *Les carabiniers* – 1962, the latter featuring the repetition of the same camera movement in the execution of the partisan girl); and, ultimately, his ongoing polemic with Bazin, as he recalled it in an interview with Alain Bergala, in 1985:

> I have always had, through my education, the spirit of contradiction. I said to myself: they are sharp-tongued, but couldn't one say the opposite? Bazin was saying: sequence-shot, and I was asking myself whether continuity editing was not good, after all. (Bergala 1985: 10)[3]

This statement aptly captures Godard's stand in his two other articles on editing in relation to *mise en scène*: 'Defense and Illustration of Classical Construction'/*Défense et illustration du découpage classique*, and 'Montage, My Fine Care'/*Montage, mon beau souci*, which were published in *Cahiers du cinéma* in September 1952 and December 1956, respectively. Bazin had argued, for instance, that Orson Welles's montage, unlike that of the early avant-garde film-makers of the 1920s, 'is not trying to deceive us; it offers us a contrast, condensing time, and hence is the equivalent for example of the French imperfect or of the English frequentative tense' (Bazin 2005a: 36). Contrary to Bazin's indictment of German expressionism and the use of optical effects and montage otherwise than to enhance the inherently realist vocation of narrative cinema, Godard argued that American comedy, as a genre, owed less to Mack Sennett slapstick than it owed to German expressionism, given that 'Expressionism had made the eye the moral focus for feeling' (Godard 1972a: 27). He then goes on to defend Otto Preminger's use of shot and reverse shot, and his predilection for 'medium rather than long shots' which revealed 'the desire to reduce the drama to the immobility of the face' (28). Whereas Bazin praised Italian neorealism for 'its stripping away of all expressionism' and, in particular, in the 'total absence of the effects of montage' (Bazin 2005a: 37), Godard endorsed the heightened realism of the close-up, despite 'the spatial discontinuity occasioned by shot changes which certain devotees of the "ten-minute take" make a point of despising' (Godard 1972a: 29).

The quintessential scene in *À bout de souffle*, as far as Godard's polemical engagement with Bazin is concerned, occurs in the second half of the film, when Patricia and Michel go to see a Western to escape the police and wait until nightfall. It is only when they leave the cinema that a long shot reveals what was playing: Budd Boetticher's *Westbound* (1959). Beyond the historical realism of the cinephile reference to the contemporary French release of an American film, the whole scene is an elaborate allusion to Bazin's articles on the Western, the latest of which, published in 1957 in *Cahiers du cinéma*, was devoted to Budd Boetticher, and was entitled 'An Exemplary Western: *Seven Men From Now*' (Bazin 1985: 242–7). In his 1953 article, 'The Western or the American Film *par excellence*', Bazin traced back the origins of the genre to 'the encounter between a mythology and a means of expression' (Bazin 2005b: 142), and signalled the correspondence between the character of the hero and the style of *mise en scène*, which explains the virtual absence of close-ups, and the pronounced predilection for travelling and panning shots 'which refuse to be limited by the frameline and which restore to space its fullness' (147). Unlike the aural quotation from Otto Preminger's *Whirlpool*, the scene filmed inside the cinema where Boetticher's *Westbound* is supposed to be playing hinges on one of the most intriguing instances of sound-image asynchrony in cinema history, relying entirely on the extreme close-up of Michel and Patricia kissing as their profiles are lit up by the flickering light coming from the screen and the following implausible version of the dialogue of the film in progress (dubbed in French and recited in monotonous, incantatory manner) is heard on the soundtrack:

> MAN'S VOICE (*off*): Beware, Jessica,
>   The beveled edge of kisses.
>   The years pass by too swiftly.
>   Shun, shun the memories that hurt.
> WOMAN'S VOICE (*off*): You're wrong, sheriff . . .
>   Our story is noble and tragic
>   Like the mask of a tyrant.
>   A drama neither perilous nor magic.
>   No cold detail
>   Can turn our love pathetic (Andrew 1990: 122).

The compelling framing of the scene (with its assumed mirror image of a situation portrayed on the screen) is visually in jarring contrast to Bazin's argument about the stylistic specificity of 'The Western or the American film *par excellence*', predicated on the virtual absence of close-ups.

Added to this layer of filmic intertextuality, however, there is a different type of confrontation between Hollywood and the new French cinema going on at the level of soundtrack where a short aural quotation is followed by an incongruous dubbed dialogue made up of extracts from love poems by two surrealist writers: Aragon's 'Elsa je t'aime' and Apollinaire's 'Cors de chasse'. This lyrical interlude is loosely connected with the expected Western story through the addition of short introductory lines, meant to identify the off-screen characters as Jessica and the sheriff (neither of whom, needless to say, appears in Boetticher's film). More than the question of a distinctly postmodern collision between 'low and high culture' (Martin 2004: 262), what strikes the cinephile viewer in this case is Godard's carefully constructed opposition between two cinematic traditions, and the manner in which surrealism is used as shorthand for the French '*politique des auteurs*' in contrast to established Hollywood genre conventions. A pastiche of the American film noir (and of Bogart's recognisable screen persona), *À bout de souffle* also engages, in parodic mode, with the assumed 'exemplarity' of the Western, its 'faithfulness to history' (*sa vérité historique*) and the realism of its *mise en scène* (Bazin 2005b: 142). If Bazin emphatically stated in the opening lines of his 1957 article on Budd Boetticher, entitled 'An Exemplary Western: *Seven Men From Now*', that 'We have here the opportunity of applying what we have said about the *politique des auteurs*' (Bazin 1985: 241), it was a different understanding of the new aesthetic and stylistic conception (based on the competing practices of the Hollywood studio system and the neorealist inspired French new wave) that Godard would reclaim and defend. Whereas Bazin invariably praised the realistic credentials of directorial styles which privileged the use of depth of field over editing (whether this happened to apply to Orson Welles, Jean Renoir or Visconti), from 1959 Godard embarked on a quest for the specificity of the French *authorial* approach to film-making which was to crystallise into the manifesto of the *Nouvelle Vague* – neither a slavish imitation of Hollywood nor a perfunctory rehearsal of neorealist techniques to mark the break with the Hollywood tradition:

> Because even when it is badly composed, badly shot, badly edited, one feels, one senses that there is an artist behind the French camera; whereas even when it is well composed, well shot, well edited, behind the foreign cameras one senses, one feels that there are only craftsmen. (Godard 1972b: 111)

It is worth recalling here that, when Godard greeted the news of Truffaut's success as the director chosen to represent France at the Cannes Film Festival in 1959, he did so under the banner of 'those [. . .] who waged, in homage to Louis Delluc, Roger Leenhardt and André Bazin the battle for the film auteur' (Godard 1972j: 147). The yardstick, however, of the artistic legitimacy that Hollywood film-makers were supposed to have achieved, thanks to the '*politique des auteurs*', appears in the shape of a reference to Aragon (rather than to the more respectable French realist tradition of the novel): 'We won the day in having it acknowledged in principle that a film by Hitchcock, for example, is as important as a book by Aragon. Film auteurs, thanks to us, have finally entered the history of art.' (147) Surprisingly, Godard's template for the new style of filming and the French *politique des auteurs* does not seek support in either Renoir's or Rossellini's *mise en scène* but in the aesthetics of the surrealist avant-garde (whether in the guise of its poetic revolution of language, illustrated by Aragon, or in respect of its ingenious use of montage, Bazin's protestations notwithstanding).

Surrealism crops up at regular intervals in Godard's articles from the 1950s, and perhaps nowhere more saliently than in his review of the 1959 Short Film Festival in Tours which mixes an approving nod to Bazin's notion of 'impure cinema' (in defence of screen adaptations) with a discussion of the specificity of the new school of 'French short film-making' (under the heading '*Vive la France*') and an enthusiastic review of Jacques Rozier's *Blue Jeans*, leading up to the quotation of the same quatrain from Aragon's love poem, 'Elsa, je t'aime', which Godard deliberately inserted and ended up reading on the soundtrack of *À bout de souffle* several months later. The common denominator of Godard's incursions into Bazin's critical territory from a surrealist angle resided in his passionate interest in documentaries and the nature of the reality captured on camera not only by the early pioneers of the medium, such as the Lumières, but also by contemporary anthropologists and amateur ethnographic film-makers, such as Jean Rouch, who left a deeper mark on the evolution of the new wave than one may first be inclined to think. If Godard admired Rouch's keen eye for the composition within the shot, in a 'search for the Holy Grail called *mise en scène*' (Godard 1972c: 129), this was because he knew Rouch's style did not derive from a conscious aesthetic decision but emerged in response to the constraints of the medium and of the amateur tools he had at his disposal: a hand-held camera, no direct-sound recording equipment, and, above all, the very short – 20 seconds – reel of film which accounted for the lack of montage, the fluidity of the shot and the unity of space achieved. What Rouch and the surrealists (epitomised by the recurrent references to Aragon, Franju, and later to Buñuel) brought to the new generation of film-makers, according to Godard, was a refreshing return to the origins of cinema, to the truthfulness of the unskilled or spontaneous recording of reality, to the early days of montage and the advent of sound, when each optical or sound effect still had the ability to disconcert the viewer, and reveal the unknown, or the disquieting side of everyday occurrences:

> In all of Franju's documentaries, even the least successful of them, a flash of madness suddenly rips the screen and forces the spectator to look at reality in another light. In *La Tête contre les murs* (1959) [. . .], this flash, this poetic illumination, has become the theme of the film. [. . .] In more modern terms, let us say that Franju demonstrates the necessity of Surrealism if one considers it as a pilgrimage to the sources. (Godard 1972j: 129–30)

The return to the origins of cinema ranked high among Godard's privileged markers of a break with tradition, which echoed his appreciation of the early Dada and surrealist dismantling of established literary codes and classical writing, most often evidenced in his references to Aragon or to *Ballet mécanique* (Fernand Léger, Dudley Murphy, 1924) (Godard 1972c: 54). In one of his retrospective interviews, he interestingly tied in his use of 'amateur' techniques in *À bout de souffle* with his understanding of the inherent realism of cinema, which happened to coincide not only with Bazin's conception (based on the indexical nature of the medium) but also with the surrealist notion of photography as 'genuine photography of thought' (Breton 1988 : 245):

> I think that cinematographers [. . .] think their eyes look *out* at a moving reality that's coming *in*, but they don't consider that maybe there's a kind of invisible camera with an eye *out there* and with the printing *in here*. [. . .] Most cinematographers are bad soldiers who don't know what they are fighting for, whether they want the enemy to come in or go out. [. . .] That is why I brought 'amateur' techniques to movies. In *Breathless*, I used the same techniques of *Life* reporters who, at that time, had nothing to do with Hollywood. I also used underexposed pictures, which were considered awful. (Godard 1998: 98)

The extent to which surrealism, alongside the new documentary tradition (illustrated by young film-makers of the 1950s such as Agnès Varda, Jacques Rosier and Alain Resnais), becomes the template of French neorealism, and of Godard's own interpretation of the *politique des auteurs*, as opposed to what he calls the *politique des metteurs en scène* (Godard 1972c: 79), can best be measured when considering the paraphrase of Breton's memorable ending of *Nadja* (1928) which provides the peremptory conclusion of Godard's review of the Tours Short Film Festival: 'Henceforth, the beauty of any short film must be that of these four (Varda's *Du côté de la côte*, Demy's *Le Bel indifférent*, Rozier's *Blue*

Jeans and Resnais' *Le Chant du Styrène*), or no beauty at all' (Godard 1972e: 116). 'To make a short film today is in a way to return to the cinema's beginnings' (112), Godard further remarked, and, in the same way in which he defended the use of montage by the new generation of documentary film-makers, he constantly sought to validate the enhanced realism derived from Eisenstein's revolutionary use of the 'montage by attraction' or optical effects, which came up in the early Dada and surrealist films, as well as in certain otherwise thoroughly plausible scenes from Hitchcock's *The Wrong Man* (1956) (Godard 1972c: 54). Godard's conspicuous references to Buñuel in his later militant productions, such as *Weekend* (1967) and *Prénom Carmen/First Name: Carmen* (1983), further highlight the new wave director's belief in the indissoluble link between social realism and its cinematic expression in a revolutionary syntax of film. The enigmatic hitch-hiker in *Weekend*, identified by means of a recurrent screen caption as the 'exterminating angel' (the title of Buñuel's iconic 1962 feature), declares in typical Dada fashion: 'I am here to proclaim to these modern times the end of the grammatical era and the beginning of an age of flamboyance in every field, especially the movies'. The savage indictment of consumer society in *Weekend* thus echoes the scathing critique of the bourgeoisie in Buñuel's surrealist parable whose theatrical *mise en scène*, coupled with a striking use of repetition, prompted Deleuze's comments on the evolution of cinematographic language in the work of the surrealist film-maker, signalling the advent of the 'time-image' from within the confines of a classical, realist construction:

> *He injects the power of repetition into the cinematographic image.* In this way he is already going beyond the world of impulses, to knock on the doors of time. [. . .] He elaborates another type of sign which might be called 'scene' and which perhaps gives us a direct time-image. [. . .] But it is from inside that Buñuel goes beyond naturalism, without ever renouncing it. (Deleuze 2005: 137)

Bazin's highly appreciative remarks on Buñuel's documentary style in *Las Hurdes/Land without Bread* (1933) and *Los olvidados/The Young and the Damned* (1950) similarly underscore the successful blend of surrealist imagery and a sociopolitical message, which is rendered all the more effective by the skilful use of montage and optical effects, despite an obvious break with the conventions of narrative cinema and psychological realism. One of the few favourable reviews of *Los olvidados* at the time of its first release in France, Bazin's article interestingly contrasts Salvador Dali's vision for the dream sequence in Hitchcock's Hollywood-produced *Spellbound* (1945), hinted at rather than explicitly designated as the worst example of Freudian surrealism, and Buñuel's subtle interweaving of continuity editing and irrational elements in the scenes referred to below involving the Pedro's and Jaïbo's characters:

> Buñuel achieves the tour de force of recreating two dreams in the worst
> tradition of Hollywood Freudian surrealism and yet leaving us palpitat-
> ing with horror and pity. Pedro has run away from home because his
> mother refused to give him a scrap of meat which he wanted. He dreams
> that his mother gets up in the night to offer him a cut of raw and bleed-
> ing meat, which Jaïbo, hidden under the bed, grabs as she passes. We
> shall never forget that piece of meat, quivering like a dead octopus as
> the mother offers it with a Madonna-like smile. Nor shall we ever forget
> the poor, homeless, mangy dog which passes through Jaïbo's receding
> consciousness as he lies dying on a piece of waste ground, his forehead
> wreathed in blood. (Bazin 2013: 54–5)

Bazin's profound affinity with Buñuel's vision carefully distinguished between
the unsatisfactory effect of iconic or pictorial elements in surrealist cinematography when used to render in too deliberate a fashion the aesthetics of
Freudian ideology, on the one hand, and what he termed the 'irrefragable
truth' of the psychoanalytical situations portrayed in Buñuel's early films: *Un
Chien Andalou/An Andalusian Dog* (1929), *L'Âge d'Or/The Golden Age* (1930)
and *Los olvidados* (55). The graphic, visceral vocabulary which Bazin marshals
in support of Buñuel's approach to rendering the inner reality of thought processes resonates well with the critic's insistence on the indexical, physical connection between the image and the object captured on film: 'his images have
a pulsating, burning power to move us – the thick blood of the unconscious
circulates in them and swamps us, as from an opened artery, with the pulse of
the mind' (55).

 Though the surrealist conception and practice of cinema seemed in every
way opposed to Bazin's conceptualisation of cinematographic realism, the
enthusiastic adoption of photography among the preferred experimental techniques in early avant-garde circles happened to arise from the same acknowledgement of the radical shift in the existing regime of visual representation
inaugurated by the photographic imprint. Bazin and Breton agreed not only
on the objectivity derived from the indexical nature of the new medium (the
former highlighting, for instance, 'the transference of reality from the thing to
its reproduction' – Bazin 2005a: 14) but also on the mechanical, non-human
process involved, which made the author of *The Surrealist Manifesto* describe
automatic drawing in terms of a type of transfer or decal (Breton 1988b: 325)
while Bazin, in turn, hailed the realism inherent in the type of 'moulding'
or 'imprinting' which photography and film pioneered (Bazin 2005a: 96–7).
The paradox of the temporal 'cast' that cinema realises by 'moulding itself
on the time of the object and [. . .] taking the imprint of its duration as well'
(97) ties in with one of the earliest and most enduring aspirations of surrealist
cinema which related to the possibility of capturing both the mere duration of

a movement in space (or what Deleuze referred to as the 'movement-image') and the expression of inner time perception. Buñuel's use of repetition in *The Exterminating Angel*, and his use of superimposition and slow motion in *Los olvidados*, fully demonstrate the potential of surrealist cinema to achieve one of the earliest expressions of the 'time-image' whose truthfulness ensues from a sustained exploration of the status of photographic images which Bazin himself defined, in relation to surrealism, as a 'hallucination which is also a fact' (16).

The return to the sources of cinema in surrealism, and in its subsequent new wave avatars, as well as in Godard's experimental and militant cinema, can thus be said to tend towards the realisation of the 'integral realism' which Bazin identified as 'the myth of total cinema'; 'a recreation of the world in its own image, an image unburdened by the freedom of interpretation of the artist or the irreversibility of time' (Bazin 2005a : 21). With the advent of digital and 3D modes of production and consumption, film language is on the threshold of a new revolution, which Bazin had foreseen, and which, paradoxically, surrealism as well as the French neorealist and new wave practitioners promised to fulfil by pledging to recapture what 'the real primitives of the cinema' had imagined. The 'complete imitation of nature', aiming, beyond mere repetition, at the recreation of the complete haptic and psychological perception of time, of processes of memory and projection into the future, freed from the constraints of linear, irreversible duration, yet firmly grounded in the corporeal experience of the viewer. If, with every new development, as Bazin remarked, film language draws nearer and nearer to its origins, then 'cinema has not been invented' (21) and every repetition and return bring it closer to the 'decisive instant' when the closed or circular movement becomes 'a repetition which not only succeeds, but recreates the model of the originary' (Deleuze 2005 : 136). In attempting to realise the myth of total cinema, which has always been and will always remain tied in with the myth of its 'integral realism', the indexicality of photography and film will no doubt increasingly tend to restore the inner objects and phenomena of spatial and temporal perception, in a symptomatic return to the surrealist 'genuine photography of thought', and to its disturbingly persuasive pictures of the mind whose 'meaning (as Bazin himself argued) is not in the image, it is in the shadow of the image projected by montage onto the field of the consciousness of the spectator' (Bazin 2005a : 26).

NOTES

1. These titles refer, in each case, to a series of articles reprinted in the French edition of *What is Cinema*, in 1958. 'Montage interdit', translated as 'The Virtues and Limitations of Montage', gathers together two articles published in *Cahiers du cinéma* in 1953 and 1957, whereas 'The Evolution of Cinematographic Language' is a compilation of three articles: the earliest published in 1950, in *Cahiers du cinéma*, the second in 1952, in a volume entitled

Twenty Years of Cinema in Venice, and the last in 1955, in the magazine *L'Âge nouveau* (see Bazin 1985: 49, 63).

2. I have slightly altered the translation of the last two words to render the connection between the instant and eternity in Godard's text.

3. All translations are mine unless otherwise indicated.

REFERENCES

Andrew, Dudley (1990), *Breathless, Jean-Luc Godard, director*, New Brunswick, NJ and London: Rutgers University Press.

Bazin, André (2013), 'Los olvidados', *L'Esprit*, XX, no. 186 (1951), pp. 85–9; quoted in English from 'Cruelty and Love in *Los Olvidados*', *The Cinema of Cruelty. From Buñuel to Hitchcock*, ed. with an Introduction by François Truffaut, trans. Sabine d'Estrée with Tiffany Fliss, New York: Arcade Publishing, pp. 51–8.

— (1985), *Qu'est-ce que le cinéma*, Paris: Éditions du Cerf.

— (1997), *Bazin at Work. Major Essays and Reviews from the Forties and Fifties*, trans. Alain Piette and Bert Cardullo, Abingdon and New York: Routledge.

— (2005a), *What is Cinema I*, trans. Hugh Grant, Berkeley, CA, Los Angeles, CA and London: University of California Press.

— (2005b), *What is Cinema II*, trans. Hugh Grant, Berkeley, CA, Los Angeles, CA and London: University of California Press.

Bergala, Alain (1985), *Jean-Luc Godard par Jean-Luc Godard*, Paris: Éditions de l'Étoile and Cahiers du Cinéma.

Breton, André (1988a), 'Max Ernst' (text written for the catalogue of Max Ernst's exhibition at *Au Sans Pareil*, and later published in *Les Pas perdus*), *Oeuvres complètes* I, Paris: NRF and Gallimard, pp. 245–6.

— (1988b), 'Le Manifeste du surréalisme', *Oeuvres complètes* I, Paris: NRF and Gallimard, pp. 309—46.

Deleuze, Gilles (2005), *Cinema 1*, trans. Hugh Tomlinson and Barbara Habberjam, London: Continuum.

Godard, Jean-Luc (1972a), 'Défense et illustration du découpage classique', *Cahiers du cinéma* 15, September 1952, quoted in English in Milne, Tom, and Narboni, Jean (eds) (1972), *Godard on Godard. Critical Writings by Jean-Luc Godard*, New York and London: Da Capo Press, pp. 26–39.

— (1972b), 'Montage, mon beau souci', *Cahiers du cinéma* 65, December 1956, in Milne and Narboni, pp. 39–41.

— (1972c), 'The Wrong Man', *Cahiers du cinéma* 72, June 1957, in Milne and Narboni, pp. 48–55.

— (1972d), 'Bergmanorama', *Cahiers du cinéma* 58, July 1958, in Milne and Narboni, pp. 75–80.

— (1972e), 'Chacun son Tours', *Cahiers du cinéma* 92, February 1959, in Milne and Narboni, pp. 107–16.

— (1972f), 'Moi un noir', *Arts* 713, 11 March 1959, in Milne and Narboni, p. 129.

— (1972g), 'La tête contre les murs', *Arts* 715, 25 March 1959, in Milne and Narboni, pp. 129–130.

— (1972h), 'L'Afrique vous parle de la fin et des moyen', *Cahiers du cinéma* 94, April 1959, in English in Milne and Narboni, pp. 131–4.

— (1972i), 'Remarquable. Georges Franju, *La Tête contre les murs*, *Arts* 715, 25 March 1959, in Milne and Narboni, pp. 129–130.

— (1972j), 'Exclu l'an dernier du Festival, Truffaut représentera la France à Cannes avec *Les 400 coups*', *Arts* 719, April 1959, in Milne and Narboni, pp. 146–7.

— (1972k), interview published in the special *Nouvelle Vague* issue of *Cahiers du cinéma* no. 138, December 1962, in Milne and Narboni, pp. 171–96.

— (1990), interview with Yvonne Baby, *Le Monde*, 18 March 1960, quoted in English from Andrew 1990, pp. 165–6.

— (1998), *Interviews*, ed. Sterritt, David, Jackson, MS: University Press of Mississippi.

Martin, Adrian (2004), 'Recital: Three Lyrical Interludes in Godard', in Temple, Michael, William, James S. and Witt, Michael (eds), *Forever Godard*, London: Black Dog Publishing, 2004, pp. 252–71.

Milne, Tom, and Narboni, Jean (eds) (1972), *Godard on Godard. Critical Writings by Jean-Luc Godard*, New York and London: Da Capo Press.

Ropars-Wuilleumier, Marie-Claire (1982), 'The Graphic in Filmic Writing: *À bout de souffle* or the Erratic Alphabet', in *Enclitic*, 5: 6, 1982, pp. 147–61.

CHAPTER 5

Multiple Indexicality and Multiple Realism in André Bazin

Seung-hoon Jeong

INTRODUCTION: BAZIN REVISITED

Recent revisits by film scholars to the work of André Bazin go beyond a nostalgic return to the Bazin legacy, and also do so despite the supposed demise of its foundational medium, celluloid film. As suggested in *Opening Bazin* (Andrew and Joubert-Laurencin 2011) and *André Bazin's New Media* (Bazin 2014a), among others, Bazin is not just reaffirmed as a canon builder but 'reopened' as an intellectual who validly articulated the specificities of cinema.[1] His critical openness to diverse arts and cultural phenomena also reappears as a seminal reference point for a film academy which has been both expanded and threatened by new audiovisual practices and an all-directional approach to media studies. The task now may be to reframe this chaotic age of explosive media growth from the perspective of cinema if this now outdated medium is to retain the potential to offer new insights into media research. Against this backdrop, to rewrite Bazin's core theory of cinematic realism could also be imagined as a prelude to understanding its (post-cinematic) evolution. This attempt should identify theoretical conundrums in his multifaceted account of realism and its reinterpretations by later critics through a sort of dialectic thinking about concatenated ideas that Bazin might have articulated had he had the opportunity to do so. In other words, the evolution of Bazin's work and post-Bazinian critique of him should be retraced to retheorise Bazinian realism in a synthetic post-Bazinian language. The result of this would be to reformulate the notion of (post-)cinematic reality. As an initial step, this chapter focuses on Bazin's own realism via the unavoidably Bazinian term of *indexicality* which, though Bazin never used it, could be deconstructed and reinterpreted anew in broadly two opposite, yet interconnected, directions: those of the gaining and losing of reality.

FROM DIRECT REALISM TO PERCEPTUAL REALISM

Let me address a series of controversial points one by one and refine Bazin's position while filling in gaps he left behind. To begin with, Bazin's 'direct realism' means, briefly speaking, that the photographic image is an 'index', a type of sign whose relationship to its referent is actual causality, according to Charles Senders Peirce (see, among others, Wollen 1998; Doane 2007b; Gunning 2007). The object in front of the camera is physiochemically imprinted on to the light-sensitive film surface so the photograph brings unmediated reality as such (whereas the painting – an 'icon' that imitates the appearance of its referent – is subjectively mediated by the artist, however similar to its model it may look). This 'index argument' can lead to the assumption that the referent of a photographic image is a non-diegetic, pro-filmic object on the most fundamental level. This is the very guarantor of the documentary value that characterised Bazin's film ontology but it poses a dilemma in narrative film. For example, the image of, say, Arnold Schwarzenegger in *The Terminator* (James Cameron, 1984) is primarily an index of his real existence as the 'hard body' actor and future governor of California which is never essential in our diegetic, filmic experience of the cyborg character that he plays (Jeong 2013, 185; similarly, see Carroll 1988, 147–9). Bazin, however, would of course have argued that the photographic material base infuses immaterial diegesis with the more direct effect of reality more than any former media since the narrative space visible looks exactly like the actual perceivable world. The classical 'suspension of disbelief' works here all the more easily because belief in diegesis as reality involves less conscious activity. But this suspension does not mean that we completely forget the mechanism of the apparatus; it is just its suspension, that is, a conventional negotiation over what is supposed to be real within the fictional. Limitations of the medium, and even the implausibility of the narrative, are willingly tolerated or overlooked when we take for granted this negotiation. The indexicality of the image only enhances and does not deny the 'fetishist disavowal' in psychoanalytic terms, the disavowal of the fact that a fetish is a fake of something absent: 'I know (it's just a film) but all the same (I believe it is real)'. In short, knowledge and belief are not incompatible.

A more serious question can be raised regarding Bazin's insistence that 'every image should be experienced as an object and every object as an image' (Bazin 2009: 9). On the level of the image this notion goes beyond what Richard Allen calls 'projective illusion', the illusion of reality that an active spectator voluntarily projects on to his mind despite medium awareness (Allen 1995: 81–106). While this projection may not necessarily require the image's indexicality it still resonates with the psychology of suspending disbelief. Bazin's claim is far more provocative than this, though; a photograph creates a 'really existing hallucination [. . .] proved by surrealist painting's use of *trompe l'œil* and its meticulous attention to detail' (Bazin 2009, 10). Noting that surrealism turned to 'the gelatin of the photographic plate to create its visual teratology' (9), Bazin may have meant that, for example, the clear-cut imagery of surreal objects in the works of Salvador Dalí and René Magritte, such as melting watches and floating castles, looks as graphic as if those objects existed right there. This paradox of realism as surrealism does not assume the dichotomy of compatible knowledge and belief because a person in hallucination, without recognising the material condition or desiring to ignore it, may just experience that the image *is* the model. How can we accept Bazin's equation of normal perception with such an hallucinatory one?

This conundrum demands a multilayered approach. Firstly, a photo as index is a trace of its object that existed 'there and then' like the fingerprint and the death mask, but the other type of index – in Peirce – purely indicates what is 'here and now' like the arrow symbol and the linguistic 'deixis,' that is, such words as 'I', 'you', 'this', and 'here'/'now', whose referent varies depending on the situation of its utterance given in the present: 'I' denotes the speaker who says 'I'; 'now' designates the moment when the word is uttered. This presentness underlies Bazin's idea of the photograph as really existing hallucination; the image here is no longer a trace of the past but nothing other than the very thing that it indicates at this moment right here and now. This evokes Christian Metz's well-known example: a close-up of a revolver signifies not simply 'revolver' as 'a virtual lexical unit' but its actualised appearance in a syntactic context: 'Here is a revolver!' – here, 'here' functions as a 'pure index of actualization' (Metz 1974: 67). Metz precisely recognises the image as a deictic index though he neither refers to Bazin nor focuses on hallucination, addressing this indexicality semiotically. That being said, hallucinatory indexicality can be reviewed in terms of, and as the expansion of, the common linguistic effect of metonymy: the trope of calling a thing by an associated other thing, primarily based on contiguity (as distinct from similarity in the case of metaphor), just as a man who wears a yellow hat can be called 'Mr Yellow Hat'. When we call a photograph of a revolver a 'revolver' in our daily language habits, the gap between the photograph and the referent is metonymically bridged without upsetting our understanding at all. This symbolic convention involves no psychological investment or pathological hallucination, and is prevalent in everyday speech and writing.

Secondly, this contiguity can bring back the indexical notion of trace in that it results from physical causality. The photographic image, the trail of light from the object, is the mechanically contiguous effect of the object as its cause. In other words, the principle of metonymy does not remain a mere rhetorical convention but is literally realised in photography which makes contiguous the 'there and then' to the 'here and now'. In a dialectic way, this overlap of the past and the present may synthesise the two temporalities embodied by indexical trace and deixis each on a different level that is neither exactly the present nor the past. The photographed object may be 'real but outside (historical) time altogether' (Morgan 2006: 452). One could say that its temporality ontologically partakes of the Deleuzian 'virtual' in which the past consists with and subsists in the present even without explicitly showing the 'time-image'. Thus, the hallucinatory effect exudes not unreality but a vivid feeling of reality that the object-image exists, as it is rooted in actual causality, while being slightly detached from our spatio-temporal co-ordination. That is why photography goes beyond its embeddedness in ordinary perception, opening a new perception 'unsullied' by 'habits and preconceived notions' (Bazin 2009: 9) – like the French impressionist notion of *photogénie* that enables new discoveries and associations of things in the tradition of what Malcom Turvey calls 'revelationism' (*Revelationism*, 2008).

Thirdly, hallucination in turn takes on a new psychological implication. Traditionally, it means 'an internal phantom which appears as external object', a visual and tactile sensation that fuses perception with imagination, forging mental images for 'psychic reality' (Chevrier 2011: 43). But Bazin's hallucination is neither supernatural nor psychotic so the negation of the object by the affirmation of its image justifies 'a broadened demand for realism' (45). The psychic reality in this case should be understood as unfolding in front of the viewer whose perception is fully immersed into that visual field and not as occurring only in his mind through distortion and deviation. In other words, it is the screen that hallucinates the world in its own version which we see as real in our cinematic perception. Daniel Morgan calls this type of realism 'perceptual realism' rather than 'direct realism' (Morgan 2006: 457). Perceptually, our world is substituted by the world of the screen in its exclusive autonomous spatio-temporal density. 'For a time, a film is the universe, the world or, if you like, nature' (Bazin 2009: 197). It brings 'a complete realism, the recreation of the world in its own image' unburdened by the artist's interpretation or the irreversibility of time (17).

INDEXICAL EFFECT AS DIEGETIC CAUSALITY

After multiple turns, we now redefine indexicality as grounding the film's fullness of its own physical reality in a perceptual virtuality. Bazin links up 'the fullness of cinema with a transcendence of the image' by passing the limit of art, thus 'realism carried to its height is an *apotheosis* of the real in the image' (Chevrier 2011: 53). His idea of 'total cinema' is comparable to Flaubert's dream book that flies high on style alone, style asserting itself over matter autonomously – 'a book about nothing, a book dependent on nothing external' in which realism and hallucination are tied and cancelled together to create a

'meticulous mnemograph' (45) of everyday facts so thoroughly that it is sufficient to be a world in itself and not a text within the world. Bazin's neorealism is 'haunted' by surrealism in this expansion of hallucination as the essence
of mimetic restitution (51). The 'reality effect' of realist novels in Roland
Barthes's terms is generated by neorealist films all the more naturally because
concrete visual details do not need verbal descriptions that are inevitably selective and subjective, no matter how comprehensive and objective they may be.
So, paradoxically, 'in the perfect aesthetic illusion of reality, there is no more
cinema' (Bazin 2005a, 2: 60). *Bicycle Thieves* (Vittorio De Sica, 1948) does not
refer to the external world but implies 'the possibility of artifice taking on a life
of its own' because 'the cinematic way of seeing and being in the world [. . .]
no longer needs actors, plots, or sets, in order to be experienced as our lived
reality's signifier of authenticity and "truth"' (Elsaesser 2011: 7).

Political critics of Bazin claimed that this experience is constructed by the
cinematic apparatus and that to derive transcendent faith in idealistic truth from
it is ideologically naive. But, according to Philip Rosen, Hugh Gray's translation of Bazin's word *croyance* into 'faith' in *What is Cinema?* has, owing to the
English word's religious connotation, excessively coloured Bazin as a Roman
Catholic idealist. 'Faith' in reality may just mean the general sense of 'belief' in
the image as real, the psychologically irrational mimetic desire dating from the
'mummy complex' up to the 'total cinema' obsession – it is anti-materialistic
subjectivity projected into objective materiality (Rosen 2011: 10–40).[2] Bazin,
however, would be still vulnerable to Jean Baudry's criticism that this belief is
the deceptive outcome of the apparatus, just as images reflected in Plato's cave
are mere shadows and not real things. Tom Gunning, then, emphasises not
the dualism of subjectivity and objectivity in human history but Bazin's own
dialectic that the ideal of the world in its image sublates illusion, 'absorbing
its techniques, yet also transcending them' in a Hegelian rather than Platonist
idealism (Gunning 2011: 124). It goes beyond the pseudorealistic *trompe l'œil*
of simulating sensation with mere tricks, and moves towards 'the worldhood of
the world' phenomenologically. While this asymptotic movement is Hegelian
in its dynamism, it is noted that total cinema, unlike its name, does not posit
a Hegelian universal totality but a 'phenomenological image of the world as
bounded by a horizon' which is to be expanded (125).[3]

To note a few points related to Gunning: First, for Bazin, the genius of surrealism lies in its near-photographic *trompe l'œil*, just as photography perfects
the iconic reproduction of the object (through indexicality) and thus opens
the phenomenological horizon so vividly. This horizon is not the result of the
sublation of the medium but the result of the medium itself. Second, although
Gunning rightly points out that Bazin's 'total cinema' essay does not depend
on the index argument (122), indexicality redefined as actual metonymic causality between the object and the image enables the very phenomenological

world of the cinema to appear in its own spatio-temporal virtuality. Then we face another conundrum: if indexical, the iconic image as *trompe l'œil* seems phenomenologically graphic enough to enable perceptual realism; but are surrealist paintings (in Bazin's age) not still paintings, that is, only iconic and non-indexical? Here, I argue that what truly matters is not indexicality per se but the 'indexical effect', that is, 'the machine-like impact of the image on our minds' which surrealist, photorealist, hyperrealist painters all create, sometimes using the gelatin of the photographic plate. Medium specificity is less decisive than has been thought insofar as the indexical effect is concerned, and occurs (Jeong 2013: 115). The aforementioned surrealist paintings of Dalí and Magritte may embody this indexical effect as if they were photos. So, again, realism is not different from surrealism in Bazin.

By extension, Bazin also endorses fantasy: '[t]he presence of a marvellous or fantastic quality in film, far from invalidating the realism of the image, is the most conclusive evidence of it [. . .] Its trick effects must be perfect in a very material sense: the invisible man wears pyjamas and smokes a cigarette' (Bazin 2009: 196). What is at stake is something that is not so much surreal as 'supra-real', that exceeds realistic boundaries through expanding, even transforming, them on a virtual plane, just like a superhero who does not exist actually but whose fashion, flight, power, and so on are so vividly alive that his fictional reality upgrades our actual reality. An abnormal world thus appears as real insofar as some 'normal' experience of it is enabled consistently according to its own natural law. Here, I expand indexical causality from the image–object relation to the relation among things happening diegetically. Since what is seen now is not a single photographic image but a cinematic succession of images, the reality effect comes out of the indexical effect of the moving image, the effect of causality between contiguous images showing concrete events as causes and effects. This indexical effect in motion, duration, action–reaction and narrative, brings cinema the full gain of dynamic reality beyond the mere appearance of the image-as-object. In other words, a certain super/natural law based on this causality – Spiderman's hands are sticky enough to sustain him on the wall, and so on – underlies fantastic realism. Similarly, the levitation scene in Andrei Tarkovsky's *Solaris* (1972) – a couple in a room are slightly lifted from the floor and slowly float along with candles and a book – in its full concreteness, is fantastically real since we can grasp the principle of the countergravitational movement there (and which looks more 'scientifically real' when set in outer space, as shown in a film such as *Gravity* (Alfonso Cuarón, 2013). Non-existent digital creatures in *Jurassic Park* (Steven Spielberg, 1993), *Harry Potter and the Philosopher's Stone* (Chris Columbus, 2001), *The Lord of the Rings* (Peter Jackson, 2001), and so on, all effuse the utmost indexical effect of reality in this sense. Dinosaurs which we have never seen in reality stroll in peace, run amok, and kill people in exactly the same way as we imagine they would have done in the distant past; while their violent attack may startle us (as is intended), nothing is surprising in the mechanism of their, to us, natural movement.

In short, multiple realisms exist for Bazin insofar as the diegetic indexical effect works regardless of the medium specificity, even without direct indexical materiality. If we recognise and accept this effect as fitting the surreal or supra-real mode of a film, it is realistic. Perceptual realism can be based on, but not limited to, direct realism here. Let's not ignore, however, a thin line that still resides between 'virtual reality' (pure fantasy) and 'the real of the virtual' (imaginary reality). While Bazin's total cinema would ultimately embrace the former, his well-known prohibition of montage highlights a certain condition of indexical effect pertaining at a level between image and diegesis, that is, the condition of spatio-temporal unity or density on which the causal chain of images can function realistically in itself without 'artificial' intervention. The real of the virtual, true reality, may emerge when this condition is not divided, damaged, fabricated or manipulated as it often is in virtual reality. That is why Bazin thought CinemaScope to be of value; it can best serve the imagery of the Western as panoramic desert by enhancing the spatial scope in its full density on a widened screen, unlike Cinerama and 3D, both of which had technical problems in his period (Bazin 2014a: 215–66). That is why Bazin would appreciate today's digital 3D cinema, if not for its 'virtual reality' effects, at least for its three-dimensional horizon of phenomenological spatiality that appears even by merging the screen and cinema space. Roughly, there are three main directions of this merging: the screen moves forwards as if the faces shot in sudden close-up in *Avatar* (James Cameron, 2009) pop up to the viewers at a tangible distance; the screen recedes backwards as if the images of the boundlessly unfolding sea and sky in *Life of Pi* (Ang Lee, 2012) open up sublime infinity; and the screen creates a circulatory space when the rotating camera in *Gravity* turns around the main character floating up in the air or around the nothingness of space as if to position the viewer in the middle of a weightless state of being.

In addition to such technically cutting-edge mainstream films, we can also understand other films, be they classical, modern, artistic or documentary films, as post-Bazin Bazinian in these terms. Leonard Retel Helmrich's 'single-shot cinema', best exemplified in *Shape of the Moon* (2004), may incarnate the most Bazinian approach in documentary aimed at getting to the core of an event through an orbital camera movement that continues to position the viewer within the surrounding milieu without cutting into the organic wholeness of that milieu. A fictional counterpart would be Béla Tarr's mesmerising circular camera movement which mingles with dancers in the dancing scenes of *Satantango* (1994) and *Werckmeister Harmonies* (2000). In addition, it could be argued that the art film tradition also includes the international succession of neorealist waves whose signature style is the Bazinian sequence shot in a long-take/deep-focus *mise en scène* that embodies spatio-temporal holism, as seen in the works of film-makers such as India's Satyajit Rai, Iran's Abbas Kiarostami, Taiwan's Hou Hsiao-hsien, and China's Jia Zhangke. This is especially so with regard to films about children, a typical neorealist trope, as Bazin noted, and which includes such films as *Bicycle Thieves*, *Germany Year Zero* (Roberto Rossellini, 1948) and *Los olvidados* (Luis Buñuel, 1951); more recent examples also include Jafar Panahi's *The White Balloon* (1995), Edward Yang's *Yi Yi* (2000) and Koreeda Hirokazu's *Nobody Knows* (2004) (Cardullo 2011b: 27–8). The phrase 'slow cinema', recently mentioned in popular journals, is, in a sense, an updated Bazinian term that embraces subdued visual schemes and a sense of mystery and adventurous provocation so as to invite the viewer's free and active interpretation without channelling that through the use of montage. The slow cinema counters the 'fast cinema' of the commercial–industrial apparatus aesthetically and politically, and includes films by Theo Angelopoulos, Alexander Sokurov, Tsai Ming-liang, Bruno Dumont, Pedro Costa, Apichatpong Weerasethakul, Carlos Reygadas, Lisandro Alonso and Lav Diaz.

THE MULTIFACETED POTENTIAL OF MONTAGE

Nevertheless, it must be noted that Bazin neither asks for the prohibition of montage nor insists upon direct indexicality over montage with regard to creating the indexical effect. In Albert Lamorisse's *White Mane* (1953) and *The Red Balloon* (1956), the staging and editing of multiple horses and balloons to show one identical horse/balloon on screen still preserves ontological homogeneity (Bazin 2009: 79–80). Indexically wrong yet effective, such montage also underlies the famous Bazinian long-take/deep-focus shot in *Citizen Kane* (Orson Welles, 1941) that shows a bottle of alcohol amplified in the foreground, Kane's wife Susan lying in bed in the middle of the shot, and Kane rushing into the room in the background. This shot allows 'the ontological ambivalence of reality directly, in the very structure of its appearance' without cutting the whole into several shots, so that the viewer can 'exercise his liberty and his intelligence' to deduce Susan's attempted suicide (Bazin 1978: 80) even though, in fact, the shot superimposes three different shots in one frame by using mattes. The sense of integrity of space produced here amounts to 'an impression [. . .] of continuous and homogeneous reality' (77) though it is in fact 'the effect of internal montage' (Morgan 2006: 456), that is, it amounts to an indexical effect of causality using non-indexical techniques – just like the sound of footsteps can be created by a drum, based on iconic similarity, which effectively mimics the indexical contiguity between a real footstep and its sound.

For Bazin, not only can this sort of internal montage within a fake sequence shot be potentially useful and effective but so also can the montage of different shots in general. Bazin objects to the rhetorical use of temporally compressed montage, that is, the 'art of ellipsis' as a logical and abstract narrative process that targets action-oriented signification by cutting out unnecessary time (Bazin 2005a: 2:81). He supports, however, the idea of montage as 'collage' where the collage presupposes that 'the equality of the elements of concrete contiguity must be privileged over the hierarchy of compositional motifs' and thus where the heterogeneity of real materials is more important than their dramatisation. Here, an 'egalitarian utopia [. . .] underpins the idea of realism' (Chevrier 2011: 47). This egalitarianism is also constitutive of experience. Heterogeneous things experienced in daily life are contiguous on a decentralised plane such that 'their ontological equality destroys drama at its very basis' while our sensitivity to them is maximised across duration (Bazin 2005a: 2: 81). So the long take itself does not necessarily promise Bazinian realism if it serves dramatic effects only by oppressing the heterogeneity of things themselves immanent in duration. Alfred Hitchcock's *Rope* (1948), essentially an eighty-minute-long sequence shot, is just a prolonged theatrical action whose temporal structure is therefore artificial. On the other hand, the multi-shot scene of the maid's morning routine in Vittorio De Sica's *Umberto D* (1952) visualises the continuity of her 'life time', with nothing in particular or singularly different happening (76). This is not the temporality of drama but 'the concrete duration of the character' (77) that makes us aware of 'what it is to be a man' – though, in this case, a woman (78); its objectivity, thus, reveals something broadly subjective that is related to the human condition. Cinema here becomes 'the asymptote of reality' (82).

Given the above, it could be argued that, by extension, Bazin seems to see two types of continuity. The 'action-proper' form of continuity establishes logical relations and significant changes in narrative. But, if this type of continuity represents 'the major points of dramatic articulation' as organised within the script, what is truly revelatory is that which underlies durational life itself (and which often deviates from the main storyline) as seen, for example, in Federico Fellini's long descriptive sequences: the nocturnal walks and senseless strolls in *I vitelloni* (1953); the visit to the convent in *La strada* (1954); the evening at the nightclub and the New Year party in *Il bidone* (1955). His characters best reveal themselves not by doing something specific but 'by their endless milling around' in ways that make us feel this revelation as not necessarily intended or calculated, predetermined or predicated (90). Certainly, in Gilles Deleuze's terms, this disoriented movement signals the crisis of the 'action-image' and the rise of the 'affection' and 'time-image' in post-war cinema. Let me just mention two extreme cases in this regard. First, Jacques Tati's *Playtime* (1967) is entirely composed of a series of long sequences with Tati only wandering around modern Paris, revealing what a sensational experience being lost in modernity is. Second, the ending of Michelangelo Antonioni's *L'Eclisse* (1962) shows, after several scenes of the heroine's roaming around, her complete disappearance followed by a bizarre montage of unrelated things which the camera captures, as it blankly drifts about on the streets, wholly embodying a sense of modern alienation. Here is an important facet of Bazinian realism that reveals a heterogeneous plane of things as such in immanent durational temporality outside of dramatisation.

Let me note here that, as Morgan suggests, realism for Bazin is not simply neorealism, which itself should be seen not as a noun but as a 'verb', an aesthetic 'activity' whose constant is the general ontological foundation and whose variable is the specific stylistic addition. It is a dialectic between 'the physical level of reality and the style that gives it meaning' (Morgan 2006: 464). But, while the style is not limited to certain techniques or dogmatic rules, this does not imply that realism is a blank term open to any cinematic style. Though Bazin called socialist realism historico-materialist realism, he did not appreciate Soviet montage, and also condemned German expressionism for being the most anti-realist form of film because cinema should acknowledge itself as a medium inherently related to physical reality. This is the 'acknowledgement' of the first level of directly indexical reality, which one can interpret by using an open set of stylistic resources, thus leading to the second level of stylistically aestheticised reality with facts developed more individually (472–5). This does not deny direct reality (as German expressionism does) but negates it in an aesthetic dialectic in order to reveal its truth.

This 'truth' is sometimes not even visible within physical reality. While watching Roberto Rossellini's *Paisan* (1946), '[o]ur mind must bestride events the way one hops from stone to stone when crossing a river' (Bazin 2009, 239). Our imagination makes use of each event, 'a fragment of raw reality, inherently multifarious and ambiguous, whose meaning becomes apparent only after the fact, through other events connected up in our minds' (241). This quotation may resonate with my argument on the indexical effect of diegetic causality that deviates from the clearly visualised contiguity between images as cause and effect in two ways (Jeong 2013: 188). On the one hand, an image can be the effect of its unrepresented cause – an object, event, or situation as a gap in the narrative – that is deduced in the viewer's mind. The bottle in the aforementioned *Citizen Kane* shot is an index of Susan's unseen suicide attempt. In Deleuze's own usage of the term, this is the 'index of lack' that indicates an implicit element of note (Deleuze 1986: 160–2). On the other hand, an image can be the cause of an effect that is not always decidable, identifiable, or representable. In *Memento* (Christopher Nolan, 2000), the tattoo of 'I'VE DONE IT', seen on the protagonist's chest when he lies with his wife, provokes us to ask what it means. For Deleuze, this could be an example of the 'index of equivocity' whose enigmatic quality can cause potentially very different results to occur. Here, our reasoning can be delayed and disrupted all the more radically than in interpreting an index of lack because, here, the resolving of the lack involved could be deferred unendingly.

Correspondingly, ambiguity, the real nature of life and the world for Bazin, can emerge not only in a deep-focus sequence shot but also through montage – what I call the 'montage of ricochet' (Jeong 2013: 189). Like a stone skipping off the surface of a body of water, or like Bazin's aforementioned analogy of people crossing a river, the 'montage of ricochet' shows the lack of successive cause and effect and involves various degrees of equivocity (thus it is different from the standard montage that maximises the efficient delivery of causality by minimising ambiguity or excessive duration as in the case, for example, of showing only the first and the last steps of a person mounting a set of steps). Robert Bresson is a master of this type of ricochet montage: *Mouchette* (1967) ends with Mouchette rolling down a slope towards a body of water but then the film does not show her falling into the water, only the indexical trace of that fall as a motion of ripples that leaves a lasting emotional trace in our mind; *A Gentle Woman* (1969) starts with close-ups of a falling chair, a falling veil, then a woman already fallen to the ground where the act of falling is not itself shown. Overall, the montage of ricochet omits dramatically decisive and traumatic moments, opening gaps and lapses that are indexically contiguous and real but visually ambiguous and virtual. Here, the virtual is not phenomenological, as in our usage of the term regarding the total cinema of fully sensible reality, but concerns an ontological dimension beyond or beneath this sensorial screen. Thus, the gap in diegetic causality can vary in montage; cause-images and effect-images can intermingle in the utmost proximity in the ideal state of Bazin's phenomenological realism – which I refer to as 'montage of amalgam' (188), whereas the montage of ricochet widens their distance to open the other, more ontological side of this realism.

FROM INDEX TO PARA-INDEX

Though almost neglected among scholars, this ontological side is also an aspect of Bazin's realism and, indeed, its hidden core, as suggested in his essay 'Cinema and Exploration' on documentary films about exploration. When discussing *Kon-Tiki* (Thor Heyerdahl, 1950), an adventurous re-enactment of the hypothetical migration of ancient Peruvians to Polynesia on small boats, Bazin does not criticise the film's poor visual quality and loss of much of its footage because of the difficulties in film-making; he rather appreciates its vivid evocation of invisible danger. He says, 'its faults are equally witness to its authenticity. The missing documents are the negative imprints of the expedition – its inscription chiseled deep' (Bazin 2005b: 1: 162). In other words, what is absent is indexically inscribed in the virtual dimension of the film so that the present image is an index of what it lacks and, where it is not possible to remove or minimise equivocity, which it is still possible to sense. The image then does not display reality in its fullness but only in part whilst indicating what is not and could not be displayed. It is 'an index of what should have been represented but couldn't [be]. An index of its own failure', which I call a 'para-index' that indicates the absence of something unseen beside it – this imperfect indexicality imbues the most objective medium with the most subjective experience (Jeong 2013: 192; Jeong 2011: 182–4). The dot-like, unclear image of a whale hurling itself at the raft and alternating between being visible, then invisible, is one such para-index of the unrepresentable animal that is a part of the extensive sea, 'apparent without appearing', like the phasmid (the stick insect that resembles its environment in perfect camouflage) whose etymology implies 'phantasm' and 'apparition' (Didi-Huberman 1998: 15–20). The whale, a dangerous beast-ghost that can sweep us into the abyss of death where no ontological boundaries exist, could thus be called a para-ontological other of the human. As such, it is only partially, impossibly traced by an imperfect para-index in the film.

Importantly, the para-index does not lose indexical contiguity to what goes beyond perceptual realism. It is rather a radical case of the deixis (the indicator of 'this, here and now') as hollowed out, empty of meaning (Doane 2007a: 2) in that it indicates only what appears at the moment of its disappearing. Phenomenological ephemerality characterises the 'para-indexicality' of 'para-ontological realism', as it were. The image is a transitory interface between actual reality and the virtual as the real where 'that obscure object' in the sea lurks, waiting suddenly to attack the boat. In Lacan's terms, the unrepresentable Real is representable in the Symbolic and can erupt to overturn the very reality through the 'object little-a', an enigmatic object that generates a desire to attain it but that is unattainable at the same time.[+] Reversing the early Lacanian Grand Theory attack on Bazin, Serge Daney catches this late Lacanian notion in Bazin's approach to 'reality on the other side', the realm of the Real: we see '[t]he screen, the skin, the celluloid, the surface of the pan, exposed to the fire of the real and on which is going to be inscribed – metaphorically and figuratively – everything that could burst them [the very screen, skin . . .]' (Daney 2002, 34–5). That is, the screen is vulnerable to the Real which it wants to show as closely as possible but which is too dangerous to be shown properly. Put in the double bind of neither fully representing nor escaping this 'fire of the real', the image barely appears as a kind of 'soot', the trace of its maximum allowable approach to the still unattainable Real. But, without this imperfect trace, we could not even sense what it could not show. 'The failure of index is thus the index of failure [. . .] only through which are we confronted with its beyond' (Jeong 2013: 196). This, at one and the same time, represents the impotence and power of the image.

We should be careful, however, not to suggest some easy transcendentalism regarding the status of the Real or, more ontologically, the Deleuzian Virtual which is not limited to psychoanalytic trauma or the sublime but open as the immanent horizon of the actual. It is worthwhile to examine Bazin's enigmatic religious aspect here. Rosen argues that cinema, like the mummy, embalms time, defeats death, and is thus a kind of 'miracle' realised by the human's subjective transcendental 'investment in something everlasting, which means something beyond the sensible, beyond the worldly constraints of space and time' (Rosen 2011: 111). But Bazin condemns the 'psychological' mimicry of appearance as 'pseudo-realism' while praising 'true realism' as 'aesthetic' in its concreteness and essence, realist and spiritual at the same time (Bazin 2009, 6). To attend to an ephemeral thing does not necessarily lead to the spiritual essence of the thing. The uniqueness of photography does not lie in its perfect reproduction of iconic appearance through direct realism but in its spiritual revelation of essential thingness through perceptual or even para-indexical realism. And this revelation, even if partial, is achieved through the objective mechanism of photography outside the artist's subjectivity. Meaning comes out of the machine like divine providence, like *deus ex machina*, not as predetermined by the hand of the director/creator who ambitiously takes over God's power, but as mystery to be revealed to the audience which just encounters the truth of the real. This also means that auteurism, in Bazin, is a contradictory construct, as it implies a self-renouncing authorial authority. Cinema 'humbly renounced the hubristic display of authorial personality and thus enabled [its] audience to intuit the numerous signification of people, things, and places' (Cardullo 2011a: 8).

Is the invisible thingness of the visible thing religious? How could we better characterise Bazin's emphasis on spirituality or even reinterpret it from a post-Bazinian angle without simply calling it Catholic? Let me turn to examples from Bazin himself. On Henri-Georges Clouzot's documentary, *The Picasso Mystery* (1956), Andrew rephrases Bazin's idea: 'the camera looks deep into the frame as a site of "vertical" movement, tunnelling into time as paintings appear [. . .] during the course of the shooting and the projection' (Andrew 2011: 163). The film is a palimpsest of 'the paintings underneath the paintings' (Bazin 1997: 213), a kind of 'mystic writing pad constituting the painter's "image-temps"' in that it 'could make us see duration itself' (213) through 'the gap between subjectivity and objectivity, a gap across which the spark of creativity leaps' (165). This Bergsonian duration is not simply subjective or objective; it transcends that dichotomy spiritually, yet is fully immanent in actual reality as the condition of thingness from which things emerge and submerge. The screen appears as an image of this time, an index of the Deleuzian 'plane of immanence' where things are in a constant process of becoming.

Likewise, we now understand Bazin's attraction for the shot of a 'white screen' with only a black cross and a text being read over it in Bresson's *Diary of a Country Priest* (1951). It appears like a 'negative hallucination, one that does not produce an additional reality, but an empty actuality'. This shot then draws attention to three immanent planes. The first is the actual film screen as part of the cinematic apparatus, 'the support for any projection and the condition of cinematic realism' (Chevrier 2011: 45). The second is the white page of the film's original novel that only has words in black (evoking the Bible: 'in the beginning was the word'). But how should we interpret Bazin's claim that this image-free screen handed back to literature is 'the triumph of cinematographic realism' (Bazin 2009: 156)? What is the real within this realism? This final conundrum leads to the third plane. The black cross is 'the only visible trace left by the assumption on the image, bears witness to something whose reality was only a sign' (141). This sign in/as physical reality is thus an icon of 'spiritual grace or transcendence' or, rather, 'an inner state without exterior form' (Morgan 2006: 472–4). Put in another, less religious, way, it could be a para-index of the very ontological plane on which some spirituality, a sense of transcendence beyond actual physicality, may have potential to appear like a religious epiphany. Here may be the most fundamental and ultimate facet of Bazinian realism.

REWRITING BAZIN

Like these three planes, the multifaceted notions of realism and indexicality suggest Bazin's ever-evolving view of the cinema. In some sense '(e)ach metaphor captures something important about what a photograph is, but each fails in some way' in Bazin (451). Many commentators focus on a certain understanding of Bazin, and his value or limitations. But we could see that each Bazinian idea has a certain validity on which Bazin is able to build another that both challenges and also encompasses this validity which is thus overlapped with other validities in multiple negotiations and evolving expansion. The old criticism of Bazin 'the realist' for being 'idealist' is thus not only oxymoronic (Gunning 2011: 119) but also inadequate. It also implies that the constructivist view of realism as fabricated, wrongly idealised, and thus not real, is not sufficient. Bazin is truly realistic, however. He shows the link between realism and the real while the attention to reality as ideologically constructed is not really missing in his criticism. He is sensitive to the media apparatus more than anyone else, and does not jump into clichéd religious transcendentalism. Notably, Deleuze sees much less significance in the constructivist Grand

Theory than the Epstein–Bazin line of Bergsonism in his taxonomy of cinematic signs, including the new notions of index discussed here, that is, lack and equivocity, which are different from many notions commonly mentioned within Bazin studies. To rewrite Bazinian realism in terms of multiplied indexicality would, thus, be realistic.

NOTES

1. Also notable are Bazin's essay collections (Aitken 2006; Bazin 2014b) and the special section in *Cahier du cinéma* (Delorme et al. 2014) that features the English/French publication of *Opening Bazin*, winner of the 2012 SCMS best anthology award. This book is an outcome of a transatlantic double conference on Bazin in 2008, his fiftieth memorial year, and many papers in it are owed to its main editor and lifetime Bazin scholar Dudley Andrew's Bazin archive at Yale University. I refer to some of them as main references. I also note that this essay consults and updates some points made in the chapter on indexicality in my book (Jeong 2013).

2. As the Egyptian mummy shows, mummification is the process of preserving the human body, embalming its appearance against post-mortem decay. For Bazin, this ancient technique prefigures plastic arts driven by the mimetic desire, the 'mummy complex'. It implies the psychological, artistic aspiration to immortality that 'crystallizes subjective obsession and temporality' as Rosen says.

3. In the Hegelian dialectic, a thesis both negates and assimilates, that is, 'sublates' its self-generated antithesis into a larger synthesis, and this dynamic process goes on to reach an ideal state into which everything is sublated in perfect totality. Bazin's 'total cinema' asymptotically approaches the ideal representation of reality in this way, though it does not construct a total system.

4. Lacan's terms are dispersed throughout his work with different implications, but very briefly, the object little-a (*objet petit a*) is the remnant left behind in the Real by the introduction of the Symbolic order. This order shapes our normal reality through sign systems like language that basically replace the Real, which thus remains unrepresentable and only sensible in the form of this little object appearing on the border of the Symbolic and the Real.

REFERENCES

Aitken, Ian (2006), *Realist Film Theory and Cinema: The Nineteenth-Century Lukácsian and Intuitionist Realist Traditions*, Manchester: Manchester University Press.

Allen, Richard (1995), *Projecting Illusion: Film Spectatorship and the Impression of Reality*, Cambridge: Cambridge University Press.

Andrew, Dudley (2011), 'Marlaux, Bazin, and the Gesture of Picasso', in Andrew, Dudley and Joubert-Laurencin, Hervé (eds), *Opening Bazin: Postwar Film Theory and Its Afterlife*, New York: Oxford University Press, pp. 153–66.

Andrew, Dudley, and Joubert-Laurencin, Hervé (2011) (eds), *Opening Bazin: Postwar Film Theory and Its Afterlife*.

Bazin, André (1978), *Orson Welles: A Critical View*, New York: Harper & Row.

— (1997), *Bazin at Work: Major Essays and Reviews From the Forties and Fifties*, ed. Cardullo, Bert, New York: Routledge.

— (2005a), *What Is Cinema?* translated by Hugh Gray, Vol. 2, Berkeley, CA: University of California Press.

— (2005b). *What Is Cinema?* trans. Hugh Gray, vol. 1, Berkeley, CA: University of California Press.

— (2009), *What Is Cinema?* trans.Timothy Barnard, Montréal: Caboose.

— (2014a), *André Bazin's New Media*, ed. Andrew, Dudley, Oakland, CA: University of California Press.

— (2014b), *Bazin on Global Cinema, 1948–1958*, trans. Bert Cardullo, Austin, TX: University of Texas Press.

Cardullo, Bert (2011a), 'Defining the Real: The Film Theory and Criticism of André Bazin', in *André Bazin and Italian Neorealism*, New York: Bloomsbury Academic, pp. 1–17.

— (2011b), 'What Is Neorealism?', in *André Bazin and Italian Neorealism*, pp. 18–28.

Carroll, Noël (1988), *Philosophical Problems of Classical Film Theory*, Princeton, NJ: Princeton University Press.

Chevrier, Jean-François (2011), 'The Reality of Hallucination in André Bazin', in Andrew and Joubert-Laurencin (eds), pp. 42–56.

Daney, Serge (2002), 'The Screen of Fantasy (Bazin and Animals)', in Margulies, Ivone (ed.), *Rites of Realism: Essays on Corporeal Cinema*, trans. Mark A. Cohen, Durham, NC: Duke University Press, pp. 32–41.

Deleuze, Gilles (1986), *Cinema 1: The Movement-Image*, trans. Hugh Tomlinson and Barbara Habberjam, Minneapolis, MN: University of Minnesota Press.

Delorme, Stéphane, Béghin, Cyrill, Andrew, Dudley and Elliott, Nicholas (2014), 'Réouvrir Bazin', *Cahier du Cinéma*, no. 697 (February), pp. 58–75.

Didi-Huberman, Georges (1998), *Phasmes: Essais sur L'apparition*, Paris: Éditions de Minuit.

Doane, Mary Ann (2007a), 'Indexicality: Trace and Sign: Introduction', *Differences* 18: 1, pp. 1–6.

— (2007b), 'The Indexical and the Concept of Medium Specificity', *Differences* 18: 1, pp. 128–52.

Elsaesser, Thomas (2011), 'A Bazinian Half-Century', in Andrew and Joubert-Laurencin (eds), pp. 3–12.

Gunning, Tom (2007), 'Moving Away from the Index: Cinema and the Impression of Reality', *Differences* 18: 1, pp. 29–52.

— (2011), 'The World in Its Own Image: The Myth of Total Cinema', in Andrew and Joubert-Laurencin (eds), pp. 119–28.

Jeong, Seung-hoon (2011), 'Animals: An Adventure in Bazin's Ontology', in Andrew and Joubert-Laurencin, pp. 177–85.

— (2013), *Cinematic Interfaces: Film Theory after New Media*, New York and London: Routledge.

Metz, Christian (1974), *Film Language: A Semiotics of the Cinema*, trans. Michael Taylor, New York: Oxford University Press.

Morgan, Daniel (2006), 'Rethinking Bazin: Ontology and Realist Aesthetics', *Critical Inquiry* 32: 3, pp. 443–81.

Rosen, Philip (2011), 'Belief in Bazin', in Andrew and Joubert-Laurencin (eds), pp. 107–18.

Turvey, Malcolm (2008), *Doubting Vision: Film and the Revelationist Tradition*, Oxford: Oxford University Press.

Wollen, Peter (1998), *Signs and Meaning in the Cinema*, London: British Film Institute.

CHAPTER 6

André Bazin, or the Ambiguity of Reality

Pierre Sorlin

M ost of the time the biography of film theoreticians is of little help in interpreting their thought. Such is not the case where André Bazin is concerned because the man himself, his friendship, activities and beliefs interfered directly in his thinking. Tireless teacher, enthusiastic film analyst, keen on imparting his passion for culture and especially for cinema, he introduced movies in film societies, schools, enterprises of various kinds, talked on radio and television, and provided articles for daily newspapers and magazines. His ceaseless dedication to the spreading of high culture (Andrew 1978: 90–5) has long aroused admiration: people born after his death consider him an exceptional populariser whose articles, serious but always comprehensible, modified the dominant approach to cinema and put film analysis at an accessible level.

Not insensible to the admiration that surrounded him, Bazin made it a point of honour to write for the general public. Faithful to his friends, he could leave aside his convictions to stand up for them when necessary. On intimate terms with Roger Leenhardt, he reviewed at length the second-rate film the latter had directed, expanding on stylistic reflections even though the film was at variance with his own conception of film-making ([1948] 1997: 141–9). His close friend Jean Renoir had, as we shall see, a crucial influence over his thought. Buñuel's potboiler films bothered him and he was bewildered by what he saw as the hopelessness of Rossellini's *Germania anno zero / Germany Year Zero* (1947) but, having a liking for both directors, he commented favourably on their works, praising Rossellini for his ability to 'get us interested in an action while leaving it in its objective context' ([1949] 2011: 60) though elsewhere he was also very critical of any attempt at over-objective placement and would eventually state that, with a 'true' realism 'the accuracy of exterior social reality becomes unimportant' ([1954] 122).

The Rossellini article was an occasional text brought about by the advent of new film releases and so were a great many of Bazin's writings which, beside cinema, dealt with varied topics including archaeology, literature and even bullfights (Tweedie 2011: 276–7). If he thought of drawing up a general, all-encompassing treatise of cinema (Andrew 1978: 73), in which he would have systematically articulated his views, he never had enough time even to start that. He prepared the collection of papers which he titled *What is Cinema?* but died before the publication appeared and his purpose was to make available ideas or propositions, not to offer a well-argued theory. His thought evolved during his twenty years of active life. His first texts (Bazin 1984) used 'realism' as a mere qualifier attributed to films he had appreciated, and his conception of the notion was faltering; readers could, according to their personal opinion, call it 'resemblance or if you will [. . .] realism' ([1945] 2004a: 10) – a likeness he would later condemn as pure illusion, mere similarity not amounting to art ([1953] 53). He welcomed 'every new technical development aiming to add to the realism of cinema' ([1948] 38), including sound, but, a few years later, he deplored the artificial effect that sound added to the straightforwardness of images by offering its public an 'illusion of objective representation' ([1955] 40). In an early paper he affirmed categorically that 'realism in art can only be achieved in one way – through artifice' ([1948] 2004b: 38) while, in the 1950s, he condemned any device modifying 'this part of reality that comes to light' ([1953] 2011: 80). These were the years in which he also clarified the views on realism that will be discussed subsequently in this chapter. At the end of the decade, under the influence of the illness that would carry him off at the age of forty (1958), he dwelt on 'the objective cruelty of the world', a recurring theme of *The Cinema of Cruelty*, a collection of essays by Bazin edited by François Truffaut. It is therefore misleading to approach his writings indiscriminately without considering the date at which they were written. Peremptory statements issued in 1945–48 were modified, at times opposed after 1949. The year of the publication must always therefore be borne in mind.

Another fundamental influence on his work was his Roman Catholic faith, acquired while he was very young (Andrew 1978: 22–3), then deepened in the course of his adult life. In many instances, he had spontaneous recourse to a religious vocabulary, perspective in painting was for him an 'original sin' and photography a 'redeemer' ([1945] 2004a: 12). At times, he decided whether fictional characters deserved to be redeemed or were doomed to damnation ([1956] 2011: 182–3). His review of *Journal d'un curé de campagne/Diary of a Country Priest* (Robert Bresson, 1951) was a mystical meditation about sin, the soul, and the transcendence of divine grace and eternal salvation. This is an aspect of his personality that we cannot disregard (Cardullo 2010: 203-4). For him, the world, however dreadful it was, had been created by God for humankind and should be appraised from that angle: what mattered was 'the transparency or the opacity of human soul, a certain perviousness to grace' (ibid.).

'THE ONTOLOGICAL AMBIGUITY OF REALITY'

Two terms, 'reality' and 'realism', recurred frequently in the texts written between the end of the 1940s and the mid-1950s. Bazin did not define them; he believed that everybody had some inkling of their signification and that too precise an elucidation might put off some readers. Realism is etymologically linked to reality but Bazin hesitated over the relationship between these notions. Realism, he insisted, should be a 'representation of reality' ([1957] 2011: 199) but, instead of being a 'simple copying from life', it should rather be 'dialectically fused with reality' ([1952] 1973: 106). The connection looks quite complex; we cannot clarify it without finding out first how Bazin conceived of reality. One term, 'ambiguity', was habitually associated with reality, and not only in a phrase such as 'the ontological ambiguity of reality' ([1953] 2011: 80); the same word also appeared frequently to qualify events, facts and forms of expression. Such persistent application of this term is not surprising, though, as it was used recurrently in philosophical debates taking place both then and before. For example, by confronting notions of being and time, Martin Heidegger had questioned the notion of human 'being': individuals constantly evolving through time cannot 'be', their unceasing transformations made them indefinable, ambiguous. Well informed about the problems debated in intellectual circles, Bazin had recourse to a common vocabulary here but, unlike some philosophers, he did not worry about the ambiguity of human being because his main concern was the uncertainty that characterises reality.

Ambiguity is a category of thought that indicates a lack of decisiveness regarding a question. We are not in a quandary about inanimate matter: it can be inexplicable and baffle our understanding but there is no doubt about its material being. Ambiguity happens when we must propose an interpretation and, within this, individuals, behaviour and discourses may be ambiguous. Where does their indeterminacy lie? Bazin wavered between two answers. Some indications suggest that he had in mind an ambiguity of the world itself: the adjective 'ontological' we have met above implies that it is inherent to the world, belonging to it as a part of its nature, and so the cinema 'cannot make reality entirely its own because reality must inevitably elude it at some point. One is compelled to choose between one kind of reality and another' ([1948] 2011: 41). Yet such a statement is not satisfactory because 'the world *is*, quite simply' ([1948] 2004a: 43). Various sentences suggest that Bazin ascribed ambiguity to the intrinsic limitations of human perception: we live in 'a world that we neither know nor can see [. . .] piled-up preconceptions, spiritual dust and grime' have made reality unreadable ([1945] 15), 'the knowledge we have of reality is limited by its nature' ([1953] 78). Uncertainty relating to the essential qualities of the world or the weakness of our senses: the two propositions do not contradict each other; they are mere hypothesis which converge on our difficulty of becoming acquainted with our surroundings. As a result, Bazin's realism cannot be 'a recreation of the world in its own image', an image that would also fail to evidence 'the irreversibility of time' ([1946] 32).

It is likely that 'The Ontology of the Photographic Image' ([1945] 9–16) is Bazin's most often quoted essay, for the reason that its argument, sharp and clearly designed, seems to settle the problem of realism. Human beings have long drawn or painted landscapes, portraits and indoor scenes in the hope of catching a likeness of the world. For Bazin, the endeavour was vain: such handmade images translated their authors' personal sensations and did not show what they actually had in front of them; they were emotional representations giving a false version of reality. The invention of photography has radically modified the situation, 'the impassive lens' strips what it brings into focus of any personal interpretations; photography, being 'a mechanical reproduction in the making of which man plays no part', 'presents [the world] in all its virginal purity to my attention'. At last we have obtained a 'true realism', which grants 'significant expression to the world both concretely and in its essence' ([1945] 9–16).

Bazin was twenty-five years of age when he published this paper. During the two previous years, he had written extensively about films in circulation but this was his first speculative publication. He enlivened it with superficial anthropological references and did not shrink from using peremptory statements: 'All the arts are based on the presence of man, only photography derives an advantage from his absence. Photography affects us like a phenomenon in nature.' The thesis was simple: photography 'laying bare the realities' provides an image of things as they are. Bazin inserted the text in *What is cinema?* because it had been a first step in his thought but it had not taken him much time to discern the objections that arose from his assertions. With different tools, specific to the camera, photographers or film operators can modify the real effectively, 'the style of the set, of the make-up, performance, lighting, framing' allow presentations of countless different renderings of the same thing ([1946] 2004a: 24); the cinema 'has a thousand ways of acting on the appearance of an object' ([1951] 62), many means 'of manipulating reality and modifying it' ([1955] 40). The 'irrefutable objectivity' of the cinematic image can even evidence 'the relativity of realism'; superimposition and other optical effects confront the audience with shots that are, at the same time, realistic and incredible ([1946] 1997: 75–6).

Another difficulty appeared when Bazin began to think further about ambiguity: if the world is uncertain, be it out of its nature or because of human incompleteness, photography and film are unable to apprehend its indefinite truth. *Citizen Kane* (Orson Welles, 1941) forced the French critic to reconsider his initial statements. A shallow glance at the film does not perceive how unsettled its universe is: spectators must put all their strength into noticing how slow modifications and camera motions, which are barely noticeable, institute an atmosphere of unevenness around the characters and their environment ([1955] 2004a: 36). Welles's realism does not lie in the unquestionable 'authenticity' of his shots ([1948] 2011: 39–41), 'the impassive lens' is itself a source of ambiguity because all films, inasmuch as they resort to a mechanical process, tend 'to give the spectator as perfect an illusion of reality as possible' (38). The cinema is 'committed to communicate only by way of what is real' ([1951] 2004a: 110); even films which are falsely realist, mere copies of life content with illusory appearances, rely 'entirely on the outside world for [their] object' ([1951] 62), 'the greater part of their constituent elements [derive] from the reality' ([1955] 25), their 'illusion of reality' is 'composed of a complex of abstraction and of authentic reality' ([1948] 2011: 39). 'Art aims to go beyond reality, not to reproduce it. And this is even truer of film because of its technical realism, its ability to reproduce reality so easily.' ([1952] 107) The objectivity of the takes does not automatically entail realism.

Then, what distinguishes a photographic or cinematic image from all other sorts of pictures? At one level, it is the fact that the operator and his/her device must be present in front of the object that is filmed. It is easy to draw an absent item: suffice it to have a few sketches or a good memory. On the contrary, however, a camera cannot film an absent thing: the cinematic image is physically linked to its subject matter. The photograph and the object it reproduces 'share a common being'; a fingerprint is independent from the person whose fingers have been printed but is also closely associated with that person and, in the same way, the photographic image is 'an imprint of the duration of the object' ([1951] 2004a: 96). Bazin hesitated over the most convenient word: was it tracing, mould or transfer? The precise term does not matter: what counts is the idea of an indispensable junction; the realism of photography does not follow from a resemblance that is within a draftsman's reach, it is the outcome of a co-presence at the moment of the shooting. The connection between the shooting device and its subject/object is spatial–temporal: they were together in the same place, the same day, at the same minute; the operation occurred in 'the time-space perimeter, which is the definition of presence' ([1951] 98); the specific effect of photography is 'derived from unity of image in space and time' ([1955] 35). The trouble with photography is that it catches only an instant and freezes it. Human beings do not comprehend their surroundings instantaneously and, at first sight, they get acquainted with it progressively. Whereas the photographic image is static, the cinema, because it moves forward, 'makes a moulding of the object as it exists in time' ([1951] 98), bringing thus 'together real time, in which things exist, along with the duration of the action' ([1955] 40).

In the last decades of the twentieth century, philosophers and film analysts took a keen interest in the question of cinematic time. A film, they noted, is a

film only through its unfolding; characters, events, landscapes pass by spectators' eyes as in life, making it difficult to observe them closely. Bazin had
anticipated such considerations without ever trying to systematise his ideas.
While enunciating observations that would be resumed and extended long
after his death, he was mostly concerned with the arduous elucidation of what
realism was. The fluidity of time was central in his view but all films, realistic
or not, progress in time. He imagined once a ninety-minute film shot in continuous real time ([1951] 2004a: 82) but he knew that this was only a flight of
his imagination which left him confronting another ambiguity: there is never
an uninterrupted succession of shots in film; continuous sequences are always
separated by ellipses. Reluctantly, he acknowledged the necessity of cuts,
which break the current of time, 'ellipsis is a lacuna in reality or rather in the
knowledge we have of it, which is by its nature limited' ([1953] 2011: 78).

Before exploring Bazin's conception of realism, it was essential to delineate
the intellectual background covered in the last several pages. As a teacher and
as a dedicated believer, Bazin wanted to make people aware of their being in a
complex, ambiguous world. What could be done to overcome ambiguities, at
least partially? The solution was to cast a clear-minded look at what could be
observed and this takes us on to Bazin's conception of realism.

REALISM IN FILM

Obliged to review films which, during World War II, dealt with private,
mostly sentimental affairs and, after the conflict, avoided ongoing issues,
Bazin, in about 1945, was looking for scripts that were less superficial and
more true to everyday concerns. His first step in that direction was a relentless
criticism of the mainstream cinema. Initially, the notion of realism appeared
negatively: it was used to condemn operations that, according to Bazin, should
be absolutely ruled out. Such disapproval was far from sterile as it enabled
the young analyst to be more specific about the part cinema should play in his
project of popular education.

  Bazin's main charge against the dominant cinema was that, by allowing
no liberty of judgement to its public, it imposed pre-established interpretations. What film-makers working within dominant cinema called 'realism'
was merely the use of factual data illustrating their thesis and imposing 'only a
passive adhesion' upon the audience ([1951] 2004a: 99). Spectators, it is true,
could express their opinion about the characters or the technical qualities
of the movie but, trapped within the parameters of the narrative, they were
obliged to take heed of all incidents, and were therefore prevented from linger-
ing on side aspects of the plot or particulars of the scenery. Though he did not

use the word 'ideology' in the limited sense of deliberately manipulative ideas, Bazin was very near to the film theoreticians of the 1960s and 1970s who taxed the mainstream cinema with being an 'ideological device' channelling people's minds towards purely individual troubles or dilemmas instead of opening up those minds to the concrete problems of the society in which they lived. Less overtly political than those theoreticians, Bazin's arguments used, in advance of them, many significant ideas that would resurface in the following decades.

In his view, the chief blame should be put on montage. 'Montage interdit' ('Editing Prohibited'), an essay he wrote in 1953 and later revised in 1957, has thrown a good many readers into confusion. The first English translator of *What is Cinema?* was well advised when he chose as the English title of this essay 'The Virtues and Limitations of Montage' for, in moving away from the forceful accent afforded by a literal translation of the French title, he succeeded in insightfully rendering the deeper meaning of the text. In his article, Bazin did not 'forbid' montage: on the contrary, he recognised its intrinsic value; and, in his 1957 revised version, he insisted that 'It is in no sense a question of giving up convenient ways of varying the shots' ([1957] 2004a: 50) and was content with advising against an excessive fragmentation of sequences. Many of the film-makers he admired – Renoir, Dreyer, Buñuel, Bresson – had currently recourse to some form of editing and, implicitly, theirs was a 'permitted montage'. Amazing, at times tortuous, explanations justified such practices: 'Cocteau [in *Les parents terribles*/*the Storm Within* (1948)] remains faithful to the classic pattern of cutting but gives it a special significance by using practically exclusively shots [that give] *a psychological analysis from the point of view of the spectator's interest.*' ([1951] 92)

Whereas he had a clear notion of the realism he advocated and illustrated with detailed, subtle analysis, Bazin did not provide concrete examples of 'false realism'; his accounts were extremely general and concerned a speculative category related to films. 'The traditional realist artists', he asserted, tell stories. Instead of letting events take their course in the 'fabric of life', they select unusual facts to construct an arbitrary tale illustrating, in political, moral or social terms, their own conception of the world. They pretend to be realist through using multiple, tangible images of people, sites, objects but such quick glances at the scenery are 'illusions of reality' and conceal the will to force 'an a priori significance' on the public ([1955] 2011: 167, 174); 'analytical montage only calls for him [the spectator] to follow the guide' ([1955] 2004a: 36). What most irritated Bazin was the 'division of reality into successive shots', which are 'just a series of either logical or subjective points of view of an event' ([1948] 2011: 39). The 'chopping' of images into short elements 'insidiously' substituted a mere juxtaposition of shots for 'an objective content'. Screening dramatic events in oversimplified form, montage presupposed that their origin and consequences were unequivocal. By ruling out any trace of an ambiguity inherent to reality, it imposed its 'mediocre value' between 'the spectator and the object, like a set of prisms and filters designed to stamp their own meaning on reality' (1952] 1973: 105).

A sentence sums up Bazin's standpoint: 'Accelerated montage' plays 'tricks with time and space' ([1955] 2004a: 36). Facing an ambiguous reality, human beings, he contended, behave in two opposed ways: some essay to stick on it a pre-established interpretation; others, before voicing the slightest thought, open their mind and senses to the world. What can they observe? The continuity of the sphere where they live, time which passes inexorably, without any pause, space that surrounds them ([1951] 108). Both time and space are elusive but their uninterrupted presence is not so that people must become aware of such permanence. Bazin had been long convinced that a priori ideas blind people, preventing them from paying due attention to their environment. His reflection on montage (perhaps his excessively radical conception of how film editing was currently carried out) persuaded him that a speedy concatenation of images was likely to dim human sensibility. His characterisation of realism in films came, at least partially, as a reaction against the prevalent system of montage. In this respect a few films, *Citizen Kane*, William Wyler's *The Little Foxes* (1941) and *The Best Years of our Lives* (1946), had a significant influence on the young critic. Welles, Bazin recognised, was not a 'realist' film-maker, he ruled out 'all recourse to nature in the raw, natural settings, exteriors, sunlight and non-professional actors'; the director had even rejected 'those qualities of the authentic document [. . .] which, being a part of reality, can themselves establish a form of realism' ([1948] 2011: 41). Nevertheless, by means of long takes and depth of focus, Welles and Wyler had 'restored a fundamental quality of reality – its visible continuity' (39). In the 1948 essays, the first to focus prevalently on depth of field, Bazin was content with noting that such process, taking in 'with equal sharpness the whole field of vision contained simultaneously within the dramatic field', freed the audience from a narrow framing, while montage, enclosing the characters inside a limited plane, channelled attention towards the plot. By rejecting 'subtraction' and making setting and actors simultaneously visible, Welles's films managed to hand to the public the responsibility of looking and interpreting. Realism, by then, was an incitement directed towards spectators invited to gaze actively, instead of following a prearranged chain of images, and to become aware of their being enveloped by a continuous, vast area ([1948] 2009: 54–5).

It is later, in the mid-1950s, after his views about realism had evolved, that Bazin dwelt on the importance of depth of field. Showing a series of characters lined up at intervals from the far background to the foreground and involved in different activities, instead of presenting them separately, depth of field obliges viewers to make a personal choice, either to divide their attention between several occurrences or follow them simultaneously. Thanks to depth

of focus, films require 'a more active mental attitude on the part of the spectator and a more positive contribution to the action in progress'. Not guided by
montage, viewers find themselves uncertain about the sense they should put
on the film; depth of focus reintroduces 'ambiguity into the structure of the
image if not of necessity, at least as a possibility' ([1955] 2004a: 36).

BAZIN AND NEOREALISM: 1948 TO MID-1950S

Today, cinema historians think that what has been gathered under the term
neorealism was less a group of film-makers striving towards the same ideal
than the simultaneous release of independent films shot by directors who had
little in common except their will to put aside the conventional cinema. Bazin,
however, had not the slightest doubt about the existence of an 'Italian school
of the Liberation'. In his view, neorealists were careful in their research of
reality, but did not conceive it like documentary film-makers who look for
characteristic data. What they sought were the things themselves, in their
original, ontological manifestation, things 'inseparably one', which could only
be reached in their 'continuum', their total and indivisible continuance in time
and space. Too many directors wanted to explain the 'meaning' of objects or
occurrences whereas these, in themselves, in their full development, carry
'their own weight, their complete uniqueness, that ambiguity that characterises any fact' ([1949] 2011: 65). Let events expand 'as the hours roll by' and
they will turn out to be plain, luminous, natural; the impression they will make
will be 'unfailingly that of truth' (70). The main quality of neorealism 'lies in
not betraying the essence of things, in allowing them first of all to exist for their
own sake, freely [. . .] in their singular individuality' (81).

Bazin's neorealism was much more than a different manner of constructing images, it was 'an attitude of mind' implying moral change. Directors and
actors should renounce forcing their point of view on spectators. The neorealist directors could not film everything; they were obliged to 'filter' a complex,
uncertain reality. Their selection, however, was 'neither logical, nor [. . .]
psychological' but 'ontological, in the sense that the image of reality it restores
to us is a whole [. . .] a true imprint of reality' ([1955] 2011: 168). Instead of
inventing 'stories in the margin of everyday reality', they 'throw light on that
reality, to illuminate it from within in order to make of it an object to witness
and to love' ([1954] 142). As for actors, instead of translating the emotions,
passions or desires supposedly felt by the characters, they managed 'to be,
before expressing' and make themselves 'transparent' ([1953] 77). In such
prospect, the dramatic organisation of the plot is banned, the story, 'immanent
in the events themselves, contained in each instant of each of these events,
inseparable from the fabric of life' (1955] 2011: 174), is fully exposed to the

gaze. A trite operation, a person rolling a cigarette, is entirely visible because it is life in its immediacy and, more importantly, 'duration itself' ([1956] 1997: 212). Any gesture, filmed during the full time for which it lasts, is 'the simple continuing to be of a person to whom nothing in particular happens'. The slightest action, possibly carried out without thinking about it, evidences a way of behaving; people, absorbed in the completion of their task and observed as long as they are fulfilling it, disclose something of their being and of their adherence to the world ([1952] 2011: 112).

In *Viaggio in Italia/Journey to Italy* (Roberto Rossellini, 1954) a couple, engrossed in emotional problems are all of a sudden brought face to face with fortuitous happenings that compel them to overcome their inward-looking preoccupations and pay attention to that and those who surround them. Unexpectedly, the real has been imposed on them, and this is what cinema can do, stir people's consciousness ([1954] 2004b: 100); 'the screen restricts itself to showing us [. . .] or even better it enables us to see' ([1955] 2011: 149). In a neorealist perspective, the activities in which individuals are engaged are not figures used to enliven a fiction, they are moments of life, mere facts that, through their presentation on a screen, become events. Like the characters of *Journey to Italy*, spectators witness a process in which they are not involved; watching the occurrence from outside, instead of living it, they are permitted to appraise it fully; it is not a paradox to state that they form 'a relation with the image closer to that which [they enjoy] with reality' ([1955] 2004a: 35).

'It is in this way that the cinema achieves fruition as the art of the real' ([1955] 150). Art of the real does not mean that the cinema mirrors a reality far too ambivalent to lend itself to a copy. On the contrary, by preserving such ambiguity, it opens up an access to the real. Painting and photography fix a particular instant which, being motionless, is outside of time. Theatre and radio are unable to render the amplitude of space. It is only in film that both time and space obtain a simultaneous representation. Provided it is not intrusive, the camera places the audience in front of human characters sharing a condition analogous to theirs. Allowed to observe freely, they come to a personal conclusion: it is from their attention and their will 'that the meaning of the image in part derives'. What they discover are not 'realia', material, objects, places, but the fundamental order of their own life, the area in which they move, the duration through which they evolve ([1955] 2004: 36–7; 1997: 78–80).

'FILM IS LIKELY TO VANISH IN THE THIN AIR'

Lecturing or introducing films in various circles, Bazin was in touch with extremely diversified audiences (Tweedie 2011: 276–7). Surprisingly, he has left no comprehensive account of his experiences, and it is owing to indirect clues that we understand how disappointed he was by cinema audiences' response: people, he observed, were too concerned with accuracy, details, and objective data; 'documentary objectivity' ([1956] 2004a: 156). Despite his relentless efforts, the public had not come up to his expectations. He was especially keen on *Umberto D.* (Vittorio De Sica, 1951), a true epitome of neo-realism in which there is neither a hero nor a well-built plot leading to a logical epilogue; just bare periods of life. Unfortunately, it was a flop in Italy and elsewhere. Many saw this failure as the end of neorealism. Bazin himself was shaken; he wondered whether the Italian cinema was 'going to disown itself' ([1953] 2011: 142). Later he acknowledged 'the end of neorealism' ([1957] 199). His article on CinemaScope ([1953] 1997: 82) was, in fact, a reflection about the future of cinema which, being 'the result of the happy conjunction between a virtual need and the technological–economic state of civilization', having been born in particular circumstances, was 'likely to vanish in the thin air'.

Such possible transience did not come as a surprise for the critic who was used to contrasting plastic and 'mechanical' arts. The former, subjective interpretations of reality would last as long as humans would try to decipher their universe, that is to say, forever. The latter, produced thanks to a machine which, recording mechanically what was in front of it, did not alter this frag-ment of the real, was at the same time at risk itself from technical progress. The threat materialised with the development of television. The new medium was 'cruder' than cinema but its images were transmitted immediately, at the very moment of the occurrence; the gaucheness and hesitations of live broad-cast gave viewers the impression that they followed close on the cameraman's heels (Cramer 2011: 268–9). Direct, always at one's disposal, television did, however, introduce in the domestic area a feeling of closeness and adherence to daily reality that left no room for ambiguity. The challenge of television and eclipse of neorealism brought the cinematic realism, which Bazin had sketched out in the early 1950s, into question. In consequence, during the last period of his life, he followed the cinematic path of Renoir, on whom he was then writing a book, and also endeavoured to rethink a notion that, for him, remained fundamental.

In 1948, Bazin had noted that, instead of merely one, there were many forms of realism but he was content with ascribing the various configurations to aesthetical or technical parameters (2009: 52). Ten years later, going back over this observation, he qualified and completed it (1973: 85). Most films are realist but the 'quality' of their realism rests on their capacity of abstraction, that is to say, in their aptitude to go beyond description in order to 'signify more'. We must pay attention to the words used by Bazin the critic here: realism must not be a 'photograph' but an 'invention' based on a careful observation of human relationships in the environment where the story takes place ([1958] 62–3). The location shots have to be filmed in actual places or natural settings because studio sets look artificial, whereas indoor sequences will have to give way to imagination, not describe people or things, but reach their truth in outward appearances.

Previously, Bazin seldom used the notion of truth and, when he did, he referred to it in terms of an unequivocal verity opposed to the ambiguity of reality ([1953] 2011: 80). In the late 1950s, however, truth becomes an objective that will be achieved through its antagonistic/complementary association, its 'creative conflict', with realism. Realism obstructs the manifestation of truth if it is 'psychological verisimilitude' because psychology imparts a predetermined signification on reality. Conversely, realism makes way for the verity if it is 'not the result of simple copying from life' but 'the product of a careful re-creation' of characters through the use 'of detail which is not only accurate but meaningful' ([1958] 1973: 63). In such prospect, verisimilitude or implausibility do not matter; what counts is 'the singularity' of a person, a thing, a fact, which can be conveyed by a detail, a peculiarity, possibly false or exaggerated, but revealing ([1957] 77). The world is nothing but interdependence between living creatures, amorphous objects and space–time; human beings inhabit a universe of relations so that realism must display these perpetual exchanges (91).

There also seems to be some discrepancy in terms of 'truth' between the realism of the 'neorealism years' and that developed under the influence of Renoir. The former, preserving the continuity of time and space, helped spectators to realise their life environment. The latter goes much further and opens the way to a formulation of truth which is almost metaphysical. Actually, though, there is no fundamental contradiction here. On the one hand, Bazin considers Renoir a forerunner and inspirer of neorealism who has explored, a decade earlier, the advantages of depth of field and the long take ([1954 and 1958] 1973: 37–8, 62). On the other, the apprehension of one's involvement in time and space is a step towards a superior comprehension of the world. Both stages of Bazin's reflection on this issue also aim at the same target: to make people discover what in humanity transcends humanity ([1958] 117). The discourse of the late 1950s is simply more spiritual than the previous one.

A THEORY IN PROGRESS

If we call 'theory' a scheme intended to provide a systematic explanation for an object, an entity or a phenomenon, there is no 'Bazinian' theory. The trajectory I have delineated sets out the manifoldness of Bazin's writing which seldom puts forward conclusive statements. Instead, that manifoldness blends ideas together, returns to antecedent notions, and reveals a mind engaged in a permanent process of reflective research. The French critic was adamant on two points, however. Thinking that many have an artificial, illusory view of their surroundings, he found it necessary to help them look around and reach an enhanced consciousness of their involvement in the universe. He considered also that the cinema, realist thanks to its mechanical production, was capable of manifesting 'the hidden meaning in people and things'. Yet realism was not an exact copy of reality for the reason that reality, being fundamentally ambiguous, eludes representation. Realism was not a quality of some films, it was a process that made viewers overcome their daily routine and open their mind to 'the supernatural – or poetry, or surrealism, or magic – whatever the term that expresses the hidden accord which things maintain with an invisible counterpart of which they are merely the adumbration'. Bazin did not propose realism recipes, nor did he declare what realism was because, for him, it was mainly a means to pass 'to the other side', from 'the surface' to the 'here and now' of human beings.

REFERENCES

Posthumously published collections of writing by Bazin:
Bazin, André (1973), *Jean Renoir*, trans. W. W. Hasley and W. H. Simon, New York: Simon & Schuster.
— (1978) *Orson Welles*, trans. J. Rosenbaum, New York: Harper & Row.
— (1982), *The Cinema of Cruelty*, trans. S. d'Estrée, New York: Seaver Books.
— (1984) *French Cinema of the Occupation and Resistance: The Birth of a Critical Esthetic*, trans. S. Hochman. New York: Frederick Ungar.
— (1997), *Bazin at Work: Major Essays & Reviews from the Forties & Fifties*, trans. A. Piette and B. Cardullo, New York and London: Routledge.
— (2004 a and b), *What is Cinema ?* two volumes, revised edition trans. H. Gray, Berkeley, CA: University of California Press.
— (2009), *What is Cinema ?* trans. T. Barnard, Montreal: Caboose.
— (2011) *André Bazin and Italian Neorealism*, ed. Cardullo, B., New York: Continuum International.

Critical writings on Bazin:
Andrew, Dudley (1978), *André Bazin*, Oxford: Oxford University Press.
— (2011) (ed. with H. Joubert-Laurencin), *Opening Bazin. Postwar Film Theory and its Afterlife*, Oxford: Oxford University Press.
Cardullo, B. (2010), 'Divining the Real: The Film Theory and Criticism of André Bazin', *Midwest Quarterly*, winter, vol. 51, pp. 200–16.
Cramer, M. (2011), 'Television and the Author', in Andrew and Joubert-Laurencin, pp. 268–74.
Tweedie, J. (2011), 'André Bazin's Bad Taste', in Andrew and Joubert-Laurencin, pp. 275–87.

CHAPTER 7

Realism is to Think Historically: Overlapping Elements in Lukácsian and Brechtian Theories of Realism

Angelos Koutsourakis

THE BRECHT–LUKÁCS DEBATE

Within film studies there has been an increased interest in rethinking the debates of classical film theory. The discipline is revaluating its history with the view to the first half of the twentieth century. As David Rodowick rightly observes, this shift to past theoretical debates can be interpreted in part as a response to recent technological developments; the shift from the analogue to the digital has reawakened the shocks of modernity encountered by film scholars in the 1930s and has stimulated an increased interest in early film theory (Rodowick 2014: 3). For Rodowick, even debates on the 'end of theory' can be seen from a different perspective, not as a simple teleological consequence but as a desire to reflect on the past while also showcasing anxiety concerning an ambiguous future. Rodowick cites Vincent Leitch's point that, despite mourning related to the end of theory, theory has the potential to 'return like a ghost in unexpected forms' (207).

The question of realism was one of the central topics in early film theory and, despite the period of time that has elapsed, remains a pertinent issue precisely because of the constant development of technologies of mediation which also imply and indicate the mediated aspect of social reality. In this chapter, I intend to return to one of the major theoretical debates in the discipline of film studies: that is, the realism versus modernism one which was manifest in some of the first writings on the medium during the 1920s and 1930s, as well as in the years of the 'apparatus' (or grand) theory practised by *Cahiers du Cinéma* and the British journal *Screen* in the 1970s. The fact that realism and modernism are not necessarily antithetical categories has been the subject of recent scholarship in the field; yet, to get a better understanding of this, I propose a reconsideration of the Georg Lukács and Bertolt Brecht debate which was one of the most important theoretical disputes in film theory and

Marxist criticism. I intend to identify the corresponding elements in Brecht's and Lukács's understanding of realism by focusing on questions of theory and practice.

To begin with, it is important to acknowledge that both theorists understood realism beyond the parameters of reflectionist theories of art. Furthermore, both considered realism as a practice which is: 1. inextricably linked with the dialectical method; 2. in direct opposition to naturalism and psychologically defined characters; 3. and against the orthodoxy of socialist realism. Another crucial matter to point out is that their interpretation of realism is predicated on Friedrich Engels's definition of realism as 'the reproduction of typical people under typical circumstances', which they both quote (Lukács 1970: 77; Brecht, Berlau, Weigel: 1952: 433). One also needs to acknowledge that both accept Marx's point that social reality under capitalism is reified and disguised, and thus realism needs to reveal the social, political and historical processes that have been camouflaged in everyday life.

This revelatory principle points to the importance that Brecht and Lukács laid on the dialectical method as a process of demystification. For Lukács, dialectics is a process that aims to understand social facts and appearances in their interaction and not as isolated static phenomena. One of the key principles in his thinking is the idea of totality, that is, the ways that specific social and historical phenomena can be understood as part of a broader whole; as he says in *History and Class Consciousness*, 'only in this context which sees the isolated facts of social life as aspects of the historical process and integrates them in a totality, can knowledge of the facts hope to become knowledge of reality' (Lukács 1967: 8). Brecht also shares the idea that dialectical thinking can demystify a distorted social reality and defines dialectics as 'the science of general laws of motion and development in nature, in human society, and in thought' (Brecht, Berlau, Weigel: 1952: 431). He shares with Lukács the Marxist principle that social reality is a product of a series of interconnections and not something set and unchangeable. Therefore, the starting point of realism, for both, is to show how individual behaviours can be seen in the context of a social and historical reality that is not fixed but subject to change.

This is also why both of them disregarded naturalism practically for the same reasons. Naturalism offers a fixed image of the world without indicating that social life is the nexus of mutable divergent forces. Lukács thought that the modus operandi of naturalism was a 'pseudo-objectivity' that fails to capture 'the dialectics of conflicting social forces' and proposes instead some ahistorical 'sociological abstractions' (Lukács 1970: 167). According to Lukács, realism should capture the social phenomena in their changeability and 'only the dialectical conception of totality can enable us to understand reality as a social process' (Lukács 1967: 13). Similarly, Brecht thought that naturalism prioritised an abstract humanism which was communicated through strategies of representational verisimilitude. In its attempt to portray things with photographic accuracy, naturalism gave rise to images of the world 'as dead things' and, even when naturalism elaborated on issues that were political *tout court*, it relied heavily on strategies of individuated psychological explication. Consequently, the representation of the individual was unrealistic because it failed to show characters as part of a group reality – as the product of social interactions and human coexistence (Brecht 2014: 54).

It is not accidental that both Brecht and Lukács considered socialist realism, the official artistic doctrine of the Soviet Union under Stalin, to be an insufficient artistic method. In an essay titled 'Marx and Engels on Aesthetics', Lukács indirectly points to the weaknesses of socialist realism by explaining that the mechanical reproduction of ideological conflict as 'passive product of the economic process' is mistaken because it reduces complex social conflicts to one-dimensional 'cause and effect relationships' (Lukács 1970: 64). Elsewhere, he states that socialist realism fails to capture reality in its contradictions. Socialism turns into a dogma and the socialist solutions 'became the illustration of an abstract "truth"' (Lukács 1962: 119). In this context, Lukács clarifies that the Marxist concept of typicality, which, as was mentioned earlier, is the basis for his definition of realism, does not imply a schematic representation of individuals but aspires to capture the historically determined element of individuality as well as 'the most significant directions of social development' (Lukács 1970: 78). Brecht was also sceptical with respect to socialist realism and believed that the transition from bourgeois-literary techniques to socialist realism was not real progress because the only change was that the bourgeois standpoint was replaced by a proletarian one. In this respect, the empathetic mode of representation was retained with the only difference being that the bourgeois universal individual – Brecht, following Marx and Engels in *The Communist Manifesto*, thought that, in capitalist reality, what is taken to be 'human' is nothing but the bourgeois individual, universalised by the dominant class – was substituted by the proletarian dramatic character. Therefore, the mechanical duplication of social relationships based on class struggle could not capture the complexity of societal processes. Brecht dismissively described socialist realism as 'the banality of new wine in old bottles' (Brecht 2003: 232).

From the foregoing comments one can see that Brecht's and Lukács's views on realism share many similarities. Yet the difference is that Lukács suggested that Marxist criticism and art could benefit from looking at the masterpieces of bourgeois literature, such as those by Balzac and Tolstoy, while Brecht suggested that the changes brought about by industrial society called for new means of representing reality: realism should thus become polemical, a form of negation of: 1. conformist artistic practices; and of 2. habitual understandings of social reality. While Lukács shared Brecht's call for objects which can shift emphasis from the individual storyline to broader collective social and historical structures, he disagreed with the latter's method and valorisation of modernist representational strategies. His critique of modernism derived from his understanding of it as mere naturalism; modernism points to the angst of modern reality though its formal abstraction does not show this anxiety as part of a 'disintegrating society' (Lukács 1962: 40) but rather as a static condition of certain alienated individuals who seem to be dissociated from their social environment.

Lukács was a keen reader of Hegel's *Phenomenology of Spirit* and agreed with Hegel that the modern subject is not at home in the world (Aitken 2006: 77). Unlike Hegel, he did not believe that theory in itself can turn into knowledge of reality but saw theory as the route to praxis, that is, to social transformation. In this respect, Lukács also believed that Marxism was able to expose the social interactions and hierarchies that generate alienation and thus lead to such alteration. He viewed writers, such as Joyce and Kafka, as naturalist because he thought that they could not go beyond reproducing alienation and so overlooked the social totality. For Lukács, modernist fragmentation produced ahistorical narrative characters who had not developed from their interaction with social reality and who appeared to have been merely 'thrown into the world'. It is on account of this *Geworfenheit* (thrownness) (Lukács 1962: 39) that Lukács criticised modernist negation; for he suggested that this negation could not be understood historically. It is an abstract gesture that does not propose any alternatives on how to overcome the impasse. Illuminating in this respect is the following commentary:

> In realistic literature each descriptive detail is both individual and typical. Modern allegory, and modernist ideology, however, deny the typical. By destroying the coherence of the world, they reduce detail to the level of mere particularity (once again, the connection between modernism and naturalism is plain). Detail, in its allegorical transferability, though brought into a direct, if paradoxical connection with transcendence, becomes an abstract function of the transcendence to which it points. Modernist literature thus replaces concrete typicality with abstract particularity. (Lukács 1962: 43)

In this respect, modernist fragmentation produces pseudo-objectivity, and here the reader can notice the similarities with Lukács's critique of naturalism. Brecht, on the other hand, thought that Lukács's dismissal of modernism as empty formalism was oversimplistic. For Brecht, the distinction between form and content was a red herring, and he thought that numerous works were 'unrealistic' not because of their dependence on formal innovation but, antithetically, owing to their reliance on reproducing political content without changing the means of expression (Brecht 1974: 42). He thought that changes in industrial society, the division of labour, and the rise of capitalism demanded new ways of representing reality, and he disagreed with Lukács's viewpoint that the masterpieces of bourgeois literature should be the models of any future realistic art. Unlike Lukács, Brecht saw in the modernist experiments of James Joyce and Alfred Döblin an emphasis on the representation of a prevailing dehumanisation and the fragmentation of modern life produced by industrial capitalism. While he acknowledged that there should be a dialogue between past artistic forms and new ones, Brecht suggested that the bourgeois realism espoused by Lukács captured only the surface of things and not the social structures that can account for such surface. Additionally, he considered that Balzac and Tolstoy's overemphasis on individual characters was not necessarily realistic because those characters occupied too much space in the narrative whereas, in reality, characters emerge from processes of social relations which cannot be captured by formal motifs that privilege the notion of the individuated – and also unified – character (47).

The positions adopted by Lukács and Brecht often appear to be starkly opposed. But is that the case? Ezra Pound's view of Joyce's work can help us understand the ways in which modernism draws on the realist novel's emphasis on typicality – a quality that was a key aspect of realist representation for both Lukács and Brecht. Pound argued that Joyce was a realist because 'he deals with normal things and normal people' (Pound 2013: 67). To this we should add that Lukács does not always argue that modernism is unrealistic. Telling, in this respect, is that he praised Kafka for 'his sincerity' and 'simplicity' arguing that he reveals 'the diabolical character of the world of modern capitalism, and man's impotence in the face of it' (Lukács 1962: 77). One also needs to draw attention to the fact that one of the key aspects of Brechtian dramaturgy, the undermining of the individual character as a narrative and historical agent in favour of situations that reveal the individual as an ensemble of social, historical and political circumstances, was a key characteristic of certain realist novels. Fredric Jameson explains that the 'effacement of protagonicity' in the novels of Tolstoy was subsequently mobilised by modernist artists (Jameson 2012: 88, 111). For Jameson, bourgeois realism's commitment to Enlightenment ideas of 'demystification' was also a major influence for modernism in its desire to represent typical situations, individuals and cities, 'which make up the reality of a given moment, nationality, and history' (Jameson 2013: 144). Lukács thought that the key innovation of the realist historical novel was precisely this valorisation of typicality at the expense of dramatic concreteness; commenting on Tolstoy's radical questioning of protagonicity, he writes that 'characters come and go, but nothing happens as a result of this constant flux because each figure is as insubstantial as the next, and any one can be put in the place of any other' (Lukács 1971: 150). These observations open up alternative strands of inquiry into the Brecht and Lukács debate that can help us identify similarities between Brecht's political modernism and Lukács's advocacy of critical realism.

LUKÁCS AND BRECHT ON FILM

As mentioned, in terms of method, Lukács's and Brecht's ideas share many parallels, and these are even more palpable in their writings on film. Both dismissed psychological realism as a representational stratagem. Lukács suggested that psychological explanations do not 'encompass ideology' and convey a sense of 'pseudo-objectivity' (Lukács 1970: 151, 167) while Brecht thought that psychological characterisation could not capture the historically and socially determined aspect of human interactions. As David Barnett explains, for Brecht, successful characterisation is motivated by the Leninist motto 'who does what to whom' and 'for what reason' (Barnett 2014: 35). It is therefore no surprise that both he and Lukács were aficionados of Charlie Chaplin whom they considered to be a great realist. Both suggested that Chaplin's acting style embodied the qualities of typicality, which they favoured. In a chapter from *The Specificity of the Aesthetic*, entitled 'Film', Lukács mentions some actors who exemplify the features of typicality in their acting style. He mentions Greta Garbo, Asta Nielsen, Buster Keaton and Chaplin. As he says:

> Given our observations up to this point it may appear as obvious that we see in Chaplin the highest manifestation of this tendency . . . Rather it is in his physical existence, in his gestures and mimicry, carried through in inexhaustible variations, that the typical behaviour of the 'little guy', the man of the masses within the context of contemporary capitalism, becomes sensuously and symbolically expressed. Thus, he is able to express the socio-historic condition at a high level of typicality, and few of his contemporaries in other arts have been able to match such an achievement. One should not come to forget how close the emotional field fashioned by Chaplin, as well as its social triggers (*Auslöser*), is to the world created by Kafka. However, in Chaplin, terror and helplessness are not merely rendered sensuous from the perspective of interiority, but in an inseparable unity of interiority and exteriority. (Lukács in Aitken, trans. 2012: 207–8)

Lukács's reasoning bears considerable resemblance to Brecht's view of Chaplin as a realist actor. Tellingly, Brecht considers Chaplin to be an actor who embodies the qualities of epic acting precisely because of his ability to connect the individual character with social reality. He considers Chaplin's gestural acting to be revolutionary on account of the fact that the individual depicted is no longer seen as a static persona but as a changeable character whose *Gestic* attitudes are generated from his dialogue with the social environment. In a short essay written in 1936, he explains how Chaplin's acting in *The Gold Rush* (1936) produces *Verfremdungseffekte* (defamiliarising effects) because of the mechanical postures he adopts, postures that emphasise the changeability of attitudes towards the other characters (Brecht 2001: 10). In a journal entry on 27 March 1942 he also says that Chaplin 'historicises his subjects so that they are still enjoyable years later' (Brecht 1993: 214). Evidently, Chaplin's ability to connect the inner with the outer chimes neatly with Lukácsian ideas of totality as well as with Brechtian ideas of character as a dialectical nexus. Within this logic one also needs to mention that Lukács's admiration for Chaplin draws a direct analogy with the interrelationship between realism and modernism, and here Chaplin's modernism could well be seen in the light of what Miriam Bratu Hansen calls 'vernacular modernism': a type of cinematic modernism not predicated on notions of high art but one that takes advantage of 'popular motifs' and denaturalises them (Bratu Hansen 2010: 302). One cannot ignore the Brechtian echoes of Bratu Hansen's argument; and Chaplin's ability to represent typical social behaviour and estrange it at the same time, for example, the class divisions in *City Lights* (1931), can be viewed in terms of Bratu Hansen's formulation.

Lukács and Brecht's fascination with Chaplin, owing to his ability to externalise processes, also serves to highlight the importance they both placed on the specificity of the medium of film. Both think that film's reliance on the photographic image had simultaneously emancipatory as well as conservative potentials. Lukács aptly describes the importance of mediation in film narrative which can concurrently enhance 'the mimetic character of film' (Lukács in Aitken 2012: 210) and show things in a detached way. Obviously, his point places cinema within the logic of modernism which, as David Trotter rightly observes, was an event not in the history of representation but in the history of mediation as a whole (Trotter 2007: 11). In terms of this, Lukács does not see film as a platform for reproducing literary stereotypes, and he is quite clear that the film script can be seen only as 'instigator' for an audiovisual narrative and not as the central feature of a film's narrative (Lukács in Aitken, trans. 2012: 206). This is also stated in his first essay on film, 'Thoughts Towards an Aesthetic of the Cinema', which was published in the *Frankfurter Zeitung und Handelsblatt* in 1913, in which he discusses the difference between theatre and cinema. Praising the new medium for its 'vivaciousness', he goes on to argue that cinema needs to take advantage of its own visual means rather than producing stage drama on screen. Cinema can produce a world of 'pure externality' which is much more authentic as opposed to standardised stage drama and dialogue-driven novels (Lukács in Aitken, trans. 2012: 185). Again, Lukács's favouring of a gestural cinema has fascinating parallels not only with Brecht but also with succeeding writings on film by writers such as Giorgio Agamben and Gilles Deleuze. Lisabeth During has already acknowledged parallels between Lukács and Deleuze, setting as an example the neorealist period of Luchino Visconti which merges a 'literary realism' with a modernist 'Marxist romanticism' (During 2013).

Brecht, in *Der Dreigroschenprozeß* ('The Threepenny Lawsuit'), his most influential essay on film, argued that cinema redefines the standardised representational schemata which have their roots in the art of the novel. The revolutionary potential brought about by film's reliance on technological mediation is that 'the idea of art as an independent phenomenon of a social nature' and idealist notions of artistic individuality are radically undermined (Brecht 2001: 193). Film's reliance on apparatuses which are products of the general production process redefines the separation between art and social life. The aesthetic consequence of these developments is that film realism opposes the novelistic concepts of realism which are based upon notions of internal coherence (Giles 1998: 98). Film is not a mere reproduction of text and actions. As he says, 'gestures take the place of words as the means of expressions. Simultaneously there is a transposition into another artistic genre; the work first transformed into a dramatic mime must be transposed at the same time into a work of images.' (Brecht 2001: 186) For Brecht, gestural language or montage can undermine the organic continuity of common film narrative and focus on 'marked interruptions' that privilege external processes rather than individualised dramas (28). All these ideas are underpinned by his firm belief that cinema needs to take advantage of its reliance on photographic reproducibility, not in order to present an organically coherent dramatic world but to reflect on social processes which have a collective character. In a much-quoted sentence, Brecht explains that a photograph of a factory does not reveal anything about the social processes behind it (164). It is, however, implicit in his argument that technological apparatuses can be used differently so as to go beyond artistic concepts of *Weltanschauung* (world view) which tend to construct surface reality but do not represent reality 'as a totality' (165).

Indubitably, Brecht's employment of the term 'totality' has an interesting proximity to Lukács's ideas. What deserves special comment is that the latter also elaborated on the importance of technological mediation in the cinema, the 'deanthropomorphising' aspect of the film medium, and the fact that film is a product of capitalist processes of production. In the following quotation Lukács clearly articulates the revolutionary impact of 1. the photographic premise of the cinema and 2. mediation by means of film's 'double mimesis', that is the artistic impersonation of a human being by an actor and the camera's capturing of this mimetic process; despite some reservations, he agrees in principle with Benjamin's ideas as articulated in the 'The Work of Art in the Age of Mechanical Reproduction' essay:

Of course, photography is a reflection of reality, not reality itself; however because it depicts reality mechanically and abidingly in an [*sic*] – deanthropomorphising – way, that which is portrayed through this type of mechanically faithful depiction must also seek to preserve, as mimesis, this authenticity of reality. Even though the aesthetic means of film order and organise, and exceed, in their general effects, the immediacy of everyday life, they do not revoke – the photographic – depiction of reality, but, instead, merely place it in completely new contexts (by means of the choice of particular moments, of joining these together by means of tempo and rhythm, and through other ways of connecting them, etc.). This authenticity has to be continually retained; it has to be and ought to be an essential element of the homogeneous medium of film art. But the source of authenticity is reality itself: what is captured in the photograph can only make the objectively existing, specifically visual being-real of its respective object manifest. (Lukács in Aitken, trans. 2012: 192–3)

The foregoing passage enables an approach to thinking about Lukácsian realism both as a representation and demystification of reality. In principle, Lukács agrees with Brecht that film's innovative potential is contingent on its reliance on mediation and, not unlike Bazinian film theory, he shows preference for films that retain the medium's photographic capacity rather than theatrical films in the expressionist tradition. On the other hand, as Ian Aitken observes, he is aware that this quality of the medium can be used as a means of manipulation (Aitken 2006: 90). This is the reason why he insists that film realism is not just a matter of reflection. With reference to Vittorio De Sica's *Bicycle Thieves* (1948), he explains that realist cinema can both reveal everyday facts that skip one's perception as well as discover 'a deep poetry' that opposes the oppressive empiricism and alienation of life within capitalism (Lukács in Aitken, trans. 2012: 202). The core of his thesis is that cinema can present *der Menschen ganz* (man's totality), namely the relationships between the individual and the socially determined conditions (Aitken 2006: 74; see also Lukács in Aitken, trans. 2012: 200). This notion of totality corresponds with the Brechtian idea of the dialectic as the route to realism, which is predicated on placing individual characters in socially contextualised situations instead of treating conflict as a clash between universal individualities. But how can we address the idea of totality in film practice through the Lukácsian and Brechtian lens?

TOTALITY IS HISTORY: *SZEGÉNYLEGÉNYEK* (1965) AND *ALLONSANFÀN* (1974)

For Lukács, totality designates a synecdochic understanding of social reality in which each aspect of it cannot be understood on its own but as part of a series of interrelationshiips. Another Lukácsian term, which is useful in order to understand totality, is *die Besonderheit* (speciality) which, as Ian Aitken explains, stands for the dissolution of the general into the concrete particular, and is part of realist art's commitment to connecting the individual with the universal and the socio-historical (Aitken 2006: 79). Now the comparison with Brecht is again informative because Brecht also argued that the route to understanding unique incidents is 'by using other incidents' (Brecht 2014b: 41). Brecht viewed history as science which could connect the general with the concrete particular not by representing great historical figures but through an emphasis on historical attitudes. This is exactly what connects his view of realism with Lukács's and, indicative from this perspective, is a recent rereading of Lukácsian totality by Fredric Jameson:

> But I believe that for Lukács totality was history, and that in reality [*sic*] his conception of realism had to do with an art whereby the narrative of individuals was somehow made to approach historical dynamics as such, was organized so as to reveal its relationship with a history in movement and a future on the point of emergence. Realism would thus have to do with the revelation of tendencies rather than with the portrayal of a state of affairs. (Jameson 2012: 479)

This understanding of totality as 'revelation of tendencies' can help us clarify the dialogue between Brecht and Lukács not solely in theory but also with reference to specific films.

Miklós Jancsó's *Szegénylegények / The Round-Up*, 1965) and the Taviani brothers' *Allonsanfàn* (1974) are examples of political cinema that historicise representation through exposing a series of historical dynamics rather than simply reproducing historical incidents. Given that these film-makers are classified as representatives of modernist cinema (which has been discussed with reference to Brecht), the question is how one can approach them from a Lukácsian viewpoint. Firstly, one needs to note that Jancsó was deeply influenced by Lukács's understanding of realism and his attack on psychology as a dramaturgical vehicle (Czigany 1972: 45; Bisztray 1980: 137). Secondly, Lukács was a follower of modernist Hungarian film-makers such as Jancsó and András Kovács. While being doubtful of their modernism, he praised their commitment to history and social realism. In 1968, in an interview with Yvette Biró, he praised

Jancsó's *Szegénylegények* for its ability to engage with historical contradictions in Hungary which remained contemporarily influential (Aitken 2012: 247). Now, as far as the Tavianis are concerned, their films successfully merge modernism with a type of classical literary realism but, as Ilario Luperini explains, their view of realism originates directly from an understanding of historical reality as the product of dialectical opposites, communicated via formal elements such as 'detail/distant field, chromatic harmony/colour dissonance, intensified inner drama/slow narrative rhythm, visual fixity/animated sound modulation, and so on' (Luperini 1995: 28).

Szegénylegények is set in Hungary in 1867, years after the failed revolution of 1848, during which the Magyars, the Germans and the Poles coalesced against the Austro-Hungarian Empire. Writing on the revolution in 1849, Friedrich Engels stated that:

> For the first time in the revolutionary movement of 1848, for the first time since 1793, a nation surrounded by superior counter-revolutionary forces dares to counter the cowardly counter-revolutionary fury by revolutionary passion, the terreur blanche by the terreur rouge. (Engels 1849)

The film starts with a voice-over stating in a Brechtian didactic manner that, years after the failure of the revolution, a middle class has emerged and this class prefers a social stability that guarantees the smooth advancement of its interests. The plot is very fragmented while the characters in the film are archetypes rather than individuals whose practices are psychologically defined. Throughout the film, the boundaries between oppressors and oppressed are interchangeable as, for example, when revolutionary soldiers become informers to save their own lives. Acts of killing and humiliation are also portrayed in a cool and clinical, rather than affective, manner.

Set in the Hungarian Puszta (the name of a grassland tundra in the great Hungarian plain), the film takes place in a prison camp which houses Lajos Kossuth's (one of the key leaders of the Hungarian revolution) supporters as well as soldiers from Sándor Rózsa's (a renowned Hungarian outlaw) band who joined the revolution subsequently. Shot on location in the landscape of the Puszta, the film's *mise en scène* combines realist elements and formal abstraction which are reinforced by an overemphasis on registering group formations within a desolate landscape. While a number of characters are singled out and followed by the film-maker, any psychological explanation is frustrated as the camera follows them aimlessly; one senses that they are the carriers of dramatic *agon* but the illusion of dramatic protagonicity is stymied given that almost all the designated characters are executed once the viewer is led to assume that their individual stories can add coherence to the overall storyline. So, when the narrative focuses on one of the prisoners near the beginning of the film, the viewer is given the impression that the character will lead the story to a different path, only to realise after a few minutes that he is to be executed by the guards for no apparent reason. Similarly, when one of the rebels is identified as a murderer by the leading guard, he is given the option of saving his life by identifying one man who has killed more people than he has. Again, we follow the character's aimless attempt to act as an informer on his previous comrades. Trivial conversations are followed by mechanical group-ings of the prisoners and pointless disciplinary commands on the part of the guards. Eventually, this character is murdered by some other prisoners and then the narrative focuses on two suspected murderers.

The film also gives precedence to abstract gestural compositions over dra-matic harmony, and this formal choice, along with the absence of protagonic-ity, generates a Brechtian epic quality according to which historical forces are the real motivating factors of the narrative. The excess of gesturality is emblematised in two particular sequences. In the first one, a group of prisoners is led to the top of a building and forced to watch the torturing of a woman by the guards. She is asked to run naked through a circle of guards who whip her in a completely dispassionate way, an effect which is intensified by the fact that the soldiers are framed as an anonymous group because the camera registers their lower torsos and the viewer cannot see their faces. Immediately after this, a number of prisoners react and commit suicide by jumping from the same building. A series of low-angle shots registers the prisoners' ritualistic suicides and is followed by high-angle shots that frame another group of prisoners assembling together and protesting by attacking the guards. This sequence emphasises the dialectical quality of the film which synthesises opposites into a dialectical whole; the synthesised whole here is the idea of manipulation as a historical experience (a point to which I shall return).

Another sequence near the end of the film is also characteristic in this respect. Having managed to turn the prisoners against one another, the guards succeed in identifying Sándor's men by pretending that the last has been par-doned by the Austrian emperor. Thinking that the pardon applies to them, a group of prisoners starts celebrating and singing the revolutionary song Kossuth Nóta, only to disclose themselves to the guards. The guards explain to them that the amnesty does not extend to Sándor's men. The revolutionary song stops and the guards forcefully confront the prisoners. Evidently, the film's reference to the past points to a series of historical disappointments and to the country's failure to build a democratic socialist alternative in the light of the Soviet suppression of the 1956 Hungarian revolution. As András Bálint Kovács explains, the homogeneous landscape of the Puszta and the emphasis on gestural compositions produce a dialectical combination of realism and modernist abstraction. The openness of the landscape and the lack of dramatic development reduce the characters to 'objecthood' and all human physical interactions are defined by the historical experience of manipulation, in which victims and perpetrators are equally subordinated (Kovács 2007: 332). The historical experience of manipulation stands for totality in the film's story, not as an abstract existential denunciation of the evils of history, but as a concrete reality of the present.

In *Allonsanfàn*, totality emblematises the historical defeat of utopian visions as well as the need to recover utopia. Set in Italy in 1816, the years of the Restoration (the re-establishment of monarchy in France following the defeat of Napoleon), the film follows Fulvio Imbriani a former anarchist who decides to forget his revolutionary past and return to his bourgeois family. His former comrades are members of an underground group, 'the Sublime Brothers', which refuses to surrender. Along with his wife, they force him to follow them and leave the security of his family mansion behind. Trying to keep him in the house, his sister informs his comrades to the authorities. Many members of the sect, as well as Fulvio's wife, are then shot dead by the army. Fulvio successfully escapes from the armed forces and his former comrades who try to convince him to join an uprising in the south, which he considers to be pointless. Eventually, he is forced to join them only to betray them to a local priest. The latter convinces the peasants – whose support has also been sought by the Sublimes – to attack and kill the idealist rebels. Fulvio escapes while the Sublimes are slaughtered by the peasants and the army. *Allonsanfàn*, one of the few true believers in the utopian cause, survives and meets Fulvio in a feverish state telling him that the peasants have joined the rebels' cause. Fulvio, who is an opportunist, believes his delirious rant and puts on a red shirt to join – what he thinks to be – the winning camp, only to be shot dead next to his comrades.

Not unlike other Taviani brothers' films, *Allonsanfàn* treads the line between literary classicism and modernism. While Jancsó's *Szegénylegények* conveys typicality through a complete denial of the trope of the dramatic character, the Tavianis in *Allonsanfàn* use archetypal characters standing for larger historical forces. Fulvio represents the former dreamer who has been disappointed by the failure of the revolution. His disillusionment is also an index of the fact that he joined the revolution only out of romantic idealism instead of class consciousness. His friend Tito stands for the committed rebel who does not necessarily have a realistic strategic plan while Allonsanfàn is the true utopian idealist who refuses to give up hope even when everything seems to have been lost. The peasants towards the end stand for the masses whose enslavement to religious superstitions and lack of class consciousness make them oppose their own social interests. The film's stress on character typology thus privileges what William Guynn identifies as a key motif in historical films, the 'extrapersonal' dimension according to which 'the individual embodies a whole social position' (Guynn 2006: 109).

Notably, the fusion of realism and modernism extends also to the film's formal texture. Comparable with their subsequent films, *Allonsanfàn* merges what Lorenzo Cuccu describes as 'iconographic stylization and "gestural theatricality"' (Cuccu 2001: 63). While the former has its roots in classicist figurative representational schemas, the latter is more aligned with modernist stylisation. Illustrative here is one of the last and most celebrated sequences of the film. When *Allonsanfàn* encounters Fulvio and, in an agitated state, dreams that the Sublimes and the peasants have joined forces, a Saltarello (a Neapolitan folk dance) performed by the group of the rebels and the peasants interrupts the dialogue of the two dramatic characters; we get to see an imaginative visual of their dance/march which gains an affective impact by means of Ennio Morricone's epic soundtrack. This visual is part of the narrative (*Allonsanfàn*'s fantasy) but also an affirmative commentary in a Brechtian fashion. It operates as a statement for the importance of utopia. Not unlike Jancsó's *Szegénylegények*, the Tavianis focus on the past only to comment on the present. The film was made in a period of political disillusionment generated by the Italian Communist Party's integration into the mainstream political establishment, as well as the frustrations of the post-1968 years. While *Allonsanfàn* seems to acknowledge the historical discontent of the time, it also recognises the historical necessity to reinvent utopia and, as the Tavianis say, 'to face utopia as truth, as a specific plan, and hope that hopelessness will turn into a new motive force of change' (cited in Rafailidis 2003: 372).

CONCLUSION

A key motif underlining both films discussed here is the post-heroic narrative and, despite the antitheses between Lukács and Brecht, this is surely something that features importantly in their views on realism. In a conversation with Alexander Kluge, Heiner Müller once mentioned a story favoured by contemporary management consultants, the story of the cooked frog. If one throws a frog into boiling water the frog will try to jump out of it immediately. Something more interesting happens when one throws a frog into lukewarm water and increases the temperature gradually. The frog ends up being cooked alive without noticing it. As Müller aptly explains, this is not a dramatic incident; it would be dramatic only if the frog was conscious of what was taking place (Kluge 1996). Since it is unaware of what is happening to it, this is 'epic material' because it is the product of collective processes which are, of course, valorised by both Brecht's and Lukács's theory of realism. Lukács's and Brecht's writings on cinema, their acknowledgement of the role of technological mediation, their endorsement of typicality as the road to realism, and their view of history as science, make us see realism and modernism as complementary categories. Furthermore, the

Lukácsian concept of totality and the Brechtian understanding of realism –
according to which the individual can be seen only as part of a collective reality
– acquire new significance in the present, given that technologies of mediation
have been developed which further privilege ephemeral and fragmented visual
experiences that may deprive us of a comprehensive view of the totality of social
coexistence. In Fredric Jameson's words, 'mapping the totality is still one of the
most vital functions and ambitions of art at the present time, as it was under the
very different conditions of the modern period' (Jameson 2010: 315).

REFERENCES

Adorno, Theodor (1997), *Aesthetic Theory*, trans. Robert Hullot-Kentor, London and New
York: Continuum.
— (2007), 'Reconciliation Under Duress', Taylor, Ronald (ed.), *Aesthetics and Politics: the Key
Texts of the Classic Debates within German Marxism*, London: Verso, pp. 151–76.
Aitken, Ian (2006), *Realist Film Theory and Cinema: The Nineteenth-Century Lukácsian and
Intuitionist Realist Traditions*, Manchester and New York: Manchester University Press.
— (2012), *Lukácsian Film Theory and Cinema: A Study of Georg Lukács' Writings on Film,
1913–1971*, Manchester and New York: Manchester University Press.
Barnett, David (2014), *Brecht in Practice: Theatre, Theory, and Performance*, London and New
York: Bloomsbury.
Berlau, Ruth, Brecht, Bertolt, et al. (1952), *Theaterarbeit: 6 Aufführungen des Berliner
Ensembles*, Dresden: Dresdner.
Bisztray, George (1980), 'Auteurism in the Modern Hungarian Cinema', *Canadian-American
Review of Hungarian Studies* 7: 2, pp. 135–44.
Brecht, Bertolt (1974), 'Against Georg Lukács', trans. Stuart Hood, *New Left Review*, 84: 1,
pp. 39–53.
— (1993), *Bertolt Brecht Journals*, Willett, John (ed.), trans. Hugh Rorrison, London:
Methuen.
— (2001), *Bertolt Brecht on Film and Radio*, trans. and ed. Marc Silberman, London:
Methuen.
— (2003), *Brecht on Art and Politics*, Kuhn, Tom and Giles, Steve (eds), trans. Laura Bradley,
London: Methuen.
— (2014), *Brecht on Theatre* (2014), Giles, Steve, Kuhn, Tom and Silberman, Marc (eds),
London, New York: Bloomsbury.
— (2014b), *Brecht on Performance: Messingkauf and Modelbooks*, Giles, Steve, Kuhn, Tom and
Silberman, Marc (eds), London and New York: Bloomsbury.
Cuccu, Lorenzo (2001), *The Cinema of Paolo and Vittorio Taviani*, Rome: Gremese.
Czigany, Lorant (1972), 'Jancsó Country: Miklós Jancsó and the Hungarian New Cinema',
Film Quarterly, 26: 1, pp. 44–50.
During, Lisabeth (2013), 'A Marxist Romanticism? Visconti's *La Terra Trema* and the
Question of Realism', *Screening the Past* 38, http://www.screeningthepast.com/2013/12/a-
marxist-romanticism-visconti-la-terra-trema-and-the-question-of-realism/ (last accessed
5 March 2015).
Engels, Friedrich (1849), 'The Magyar Struggle', available at https://marxists.anu.edu.au/
archive/marx/works/1849/01/13.htm (last accessed 5 March 2015).

Giles, Steve (1998), *Bertolt Brecht and Critical Theory: Marxism, Modernity and the Threepenny Lawsuit*, Berne: Peter Lang.

Guynn, William Howard (2006), *Writing History in Film*, London and New York: Routledge.

Hansen, Miriam Bratu (2010), 'Vernacular Modernism: Tracking Cinema on a Global Scale', in Ďurovičová, Nataša and Newman, Kathleen (eds), *World Cinema: Transnational Perspectives*, London andNew York: Routledge, pp. 287–314.

Jameson, Fredric (2010), 'Globalization and Hybridization', in Ďurovičová, Nataša and Newman, Kathleen (eds), *World Cinema: Transnational Perspectives*, London and New York: Routledge, pp. 315–19.

— (2012), 'Antinomies of the Realism–Modernism Debate', *Modern Language Quarterly*, 73: 3, 475–85.

— (2013), *The Antinomies of Realism*, London and New York: Verso.

Kluge, Alexander (1996), 'Epic Theater and Post-heroic Management (transcript from a television interview with Heiner Müller), available at https://kluge.library.cornell.edu/conversations/mueller/film/106/transcript (last accessed 5 March 2015).

Kovács, András Bálint (2007), *Screening Modernism: European Art Cinema, 1950–1980*, Chicago, IL and London: University of Chicago Press.

Lukács, Georg, [1957] (1962), *The Meaning of Contemporary Realism*, trans. John and Necke Mandel, Cambridge, MA: The MIT Press.

— [1923] (1967), *History and Class Consciousness: Studies in Marxist Dialectics*, trans. Rodney Livingstone, Cambridge, MA: The MIT Press.

— (1970), *Writer and Critic and Other Essays*, trans. and ed. Arthur D. Kahn, London: The Merlin Press.

— [1920] (1971), *The Theory of the Novel: A Historico-philosophical Essay on the Forms of Great Epic Literature*, trans. Anna Bostock, Cambridge, MA: The MIT Press.

— [1913] (2012), 'Thoughts Towards an Aesthetic of the Cinema' (trans. Ian Aitken), in Aitken, Ian (2012), *Lukácsian Film Theory and Cinema: A Study of Georg Lukács' Writings on Film, 1913–1971*, Manchester and New York: Manchester University Press, pp. 181–6.

— [1963] (2012), 'Film' (trans. Ian Aitken), in Aitken, pp. 187–217.

Luperini, Ilario (1995), 'The Tavianis' "Tuscan Classicism": A Blend of Figurative Art and Cinema', in Ferrucci, Riccardo and Turini, Patrizia (eds), *Paolo and Vittorio Taviani: Poetry of the Italian Landscape*, Rome: Gremese International.

Pound, Ezra (2013), 'On *Dubliners*', in Deming, Robert H. (ed.), *James Joyce: The Critical Heritage*, London and New York: Routledge, pp. 66–8.

Rafailidis, Vassilis (2013) *Λεξικό ταινιών*, vol. 2, Athens: Aigokeros.

Rodowick, David N. (2014), *Elegy for Theory*, Cambridge, MA and London: Harvard University Press.

Trotter, David (2007), *Cinema and Modernism*, Oxford: Blackwell Publishing.

CHAPTER 8

The Moving-image Redemption of Orality and Lukács's Early Writing on the Cinema

Apple Xu Yaping

INTRODUCTION

This chapter examines Georg Lukács's early writing on the cinema, particularly his emphasis in such writing on the mimetic moving-image representation of nature and cinema's putative recovery, and even redemption, of preconceptual experience. Here, linking Lukács's thought to theories on the orality–literacy dynamic in terms of the evolution of the media, it can be argued that the early 'primitive' (Lukács [1913] 2012: 185) cinema possesses the potential to redeem orality because of the ability of the cinema to depict empirical nature and reveal the flux of the life force of temporality (Aitken 2012: 88). The exploration of Lukács carried out in this chapter both positions him as an amateur member of the viewing public of his time and demonstrates that he also identified philosophically with the critique of the problematic nature of language and celebration of redemptive gesturality which was characteristic of the intellectual discourse on film which took place in Germany between 1895 and 1918.

Though a few interpretations/translations of Lukács's 1913 essay 'Thoughts Towards an Aesthetic of the Cinema' ('Gedanken zu einer Ästhetic des Kino') ('Thoughts') have appeared (Levin 1987, Blankenship 2001, Aitken 2012), it has still 'become something of an overlooked piece within the history of film theory' (Aitken 2012: 32), partly because scholarly considerations of Lukács within film studies have tended to focus on his literary writings, and particularly those composed after his conversion to Marxism in 1917. Yet the 1913 essay differs from these and has much more in common with early literary writings such as *Soul and Form* (1910). In particular, we find in both 'Thoughts' and *Soul and Form* a critique of modernity based on the notion that the modern subject is objectified and alienated, and that knowledge is fragmented and commodified; alongside a consideration on how to re-establish a more complete understanding of self within the chaotic fragmentation of what Lukács calls reified 'ordinary life' (Lukács [1913] 2012: 183). In his 1913 film essay, Lukács hoped that the moving images of film might bring about such a redemptive possibility and this was also a hope shared by other intellectuals of the period, including his close friend and colleague, Béla Balázs.

1 THE YOUNG LUKÁCS, CULTURAL CRISIS AND THE REDEMPTIVE POWER OF FORM

The period 1908–16 has been identified as encompassing the early literary aesthetic of Georg Lukács (Aitken 2013: 9), and, as argued, 'Thoughts' can be positioned within this early aesthetic. The essay was first written and published in 1911 in a German-language newspaper in Hungary, and then revised and republished with few changes in 1913 in the *Frankfurter Zeitung* newspaper (Aitken 2012: 30). In 1911, when the essay was initially written, Lukács was twenty-six. Having published *Soul and Form* a year earlier, he was, at the time, struggling to deal with, and reflect upon, the suicide of his intimate friend and possible future wife, Irma Seidler. Heller (1983) suggests that this tragedy contributed to what became a central theme of Lukács's early writing: the quest to understand how 'the creative individual' within modernity could experience 'a *genuine* life' in the face of alienating chaos (75). In Heller's reading of Lukács's diaries, such an ideal genuine life consists in the individual experience of 'being-with-others' (75); as '*Every* person is a unique entity, and *every* person in love wants to reveal this uniqueness to the Other' (90), one has to find an authentic mode of communication and relation in order to make one's presence meaningful. What the young Lukács underwent existentially through the tragedy of his friend's suicide also manifested the problem of modern life in general, one in which human subjects are increasingly fragmented and separated from one another, and have lost the sense of a total vision of who they are and who they are authentically in relation to other human beings.

The problem of how to place individual consciousness within modern relationships, which are infused with the conventions and institutions that are structured by modernity, characterises the young Lukács's early writings and, in those writings, Lukács seeks a more organic, pre-capitalist, pre-modern, pre-rationalised experience within a variety of lived or aesthetic embodiments, or *forms* (Márkus 1983: 6). 'Thoughts' falls into this category of existential and aesthetic quest. In the essay, Lukács identified the then new medium of film as categorically different from the established word-based form of the classical theatre. The central aspect of the essay, however, lies in its celebration of film's proximity to the perceptual experience of being human. By indicating a positive attitude towards the, albeit 'primitive' (Lukács [1913] 2012: 185) and 'imperfect' (183) moving-image technology of film in achieving such proximity, the essay embodies Lukács's expectations for the medium to transcend the inauthentic nature of 'ordinary life' and recover a lost sense of 'being in the world'.

Lukács grew up in Hungary, a central European country which was then less modernised, and less fast-changing than western European states such as France, Germany and Britain. This experience endowed him with sensitivity to the imbalance and problems inherent to such fast-developing and rapidly modernising states, and the threats they posed to pre-modern cultures. Deriving a critical intellectual perspective on modernity and instrumental rationality from figures such as Georg Simmel and Marx Webber (Lukács's teacher), Lukács came to believe that individual human consciousness and autonomous selfhood had been eroded by the increasingly rationalised and objectified social relations of modernity (Aitken 2012: 3–9). Such a scenario raised up the idea in his mind of an overarching cultural crisis of the modern subject in Europe stemming from such objectification, and from the loss of an authentic encounter with *present* immediate experience. Rigid rationales permeated into everyday life, and individuals were alienated from their immediate experience of being in the life-world, or *Lebenswelt*, which can only be intuitively known by shaping meaning emanating from the concrete and transient experienced flux (Aitken 2001: 178). But that was becoming increasingly lost in the modern world. To return to 'man's deepest truth and position in the universe' (Lukács [1913] 2012: 182), according to Lukács, meant that the modern subject must have recourse to the 'immediacy and sensuousness' of the *Lebenswelt* (182), and to the natural and physical, rather than overspreading rationality and intellect. In addition, the experiential aspect that characterises the pre-modern, 'older and more intuitively vital forms of human community' (Aitken 2012: 6), might also provide a solution to the modern crisis. All of this, Lukács felt, had implications for film.

These conceptions of the modern existential status of inauthenticity and the possibility of redeeming authentic life led Lukács to locate freedom, totality, the aesthetic and authentic human experience within what he called 'soul' – the source and kernel of authenticity. But soul must be given 'form' in order to be made manifest. Form can be either objectified or non-objectified. Non-objectified form is an act of resistance to ordinary life and/or quest for authenticity carried out by the individual within the life-world, while objectified form is the embodiment of such resistance and/or quest within an aesthetic object. For example, the 'essay' as objectified literary form – and one which Lukács discussed in *Soul and Form* – is one that deploys the 'struggle to achieve absolute self-hood' (Aitken 2012: 7) through resisting the 'systematic perspective' that characterises modern science, and also through a concern with the visceral, intuitive and creative (14). Through this particular approach, the essay enacts the author's subjective *becoming*: that of 'the whole subject recreating, rediscovering and repossessing himself in a whole object' – an object that evolves but that is also nonetheless singular and complete as object (Arato, in Aitken 2012: 2). For Lukács, such artistic form invests chaos with meaning, and opposes fragmentation with totality, though not a soulless systematic sort of totality. Soul, therefore, when objectified as in the essay, implies a sense of totality constituted by human fullness and fulfilment, becoming and completeness. (Aitken 2012: 8).

The notion of totality was of considerable significance to both the early Lukács and the 1913 essay, and the notion of totality engaged with in the essay suggests a synthesis of the material world and individual consciousness, the whole and the fragment. For Lukács, the portrayal of the phenomenal world in film interacts with an individual's perceptual experience of, and intuitive understanding towards, that world, and significance emerges when the interrelation between individual consciousness and material life-world is grasped intuitively, leading to 'the pure experience of self' – in this case through the medium of film, a medium that is also experienced as a totality of sorts because it is manifest as circumscribed discrete objects (individual films) (Lukács, in Aitken 2012: 14). As Lukács pointed out in his essay, in film, 'the wordless [the ever-evolving *Lebenswelt*] is remoulded into a totality' (Lukács [1913] 2012: 184); that is, within cinema's visual, non-linguistic, evolving representation, a coherent world emerges that links fractured and changing moments/viewers to a totalising impression. It will also be argued in this chapter that the absolute or total vision which gives meaning to the human essence within the media embodiment (the form/film), as Lukács envisaged it, can be associated with oral modes of expression and communication that, as suggested by theorist Walter Ong, are, close to the authentic life-world.

II ORALITY: THE PRE-MODERN MODE OF EXPRESSION AND COMMUNICATION

The dichotomous orality–literacy model is one which has been applied to an understanding of the interrelation between the evolution of the media and changes resulting to human culture and consciousness as a whole. Generally, the model, as suggested, in particular, by American media historian Walter J. Ong, proposes a three-stage transformation effected by dominant communication technologies, from the primary oral mode of expression and communication, to writing and print, and, finally, to the contemporary electronic culture that encompasses the telegraph, telephone, broadcast, television and computer, and is, or may be, characterised by a *revived* oral mode of expression (Ong 1982). This model, in seeking to focus on the oral, also draws greatly on studies of the classics, epic forms and long-standing oral narratives in an attempt to uncover the performative and interactive aspects of texts and language.[1]

Since the appearance of the writings of Ong in the late 1960s, studies of the oral tradition have been gradually integrated into studies of media technologies and human behaviour. Though Ong's supposition of the three-stage transformation has been criticised at times as too broad and overarching, and as ignoring differentiated cultural–historical context (Scheunemann, 1996), Ong's categorisation has, nevertheless and counteractively, been frequently adopted in the scrutiny of media artefacts that highlight cultural differences. For example, and in terms of film, Marks (2000) and Naficy (2001) assert that orality, as defined by Ong, characterises culturally specific cinema and diasporic film-making within which sensory-specific memories (for example, those related to touch, smell, taste and subjective vision) embody a consciousness located in underdeveloped societies whose cultures are distinct from dominant Western civilisation. Scholars, such as Marks and Naficy, Nayar (2010), Koven (2006), Tomaselli (2006) and others, invoke orality to characterise cinemas that are, therefore, in a sense more 'organic' in terms of having their meanings rooted in local cultures and determined by the deep-seated sensory imperatives of a local viewing public. Such cinemas interact with the local viewer's 'cultural-sensorium' (Marks 2000: 215) or distinctive organisation of the senses which is anchored in the closely encountered cultural background. These studies indicate that orality can be taken as a discourse able to articulate sometimes pre-modern, non-dominant values.

To understand what constitutes the authenticity of orality, it is helpful to return to Ong in some more detail to see what encompasses orality for him. For Ong, the primary oral mode of expression and communication before writing and print culture expresses a life in which people engage with the external world through immediate physical contact. Drawing from the phenomenology of Merleau-Ponty, Ong privileges the corporeal auditory experience. Specifically, Ong believed that sound ontologically integrated one person with another, creating the Merleau-Pontyian totality of 'being-in-the-world', where individuals exist within a physically intersubjective web: 'conscious interchange of man with man, a sense of human presence, of intersubjectivity, of psychic participation' (Ong 1981: 312). Ong endorsed this notion of orality because it emblemised communal–cultural interdependence, where each 'presence' (295) of a person is meaningful, and because it places such persons within the context of the immediate surrounding life-world (295). It is not difficult to recognise the similarity here between Lukács's notion of 'authentic culture' as soul and totality and the oral being-in-the-world.

It is also important to note that Ong's emphasis on the ancient human use of pre-linguistic 'sound' within the life-world also, in effect, affirmed the gestural and performative aspects that designate the 'un-reflective', spontaneous experience existing before rational conceptualisation (Merleau-Ponty [1945] 2012: xi). It is the pre-rational and pre-analytic embodiment in sound and gesture that delineates the sensual-perceptual basis of the intersubjective life-world, and the oral mode of communicative exchange. Nevertheless, this non-conceptual communication, the Merleau-Pontyian 'initial situation' (xvi), was now, as Ong contended, 'a lost Eden' (Ong 1981: 320) because the dominance of modern technologies (writing and print) had transformed and reduced the living actions and consciousness of human beings into self-contained objects (linguistic signs and texts, books and written histories), forcing orality into decline.

In addition to his critique of a modern medium which marginalises orality, though, Ong has also pointed to the revival of orality within 'modern' – and, here, the notion of 'modern' goes back a long way into history – texts and attendant technologies which exhibit human beings' endless desire for the 'extratextual context' (Ong 1982: 102), or direct dialogue with life-world entities. This, Ong argues, can include the textually embodied dialogues of Plato and Socrates (Ong 1982: 103), the inscribed communication suggested by the 'dear diary' address in personal journals (Ong 1982: 102), the use of apostrophes indicating direct address in some nineteenth-century British fiction (such as 'Oh, Romantic Reader' in *Wuthering Heights*), the inscribed 'talk' in fictions (such as the addressing of a second-person 'you'-character in Italo Calvino's *If on a Winter's Night a Traveller*: 'Now I ask you, must a poor bookseller take the blame for the negligence of others?') (Calvino [1979] 2012: 28). These textual forms typify the way in which such literary representation aims to render the intersubjective experience of the speaking–hearing encounter. The desire to recover the 'lost Eden' has also appeared within figural media representations; for example, television's live broadcast of a conference may integrate the audience's world with the screen world when the off-screen bodies and voices of the audience are displayed on the screen and are thus perceivable (Ong 1977: 318).

Nonetheless, Ong was critical of the way that what he called 'movies' did not possess much, if any, possibility of genuine orality because of their organisation of the actualities in accordance with calculated principles of narrative and plot structure (Ong 1977: 293). It could be argued, however, that his position on this is an overgeneralisation because of its exclusive focus on forms of commercial narrative cinema whose storytelling is determined substantially according to preset rules and is also artificially self-contained. A revision of the Ongian position on filmic orality therefore needs to be conducted by focusing on what has been neglected by Ong, namely, the gestural specificity of the moving image and non-conceptual forms of linkage editing, both of which were concerns for Lukács in his 1913 essay.

III EARLY GERMAN WRITINGS ON FILM: A COLLECTIVE RECOURSE TO THE NON-CONCEPTUAL

Lukács's essay displays both an 'anxiety concerning the instrumental power of language' (Aitken 2012: 31), or 'the spoken word' (Lukács [1913] 2012: 184), and a 'celebration of the gestural and visual' (Aitken 2012: 31). Before we make a closer analysis of these two areas in the next section of this chapter, however, it deserves to be noted that Lukács's expectation that film might 'escape from conceptual or ethical perspective' (Bewes 2011: 42) in 'Thoughts' anticipated Béla Balázs's later substitution of the 'reification' of language and print culture (Balázs [1924] 2010: 84) with the *physiognomical expression* (30, original emphasis) of cinema, in his *Der sichtbare Mensch* (*The Visible Man*, 1924) and the *Der Geist des Films* (*The Spirit of the Film*, 1930). Additionally, Lukács's ideas here also precede by a long way Walter Benjamin's iconic essay 'The Work of Art in the Age of Mechanical Reproduction' (1936) which pointed out that film, while stemming from technologies of mass production, had also developed a new mode of perceptual experience and sensory memory that both favoured the experiential 'tactile quality' of things (Benjamin [1936] 1996: 118) and engaged the modern subject to discover the deeper truth beyond that surface.

These connections suggest that Lukács's idea on the oral quality of the moving image, the primitive 'new form of *beauty*', as he put it (Lukács, in Aitken 2012: 181), has to be placed against the context of intellectual discussions about cinematic representation taking place in Germany from the 1910s to the 1930s. During that time, early German writings on film became gradually consolidated as a form of 'new cultural practice' (Hake 1993: ix). This section of this chapter will now provide a brief survey of those writings, particularly focusing on arguments about the non-linguistic aspect of filmic representation within the 'kino debate' (1910–31), and Béla Balázs's writings on film, for the purpose of arguing that Lukács's optimism about cinematic transcendence was typical of, if not inspired by, an intellectual collective recourse to the redemptive moving image as a solution to the 'crisis of culture' in modernity.

III.i The problem of language and the redemptive gesture

These German writings on film were situated culturally–historically within the context of the early cinema (1895–1918) and Weimar cinema (1919–33). Here, a proliferation of film critics witnessed the then new, though rapidly changing, medium of film as part of the viewing public, and Lukács was one of these. The 'kino debate' generated by these critics encompassed an increasing concern with the specificity of the film medium and its potential cultural role and identity. This emerging culture of film and film discussion also corresponded with the emergence and aesthetic locus of the international cosmopolitan city, such as Berlin, characterised by an extensive concoction of people, rapid pace of development and the increasing demarcation of society according to the capitalist division of labour. This helped constitute what Lukács and other intellectuals saw as the chaos of the 'ordinary life' of modernity although, of course, for Lukács, the ascendancy of ordinary life was also seen as predating the rise of the metropole (Lukács [1913] 2012: 183). The popularity of film at the time, however, also suggested to some that a new cultural form had appeared which diverged from the established arts (theatre, literature, classical music concerts and so on), was especially welcomed by the urban working masses, and could stand as an antidote to the increasingly fragmentary and rationalised ordinary life generated by modernity (Karacauer 1995: 325). The new form of film, it was believed, was full of gestural and facial expression able to activate tangible, yet also suppressed, human experience, suggesting that the medium had the revolutionary power to challenge the dominance of rationalisation and the word within modernity. Identifying and encouraging such potential, the film critics at the time proclaimed that film might also have the power to transcend the limitations of linguistic signs and discourse.

This was a period when the manipulating potential of the word was a concern for intellectuals. Around 1895, the year when film first appeared in Germany, the Austrian essayist Hugo von Hofmannsthal wrote: 'People are indeed tired of hearing speech . . . [D]eep down people fear language, in language they fear the instrument of society . . . of being a powerless cog in a machine.' (Kaes 1987: 25-6). The concern here was that, through the word, individual consciousness was increasingly subjected to arbitrarily organised and manipulative systems, and the desire was to transcend such organised manipulation via non-verbal means of communication. To transcend the linguistic, Hofmannsthal proposed the importance of what he referred to as 'pure gestures', a view shared by a number of critics and essayists during the 1910s and 1920s. At this time, film was also compared with other aesthetic gestural forms. For example, the physical similarity between film and pantomime became a topic of discussion (Hake 1993: 82) because, in both, the expressive body replaced the language of abstract signs. It was also suggested that linguistic signs might play a role in the creation and consolidation of elite formations within society. So, for example, Jo Haïri Peterkirsten, writing in 1918, argued that the masses, with their low literacy skills, were 'victims of the modern civilisation' (Hake 1993: 83). In cinema, however, the 'starved senses' and 'insatiable need for spiritual community' of the masses were able to find expression (83). The lower classes found themselves more at ease with film and in the cinema than with the written or even spoken word. This scenario can be found, for example, in Alfred Döblin's *Berlin Alexanderplatz* (1929). When the proletarian protagonist Franz Biberkopf is released from prison, he finds himself to be more comfortable in the dark surroundings of the cinema where there were 'just folks, free folks, amusing themselves, nobody has a right to say anything to them, simply lovely' (quoted in Kaes 1987: 15). The sense of enchantment associated with film expressed in the above quotation was also related to the integrating tendencies of the medium. If the word created elitist separation within society, film – silent film in this case, of course – activated the optical senses to interact with gestures, surpassing linguistic barriers and engendering 'a new spiritual body culture' communicated to the mass audience (Hake 1993: 83). At least within the mass audience, a new form of integrative experience was emerging.

III.ii Béla Balázs: the gestural expression and the pre-conceptual temporality of the fairy tale

The critique of language referred to above can also be found in the writings of Lukács's once close associate, Béla Balázs. According to Balázs, modern technologies of reproducibility (print) rendered 'Words, concepts and thoughts' weightily 'timeless' (Balázs [1924] 2010: 21). In addition to such immutability, Balázs also referred to the notion of 'reification' in attributing the estrangement of people's minds within capitalist modernity to the capitalist economic rationale that separated the 'intrinsic value of objects' from their [in capitalist terms more important] 'market price' (84). Such an abstraction reduced the array of available expression, while the 'language of gesture' – as in film – did the opposite. As Balázs claimed, 'It is film that will have the ability to raise up and make visible once more human beings who are now buried under mountains of words and concepts' (Balázs [1924] 2010: 10–11). The word, for Balázs, suggests a loss of 'spirit', and privileges rationalisation over valid forms of 'irrational' and 'emotional' expression. In contrast, the visually presented, gestural 'language' in film, as the true 'mother tongue' (13) – the 'primordial form . . . of expression' (13) – relates to the 'concrete, non-conceptual, immediate experience of things' (84), and has the potential to redeem the lost spirit with its fullness of expressive elements.

Compared with the linear and sequential organisation of printed text, the moving image brings real temporal experience of 'chords of emotions' (Balázs [1924] 2010: 34). Here, the expressive elements coexist and interpenetrate in the moving image, forming a 'polyphonic' (34) combination that 'cannot be expressed in words' (34). The film gesture also animates the subjects involved in the viewing experience because the 'chords' are indeterminate, and therefore more open and inviting to interpretation than is the case with concepts. To recognise their meanings, the spectator must be actively involved in forming and transforming the 'rich amalgam' of these chords (34), reading through the symbolic appearance in order to reach the physiognomy, which relates physical expression to underlying character/spirit.

The 'physiognomical expression' in film also suggests no pre-given determination between soul/meaning and appearance because both are in a constant process of changing and becoming; the filmic representation is 'a fleeting presence within the perpetual flux of natural or organic life' (Carter 2010: xxvii). To grasp the 'physiognomical impression' (56) in both natural or organic life' and its representation in the film that lurks within 'A raging sea, a glacier above the clouds, a storm-lashed forest or the painful expanses of a desert' (41), one has to act like the pre-ratiocinative 'child' who instinctively seeks 'a deeper look' (35), deeper intuited meanings. Thus, '[T]he uncannily explicit gestures of the black shapes of trees in the forest at night can make the soberest philistine quake inwardly' (46). For Balázs, it is also the close-up in film that privileges physiognomical expressions the most because of its mimesis of the fleeting spatial-temporal momentary experience of flux. In addition, the close-up is also characterised by a temporal *division* and spatial *unity* which is akin to the pre-modern fairy tale, as for example:

Now hear the song
You look, I look at you.
Our eyes' curtain – the eyelashes – opens:
Where is the stage: outside or inside
Men and women?'
(*Duke Bluebeard's Castle*, quoted in Carter 2010: xix)

In this fairytale-ish representation, the temporally divided elements coexist in a spatial integration, giving birth to an absolute temporality that overcomes the boundaries of the past, present and future. Such simultaneity also cannot be rendered unless perceived by the spectator as such. In some close-ups, the ideal temporality rendered might also happen within constant interactions between the world of the audience and the world of the performative shot. An example Balázs took for this was the close-up of Lilian Gish's face in *Way Down East*. The shot depicts Gish's reaction towards her lover's deceit where, 'for five whole minutes she laughs and cries by turns, at least a dozen times' displaying 'the crazy rapidity with which they [feelings] succeed one another' (Balázs, quote in Carter 2010: xxix). Here, the 'crazy succession' of differing instances engages the spectator with the affective flux and emotional movement of the sequence.

IV 'THOUGHTS', THE DOUBLE MIMESIS, AND TRANSCENDENCE OF THE EMPIRICAL

The kind of cinema discussed by Lukács in 'Thoughts' had little to do with the classic narrative model because, as he contended, in a purer form, 'The "cinema" merely present actions, but not their cause and meaning' (Lukács [1913] 2012: 184), and because, in that purer form, 'There is no causality involved in such joining together' of shot to shot (183). The kind of cinema that Lukács was concerned with was also the opposite of self-sufficient forms such as the theatrical performance, which 'appears as a self-evident reality' (182) and 'something eternal' (181). Therefore, the kind of cinema that Lukács endorsed was not the 'movies' as understood by Walter Ong, namely, the commercial narrative cinema that embedded actualities drawn from the life-world within a priori conceived structures and chains of causality (Ong 1977: 293).

During the period around 1906 and 1915, Lukács studied and lived in Germany, including Berlin and Heidelberg (Gluck 1985). Around the time when Lukács wrote 'Thoughts', cinema was developing into a mass medium in Germany, and longer narrative films were emerging to constitute the predominant form of the cinema (Hake, 1993: 13). It was, however, the 'most crude and primitive' (Lukács [1913] 2012: 185) and 'imperfect', 'silent' (Lukács [1913] 2012: 182) films that Lukács appreciated most which might, in fact, have been short actualities that 'last[ed] for only a few minutes and consisted of non-fictional city vistas, news reportage, and depictions of military pageants and royal engagements' (Bock and Bergfelder 2009: 557). Importantly for Lukács, however, though primitive in terms of form, the film of actuality of that time was also able to display intensive and even uncanny visual experiences. For example, a shot of 'a factory yard [was] now at the open sea, now at a city railway station' (Brockmann 2010: 17). Here, sensual commitment was motivated by the cinematic experience as if 'standing in front of an open window, looking out' (Brockmann 2010: 17). Lukács understood that the commercial cinema operated as an apparatus 'pedagogically' (Lukács [1913] 2012: 181) and commodity 'economically' (181). It was in contradistinction to these manipulative aspects of the system, however, that he put forward his own aesthetic perspective on the cinema, within which he invited appreciation for the perceptual experience and simple 'amusement' that the new medium brought (185).

For Lukács, cinematic representation was, or should be, a 'double mimesis': the first of the vivid and vibrant experience of nature and the phenomenal life-world, the second of the humanly meaningful and trenchant substance of things and events.[2] In 'Thoughts', however, it is the first mimesis, and its particular relation to valuable and free human experience, that is of particular import to him. According to Lukács, film dwells on the everyday life that is 'so exclusively empirically alive' (183). The gestural expressiveness of the moving images is also amplified here partly because of the 'current imperfection in technology – that [meant that] the scenes of cinema are silent' (184). The cinematic representation was, as a consequence of this, 'exclusively' expressed 'through events and gesture' (184) rather than through language, and the moving image was defined in terms of verisimilitude or, what Lukács called, 'truth-to-nature' (*Naturwahrheit*) (184). Through this, the film image obtained 'maximum vivacity' (183) and was 'uncannily lifelike', 'appearing identical to nature' (182). In film:

> The livingness (*Lebendigkeit*) of nature here acquires artistic form for the first time: the rushing of water, the wind in the trees, the stillness of the sunset and the roar of the storm, as natural processes, are here trans-formed into art . . . (184)

Lukács asserted that the theatrical performance expressed via speech was an art form based on abstract language, and referred to this as 'the stage of the spoken word' (*Sprechbühne*) (185). In contrast to this, cinema, with its reliance on empirical and gestural mimesis, was closer to the experience of nature than to the experience of trenchant human meaning found on the *Sprechbühne*. As Lukács put it:

> In the 'cinema' everything that the romanticism of the theatre had sought – in vain – to achieve can now be attained: extreme uninhibited mobility of figures, the complete becoming-alive of the background, of nature and interiors, of plants and animals . . . (183)

Lukács's critique of the abstraction and arbitrariness of the word (both the written sign and its verbalisation) did not reach the high level of critique mounted by Balázs but he did take theatre as a counter-example to film in 'Thoughts', arguing that the theatre depended on linguistic norms that were less expressive than the moving image, and also less close to human experience of the external world.

Throughout 'Thoughts', Lukács continued to refer to film in relation to the first mimesis. For Lukács, 'ordinary life' is 'an anarchy of light and shadow' (Márkus 1983: 6), that is also 'the world of rigid forms (conventions and institutions) alien to man' (Márkus 1983: 6). Through the first mimesis, on the other hand, the moving image of film can capture the ephemeral vivid energy of empirical experience, a vivid energy that transcends the limitations of ordinary life. Film may, like ordinary life, fragment totality, and this might add to the existing alienation. On the other hand, as Lukács pointed out, the presentation of pure surface in the cinema, with its attendant loss of substance, 'reasons', 'motives', 'measure or order', 'essence and value' (182), provided the opportunity to configure a life that is more free, a life that is 'fantastic', that is liberating, and free (184), not mechanical as in ordinary life but indeterminate and dynamic, akin to the temporal flux of real experience which is constantly forming and being transformed. This 'fantastic' life could not be framed by reason or by linear sequential structure. In this respect Lukács found the literary models of 'fairytale and dream' most analogous to the film of 'suggestive linkage' (183). Here, fragments, past, present and future, merge into a total experience. Here also, the irrational way of organisation of the ephemeral typifies the law of filmic linkage (not 'of inexorable necessity' but 'of unlimited possibility' (183), creating a fantastic totality:

> Furniture moves around within the room of a drunkard. His bed flies with him high over the city – only in the last moment is he able to hold on to the side of the bed, while his shirt waves about like a flag, enveloping him. The bowling balls which a group of people intend to use become rebellious, and chase those people across mountains and fields, forcing them to swim across rivers, run across bridges, and climb steep staircases, until, finally, the skittles come alive and catch the balls. (184–5)

In this flow each moment is accidental; through irrational juncture, however, they come to constitute a meaningful and dreamlike whole. In recognising the interconnection between one's perceptual involvement and this whole, one's life-world experience is redeemed, and the *soul* is liberated: 'the *child* that is alive in each human being is set free here, and becomes master of the psyche of the spectator' (184). Foretelling Balázs, Lukács addressed the metaphoric 'child' image to advance the revitalisation of the life force, the pre-conceptual mind, within the cinematic experience. The filmic mimesis of the perception of temporal flux thus embodies the active participation of the individual consciousness, similar to that which occurs in the essay form, in which 'the whole subject [engages in] recreating, rediscovering and repossessing himself in a whole object' (Arato, quoted in Aitken 2012: 2).

CONCLUSION

There are parallels between Lukács's early writing on film in 'Thoughts' and Walter Ong's examination of the electronic media six or so decades later. Both assert that the pre-conceptual, unreflective experience of the life-world might be redeemed within modern technologised representation. Both believe that the orality that characterises the pre-modern, organic, immediate mode of expression and communication could be revived in the moving image. Lukács also took this further, asserting that the filmic image should relate mimetically to the natural/external world without being subjected to pre-given references; and that the connection between shots and sequences should be made according to phenomenal associations of various sorts, rather than mechanical causality. This model of film orality, or the oral mode of cinema, as derived from Lukács, and invoked by Ong, also demands an active spectatorship, that is, the viewer/modern subject overcomes the ephemeral and fragmented 'ordinary life' and arrives at a different level of experience, a 'fantastic' liberating one that discharges predetermination and instrumental divisions and casts meaning within an endless process of forming and transforming. Identifying the flux of life force, the spectator might resume his or her 'presence' and 'deepest truth and position within the universe', and experience personal value within an alienating capitalist modernity.

Lukács's positive vision of cinema's redemption of orality is also a response to his diagnosis of the 'metaphysical' and 'existential' crisis of culture in modernity (Márkus 1983: 4). The unfulfilled expectation of Lukács and the early German writers on film in general, however, and of Ong six decades later, suggests that, although modern media technologies, including film, possess the potential to retrieve the phenomenologically meaningful life, the problem of modernity and the crisis of culture remain, and that, provided the historical and social structures which manufactured the 'mechanistic bourgeois society' (16) stay unchanged, aesthetic experience, such as that afforded by film, only 'transcends the alienation of ordinary life [temporarily], but [. . .] does not abolish it' (13).

The concern with orality can be understood as a form of 'romantic' alternative to conceptually oriented materialist modernity and as falling into that overarching romantic tradition. As a discourse, it embodies recourse to being in the world as a means of coping with the alienation brought about by modernity. The difference between Ong and Lukács, though, lies with the particular aspects of alienation identified. For Ong, it is through modern media technologies that the primal dynamic knowledge becomes objectified and manipulated, becoming detached from the communicative context where it is produced and supposed to be meaningful. For Lukács, on the other hand, alienation is related to the more general condition of modernity, going back as far as the demise of classical Greek society and the loss of totality that such demise entailed. In other words, Lukács's critique of modernity goes beyond the oral/linguistic focus of Ong. The different understandings of alienation and modernity here also configure distinctive constructions of orality's counter-fragmenting nature. For Ong, in the 1960s, modern alienation can be opposed through the technologised mimesis of the communicative interdependence that characterises the oral speaking–hearing interaction; and he is thinking mainly of television here. For Lukács, in 1913, however, alienation is to be opposed not through such interaction per se but through the filmic portrayal of empirical totalities similar to the *Lebenswelt* which engage the spectator with the fleeting temporal flux, reviving the subjective experience of time, thus forming and transforming individual moments into a total experience encompassing the personally perceived past, present and future. This is a broader conception of retrievable experience than is proposed by Ong.

Admittedly, orality is an elusive concept, and has often been the subject of reinterpretation. In terms of Ong, Scheunemann (1996), for example, argues that what Ong fundamentally celebrates is 'the "great awakening" that has taken place in the scholarly world in the past few decades concerning the "oral character of language" and the basic differences between "oral modes of thought and expression" and written modes' (79). In other words, it is a celebration of the non-rational state of being in the world. Scheunemann goes on to place Ongian conceptions of orality within the general context of North American social science scholarship, seeing that context in relation to orality as encompassing work being produced in the fields of cultural anthropology and media history (79), and, more recently, visual cultural anthropology (for example, Marks 2000) and film studies (Nayar 2010).

Much of this work is concerned with the issue that orality stands for, not only as a type of knowledge (epistemology) but also a state of being (ontology); and the model of film orality, as derived from Lukács's early writing in particular and the German kino debate in general, also suggests a certain state of being: one that depends more on the subjective perception of experience within modernity. In a contemporary urban environment, where the moving image is so ubiquitous, and in a media environment in which it has become increasingly difficult to tell the difference between reality and fiction, what film orality might point to is not only a sort of active spectatorship but also the ontological state that renders subjective living more significant and visible.

NOTES

1. For example, Albert B. Lord ([1960] 1974) found that epics, such as Homer's *Iliad* and *Odyssey* were organic tales, constantly being adjusted by different singers by interplaying with their audiences, while literature was a mere consequence of the print technology with which the tales became fixed into a fixed and exclusive version.

2. The phrase is actually taken from Lukacs's 1963 work *The Specificity of the Aesthetic*, It is used here, however, to identify the double focus referred to which is operative not only in 'Thoughts' but also in *Soul and Form* (1910) and *The Theory of the Novel* (1916).

REFERENCES

Aitken, Ian (2001), 'The Redemption of Physical Reality: Theories of Realism in Grierson, Kracauer, Bazin and Lukács', in Aitken, Ian, *European Film Theory and Cinema: A Critical Introduction*, Edinburgh: Edinburgh University Press, pp. 162–202.

Aitken, Ian (2012), 'The Early Aesthetic and "Thoughts Towards an Aesthetic of the Cinema/ Gedanken zu einer Ästhetic des Kino"', in Aitken, Ian, *Lukácsian Film Theory and Cinema: A Study of Georg Lukács' Writings on Film, 1913–71*, Manchester: Manchester University Press, pp. 3–35.

Bell, Daniel (1993), *The Coming of Postindustrial Society: A Venture in Social Forecasting*, New York: Basic Books.

Benjamin, Walter [1936] (1996), 'The Work of Art in the Age of Mechanical Reproduction', in Bullock, M. and Jennings, M. W. (eds), *Walter Benjamin: Selected Writings*, Volume 3 *1935–1938*, Cambridge, MA: Belknap Press, pp. 101–33.

Bewes, Timothy (2011), 'How to Escape from Literature? Lukács, Cinema and the Theory of the Novel', in Bewes, Timothy and Hall, Timothy (eds), *Georg Lukács: The Fundamental Dissonance of Existence*, London: Continuum, pp. 36–48.

Blankenship, Janelle (2001), 'Futurist Fantasies: Lukács' Early Essay "Thoughts Towards An Aesthetic of the Cinema"', *Polygraph*, 13, pp. 21–36.

Bock, H. M. and Bergfelder, T. (2009), *The Concise Cinegraph: Encyclopaedia of German Cinema*, New York: Berghahn Books.

Brockmann, Stephen (2010), *A Critical History of German Film*, Rochester, NY: Camden House.

Calvino, Italo [1979] (2012), *If on a Winter's Night a Traveller*, trans. William Weaver, Boston, MA: Houghton Mifflin Harcourt.

Carter, Erica (2010), 'Introduction', in Carter, Erica (ed.), *Béla Balázs: Early Film Theory: Visible Man and the Spirit of Film*, New York: Berghahn Books, pp. xv–xlvi.

Garrett, Stewart (1996), *Dear Reader: The Conscripted Audience in Nineteenth-Century British Fiction*, Baltimore, MD: Johns Hopkins University Press.

Gluck, Mary (1985), *Georg Lukács and His Generation, 1900–1918*, Cambridge, MA: Harvard University Press.

Hake, Sabine (1993), 'The Literary Debates on the Cinema', in Hake, Sabine (ed.), *The Cinema's Third Machine: Writing on Film in Germany, 1907–1933*, Lincoln, NE: University of Nebraska Press, pp. 61–88.

Heller, Agnes (1983), 'Georg Lukács and Irma Seidler', in Heller, Agnes (ed.), *Lukács Reappraised*, Oxford: Basil Blackwell, pp. 27–62.

Kacandes, Irene (2001), *Talk Fiction: Literature and the Talk Explosion*, Lincoln, NE: University of Nebraska Press.

Kaes, Anton (1987), 'The Debate About Cinema: Charting a Controversy (1909–1929)', *New German Critique*, 40, winter, pp. 7–33.

Koven, Mikel J. (2006), *La dolce morte: Vernacular Cinema and the Italian Giallo Film*, Lanham, MD: Scarecrow Press.

Kracauer, Siegfried (1995), *The Mass Ornament: Weimar Essays*, trans. Thomas Y. Levin, Cambridge, MA: Harvard University Press.

Levin, Tom (1987), 'From Dialectical to Normative Specificity: Reading Lukács on Film', *New German Critique*, 40, winter, pp. 35–61.

Lord, Albert B. [1960] (1974), *The Singer of Tales*, New York: Atheneum.

Lukács, Georg, [1913] (2012). 'Thoughts Towards an Aesthetic of the Cinema', in Aitken, Ian (ed. and trans.), *Lukácsian Film Theory and Cinema: A Study of Georg Lukács' Writings on Film, 1913–71*, Manchester: Manchester University Press, pp. 181–6.

Márkus, György (1983), 'Life and Soul: The Young Lukács and the Problem of Culture', in Heller, Agnes (ed.), *Lukács Reappraised*, Oxford: Basil Blackwell, pp. 1–26.

Marks, Laura U. (2000), *The Skin of the Film: Intercultural Cinema, Embodiment, and the Senses*, Durham, NC: Duke University Press.

Merleau-Ponty, Maurice [1945] (2012) trans. C. Smith, *Phenomenology of Perception*, New York: Routledge.

Naficy, Hamid (2001), *An Accented Cinema: Exilic and Diasporic Filmmaking*, Princeton, NJ: Princeton University Press.

Nayar, Sheila, J. (2010), *Cinematically Speaking: The Orality–literacy Paradigm for Visual Narrative*, Cresskill, NJ: Hampton Press.

Ong, Walter J. (1977), *Interfaces of the Word: Studies in the Evolution of Consciousness and Culture*, Ithaca, NY: Cornell University Press.

— (1981), *The Presence of the Word: Some Prolegomena for Cultural and Religious History*, Minneapolis, MN: University of Minnesota Press.

— (1982), *Orality and Literacy: The Technologizing of the Word*, London: Methuen.

Scheunemann, Dietrich (1996), 'Collecting "Shells" in the Age of Technological Reproduction: On Storytelling, Writing, and the Film', in Scheunemann, Dietrich (ed.), *Orality, Literacy, and Modern Media*, Columbia, SC: Camden House, pp. 79–94.

Thompson, Michael J. (2011), 'Introduction: Recovering Lukács' Relevance for the Present', in Thompson, Michael J. (ed.), *Georg Lukács Reconsidered: Critical Essays in Politics, Philosophy and Aesthetics*, London: Continuum, pp. 1–12.

Tomaselli, K. G. (2006), *Encountering Modernity: Twentieth-Century South African Cinema*, Amsterdam: Rozenberg Publishers.

CHAPTER 9

The 'Naturalist' Treatment of Film in *The Specificity of the Aesthetic* (Georg Lukács, 1963) and *One Day in the Life of Ivan Denisovich* (Alexander Solzhenitsyn, 1962; Caspar Wrede, 1970)

Ian Aitken

The evaluative distinction between progressive 'narration' and reactionary 'description', that is, between realism and naturalism, is one that Georg Lukács often made in his critical writings on literature, and is encapsulated in his 1936 essay 'Narrate or Describe?'. This distinction, appearing in such an uncompromising essay, has also provided critics with reason to dismiss Lukács's position on naturalism, and also on modernism, given that Lukács argued elsewhere that twentieth-century modernism was an unfortunate and regressive outcome of the alienating tendencies found within nineteenth-century naturalism. This chapter will argue, however, that the 'Narrate or Describe?' essay, and similar, were works of polemic, related to their context in the 1930s, and that Lukács's position on naturalism and modernism began to change from the mid-1950s to the early 1960s. A key work here is *The Meaning of Contemporary Realism* (1956) in which qualified, but nevertheless real credit is given to the work of Franz Kafka and other modernist writers on the basis of the *descriptive* power of their work (Lukács 1963: 52). Lukács's ideas also began to change further after his encounter with Alexander Solzhenitsyn's *One Day in the Life of Ivan Denisovich* (1962). Lukács realised that this book fell into his overall definition of what a naturalist work was but he also understood that the novel was simply too important – and controversial – to be dismissed lightly. Lukács then revised his understanding of naturalism and this revision found expression in his *The Specificity of the Aesthetic* (the *Aesthetic*) (1963). This chapter will first explore the account of filmic naturalism given in the *Aesthetic* and then compare that with Lukács's response to Solzhenitsyn's work before applying both account and response to an analysis of the 1970 joint British–Norwegian film *One Day in the Life of Ivan Denisovich / En dag i Ivan Denisovitsj' liv*. The principal objectives here will be to assess the extent to which Lukács's positions prove expedient in understanding this film and, at least in part, the degree to which they might prove useful in application to film more generally.

THE SPECIFICITY OF THE AESTHETIC, NATURALISM AND FILM

The *Aesthetic* was originally intended to be a three-volume work though only two volumes eventually appeared. Volume I covers general aesthetic categories, Volume II more specific areas of aesthetic representation, while the proposed third volume was intended to place this study of aesthetics within a sociopolitical framework. The chapter on film appears in Volume II. In this volume Lukács continues to address the general aesthetic categories he had explored in Volume I. Chapter 14, however, entitled 'General Questions of Aesthetic Mimesis', looks at five specific aesthetic forms: 'Music', 'Architecture', 'Design', 'Landscape Gardening', and 'Film'.

In the *Aesthetic*, Lukács places considerable emphasis on the concept of artistic 'reflection' (*Widerspiegelung*), a broad-spectrum notion that stands for a formulation of 'the relationships in which men stand to the experienced world' (Pascal, in Parkinson (ed.), 1970: 148). Artistic 'reflection', therefore, consists of an *account* of the relations that persist between human beings and the world. It is an interpretation, and the use of the term 'reflection' here does not imply any sort of naive-realist objectivism. In fact, the German term *Widerspiegelung* does not translate directly into the English term 'reflection' as this is rendered more accurately by the simpler German term *Spiegelung*. With *Widerspiegelung*, the prefix '*Wider*' implies some action taken against the thing experienced so that the portrayal of the thing is different from the thing itself and that portrayal also changes our experience of the thing experienced. So, more like a combination of 'reflection against something' and 'is reflected by' the thing experienced. The Lukácsian notion of reflection therefore encloses constructivist-formative as well as veristic impulses.

Lukács also argues that, to satisfy human need, there must be a 'double reflection' (*doppelter Widerspiegelung*). The term 'double reflection' refers to an account of both intrinsic human meaning (*Wesen*) and the forms of 'appearance' (*Erscheinung* – the world of phenomenal forms and experience) (Lukács 1981, II: 477). It is not possible to go into the full meaning of these terms within this short chapter as they have a long history within classical German philosophy. Suffice it to say that the notion of the double reflection, when applied to film, implies that film would not only portray human-oriented meaning but also the *Aussenwelt*, 'outside world', of experiential empirical encounter; and this in turn means that considerable emphasis is placed on the *descriptive* powers of film and on the ability of the medium to achieve what Lukács refers to as a 'closeness to life' (*Lebensnähe*) (475). While, therefore, it should be borne in mind that the Lukácsian 'double reflection' contains a formative and reflexive, so to speak 'narrated' dimension, as well as a descriptive one, it is the latter which is given the greater emphasis and, in consequence, a foundation is laid here for overturning the rejection of the 'descriptive method' set out in a tendentious work such as 'Narrate or Describe?'

This foundation is, additionally, also reinforced by another key notion found in the *Aesthetic*, that film's ability to portray the forms of appearance in considerable detail enables the medium to capture an important aspect of human experience which is nested in the perception of those forms: the experience and perception of the 'just being so' (*Geradesosein*) of things (491). Here, whatever we experience and whatever attitude we choose to adopt towards such experience, we also at one level experience that which we encounter as simply just being so, as materials which at one level persist and are perceived by us as existing in and for themselves. Because the encounter with the just being so of things is an authentic aspect of human perceptual encounter Lukács argues that, in addition to other aspects of filmic representation, such as the establishment of diegetic content, narrative, plot and scenic design, the medium should also attempt to portray this encounter with the just being so of things. It is also because of this imperative that Lukács maintains that the relatively autonomous image must be retained as 'an essential element of . . . film art' (473).

Taken together, the imperative to portray *Geradesosein* and emphasis on the portrayal of the forms of appearance within the double reflection add up to what sounds like a delineatory, descriptive-naturalist position. Given his record of denouncing 'naturalism', however, Lukács is unable or unwilling to accept that this might be the case. For example, although, at one point, he states that 'it seems, therefore, that a naturalism, which elsewhere appears the converse of art, might be artistically possible in film' (479), he quickly refutes this stance, arguing that the approach he is advocating 'must not be referred to as naturalism' (481). Lukács does not give the approach he *does* advocate another name but it is clear that it is based on a definition of naturalism informed by his previously referred to distinction between being and appearance within the double reflection, as is made apparent when he argues that 'the philosophical-artistic meaning of naturalism consists in that, in naturalism, the being that appears wanes, or even completely vanishes, behind . . . appearance' (479). This implies that, naturalism cannot maintain the double reflection of *Wesen* and *Erscheinung*, and that, for film to achieve that essential double reflection and avoid falling into naturalism, *Wesen* must remain an integral force within the film alongside the portrayal of the forms of appearance and *Geradesosein*. Lukács does not give any detailed examples of such a film in the *Aesthetic* but he does mention the films of Chaplin more generally in this respect. According to Lukács, Chaplin provides an 'absolutely valid expression to the ordinary man's feeling of isolation against the context of the machinery and apparatus of modern capitalism' (482). No particular film by Chaplin is named here but Lukács is probably referring to *Modern Times* (1936); and here, 'being', as in Chaplin's existentially perplexed persona, remains alongside 'appearance', as in the portrayal of the 'apparatus of modern capitalism' and general auditory visuality of the film. The presence of this interaction between being and appearance in *Modern Times* means that the film would not be defined as 'naturalist' in Lukács's terms. Nevertheless, Lukács's argument is unconvincing here because *Modern Times* is clearly *not* a work of naturalism and because Lukács makes no attempt to show how a more pertinent film, which might be considered naturalist on warrantable grounds, is not so on his terms.

Lukács's argument is also unpersuasive here because, despite the accent on the need to retain *Wesen* as the basis for claiming that his position on film is not a naturalist one, the overriding account of film found in the *Aesthetic* emphasises the ability of film to portray the forms of appearance far more than the need to depict *Wesen*, and this orientation is also reinforced by the submission that film should seek *equivalence* in the portrayal of *Wesen* and *Erscheinung*. What Lukács argues here is that, because film is *able* to portray relations of being and appearance as they 'persist side by side', and in an equivalent way, as is the case with the experience of everyday life, *it should actively seek to do so* (481). When film manages to achieve such equivalence, a propitious *reciprocation* is also reinstated because the 'reciprocal relationship which exists between man and his environment is also re-established', and the 'outside world' (*Aussenwelt*) acquires the same degree of importance as the human beings who are portrayed in the film (478). When such reciprocity occurs, film also achieves an artistically 'legitimate general effectiveness', guaranteed by the fact that the medium holds to its inherent mission to portray the true character of our experience in the life-world, or *Lebenswelt*, one in which we interact with the non-human *Aussenwelt* (481). While Lukács's argument here leads to the supposition that a film could be 50 per cent constituted by portrayals of the phenomenal forms of appearance, that still leaves the other 50 per cent concerned with matters of human psychological import, and that is quite a lot. There is a problem here, however, because the idea that film should adhere to the character of the *Lebenswelt* not only implies that the medium should achieve reciprocity in the portrayal of the forms of appearance and *Wesen* but also that the portrayal of the forms of appearance should *predominate* over depictions of *Wesen*, because, in the *Lebenswelt* – the world of our everyday encounter – the experience of *Wesen* occurs less frequently than does the experience of the manifold forms of appearance. The logic of Lukács's argument here, therefore, implies a form of film in which description *predominates* and this also suggests that, what is outlined in the chapter on film in the *Aesthetic*, actually amounts to a naturalist descriptive-like theory of film, despite Lukács's denials. And, if that is so, two questions arise. First, if it was the case that, during his late period of 1955–71, Lukács developed a naturalist-like formulation of film which focused on the portrayal of the individuated forms of experience, what caused him to move in that direction? And, second, why, if he did move in that direction, did he continue to remain hostile to the notion of naturalism?

To answer the first of these questions it will be necessary to address what I will refer to as the underlying conceptual and representational model which Lukács adopted during his late period, and which is also apparent in his early period, to the extent that it can be argued that the adoption of this model in 1955–71 also marked a significant return to many of the concerns evident in the early period. In early works of literary criticism, such as *Soul and Form* (1910) and *The Theory of the Novel* (1916), Lukács used the phrase 'objectified form' to refer to the embodiment of authentic human meaning ('form') in the work of art (thus, 'objectified form'); and, in both works, Lukács explored different literary objectified forms, including the epic, novel, and essay. It has been argued by one critic, however, that, In *Soul and Form*, in particular, Lukács developed an underlying 'organic' model of aesthetic form which he then applied to the various 'forms' (Meunier in Joós [ed.] 1987: 171). In this understanding, although Lukács considered different types of the forms underlying such consideration was a view of the work of art as constituted by parts put into dynamic dialectical interaction within an overall design (171). The term 'organic' refers to this type of process which is seen as analogous to that which take place within an organism. It will be argued here, however, that a model of organic form *does not* underpin Lukács's work but is, in fact, only one modality of a deeper representational episteme which can be found in Lukács's early and late periods.

In the late period, in the posthumously published *Toward the Ontology of Social Being* (1971–73) (the *Ontology*), that episteme is embodied in the idea of the 'complex' which, Lukács argues, is the basis of social being and everyday life and, therefore, the 'primary form of existence' (Lukács in Pinkus [ed.] 1974: 17). The model of the complex set out in the *Ontology* indicates a fluid and interactive phenomenon consisting of elements and relationships which come together to form a relatively coherent, though also contradictory and mutable, clustering within social experience. These cohesions occur in an effort to make sense of the 'amorphous chaos' that characterises everyday reality but they are transient and shifting because it is never possible to make total sense of reality (Márkus in Heller [ed.] 1983: 11–12). Experienced everyday life consists of encounter with a matrix of such 'complexes', and this 'dynamically contradictory [set of] totalities', or 'complexes', makes up social being (Lukács 1982: 72). There are clear similarities here with the model of 'organic' form just referred to, and, as with that model, the model of the complex set out in the *Ontology* may also be regarded as a modality of the deeper epistemological and representational model which underpins Lukács's thought.

The key categorical term which relates to this underlying model in the *Aesthetic* is *Besonderheit*, or 'speciality'. Literally translated, the German term *Besonderheit* should mean 'singularity' though it can also mean 'special' or 'exceptional'. In the *Aesthetic*, Lukács uses the term *Besonderheit* in this latter sense, to refer to the 'special' significance of, not singularity, but the *intermediate*, that is, the artistic representation of the intermediate. *Besonderheit* is a categorical form of artistic *Widerspiegelung* ('reflection against something' – 'reflection affected by the thing experienced') and, in the *Aesthetic*, Lukács discusses three such categorical forms which, he argues, are 'the most general forms of reflection': the singular (*Einzelheit*), the universal (*Allgemeinheit*) and the 'special' (*Besonderheit*) (Lukács 1981, I: 686). These titles refer respectively to particular things, the universal type of a particular thing, and the way in which particular things become absorbed into generalities. Lukács argues that artistic reflection cannot be associated with either *Einzelheit* or *Allgemeinheit* because a work of art is neither a universal nor a particularity but is made up of parts and relations. This means that it is the third category, *Besonderheit*, which is most appropriate to aesthetic reflection. *Besonderheit* marks out the province which lies between the singular and the universal, and is character- ised by clusters of interacting terms and relations which are constituted simi- larly to the complexes found within social being; and both can be considered as manifestations of the underlying representational model already referred to. That model embodies a degree of evolving, transient coherence, and is impressionistic and fluid. It is also empirically constituted in that, even though intermedial consolidations appear within it, these eventually disappear back into the constantly evolving empirical flux. Clearly, there are many affinities with the descriptive charges of naturalism here, and this is made even more apparent when it is considered that, in the *Aesthetic*, the model of *Besonderheit* is employed alongside a focus on *Erscheinung* (the forms of appearance) and *Geradesosein* (the just being so of things). And yet, despite this, Lukács con- tinued to insist that his theory of film should not be referred to as naturalist.

It seems that, although in his late period, Lukács developed a general natu- ralist-impressionist model in both the *Aesthetic* and *Ontology*, when he came to address film and also literature in a more specific manner, he retreated to the same critique of naturalism he had routinely applied during 1930–58. In addition, and as in that period, he also applied the same critique to modern- ism because he believed that modernism was a manifestation of the naturalist 'descriptive method'. Because of this, Lukács argued that, in both naturalist and modernist works of art, 'content' (subject matter, perspective and context) was subordinate to 'form' (artistic technique), and it was this opposition between 'content' and 'form' that Lukács chose to emphasise when talking about films and novels through 1958–71. During that period, for example, this dichotomy can be found in articles which Lukács published in the Italian Marxist film journal *Cinema Nuovo*. So, in a 1958 article, he argued that 'I consider it an important and productive thought . . . to clearly separate form [the use of the term 'form' here is confusing but Lukács actually means 'content', and he is using the term 'form' in the way he applied it in early works, such as *Soul and Form*, where form stood for 'authentic human-substance'] from technique. The greatest theoretical failing of the literature pertaining to film, as far as I know, is its mixing up of the two things' (Aitken 2012: 226). Lukács not only believed that form (content) and technique should not be 'mixed up' but also that the former should take precedence over the latter. In addition, he believed that the use of modernist technique could be justified only if such technique was necessary in order to render form. So, in a 1972 *Cinema Nuovo* article on the Hungarian cinema of the 1960s, Lukács argued that, in the films of András Kovács and Miklós Jancsó, 'technical experiment' was used to express a new social content, and that such expression was far preferable to 'revolutionis[ing] form from the point of view of form, in a manner which seeks to find new modes of expression only at the level of form' (Aitken 2012: 138). In addition to films, however, this opposition between form and content was also stressed when Lukács engaged with one of the most important works of literature of the period, Alexander Solzhenitsyn's *One Day in the Life of Ivan Denisovich* (*Ivan*), and this chapter will now explore Lukács's attitude to that work before applying what I have referred to as the 'underlying representational episteme' found in the *Aesthetic* and *Ontology* to an analysis of the 1970 – and only – film adaptation of Solzhenitsyn's novel.

Though there is no direct evidence to substantiate the conjecture that the appearance of *Ivan* in 1962 influenced the approach to film adopted by Lukács in the 1963 *Aesthetic* there is enough circumstantial evidence to render such a conjecture reasonable. *Ivan* was controversial and important from the moment it appeared. Solzhenitsyn had been imprisoned within the harsh Soviet Gulag labour camp system between 1945 and 1953, and *Ivan* is based on the author's experience of imprisonment. Prior to the appearance of *Ivan*, Russian writers had not been allowed to publish on the prison camp system. Special permission to publish *Ivan*, however, was obtained from the Soviet leader, Nikita Khrushchev, who wished to distance himself from connection to, and responsibility for, the Stalinist penal system (and Stalinism in general). When the novel appeared in November 1962, its tale of one man's wretched day in a brutal prison camp had enormous impact both within and outside the Soviet Union. As a prominent literary theorist and political commentator Lukács could not, and did not, ignore *Ivan*. In addition to the status and notoriety of *Ivan*, though, a second reason for postulating the influence of the work on Lukács is that the focus on the particularity of experience in the novel fitted Lukács's then concern with particularity in the *Aesthetic*.

The argument here is not that *Ivan* had a *fundamental* influence on the treatment of film in the *Aesthetic* but, rather, that the novel contributed to the overall approach Lukács was then developing. Despite this contribution, however, when he came actually to write about *Ivan* in 1964 he did not base his approach on notions such as *Besonderheit* but on the opposition between content and form. This may have been a near automatic reflex but it might also have been the result of a felt need to stay close to the official line on *Ivan*. Lukács had almost been executed by the Soviet authorities following the Soviet invasion of Hungary in 1956 and was wary and cautious thereafter (Aitken 2012: 71). In addition, the publication of *Ivan* may have been authorised by Khrushchev in 1962 as part of the process of de-Stalinisation that Khrushchev, Solzhenitsyn and Lukács were all committed to but Khrushchev was removed from power in 1964 and replaced with the more hard-line Leonid Brezhnev, making continued support for Solzhenitsyn more perilous. Having said that, however, though he was a political reformer and anti-Stalinist, Lukács also continued stubbornly to believe in the Leninist insistence on the leading role of the Communist Party and often felt impelled to act, if somewhat masochistically, in conformity with party edicts. Such acquiescence then led him – apparently guilelessly – to endorse some of the decidedly proscriptive and disparaging criticism of *Ivan* and Solzhenitsyn emanating from leading party sources. Solzhenitsyn had been censured by such sources since the appearance of *Ivan* in 1962, and this only increased after the removal of Khrushchev in 1964. In 1968 he was also branded an 'enemy of the State' by the party-controlled journal *Literary Gazette*, and, in 1969, expelled from the Soviet Writers' Union. All this affected Lukács's response to Solzhenitsyn and *Ivan*.

Lukács wrote two essays on Solzhenitsyn. The first, 'Solzhenitsyn: *One Day in the Life of Ivan Denisovich*', appeared in 1964; while the second, 'Solzhenitsyn's Novels', appeared in 1969. In its way, the 1964 essay is as tendentious as the 1936 'Narrate or Describe?' Here, Lukács is principally concerned with the opposition between form and content, with form (meaning 'technique') now – and as in the 1936 essay – standing for 'describe' and content for 'narrate'. In this essay, Lukács attempted to distinguish Solzhenitsyn's work – which he regarded as important – from naturalism, and went as far as to assert that *Ivan* 'stands in marked contrast to all trends of naturalism' (Lukacs 1970: 19). Almost everything Lukács says about *Ivan*, however, marks it out *as* a work of descriptive naturalism. For example, it is argued that *Ivan* is a 'work which is not even symbolically conceived [but] can exert a strong symbolic effect through description', while what is symbolised – apparently *everywhere* in the novel – is 'Stalinism' (14). Whether any of this is the case is debatable. The main point here, however, is that Lukacs's endorsement of descriptive detail which is so disconnected from specific mediating contexts that it leads to general symbolic expression is precisely how, in an earlier work, and following Engels, he argued that naturalism worked (Aitken: 2006: 77). Despite this, the 1964 essay insists that *Ivan* is not a work of naturalism. Nevertheless, Lukács still remained discomfited by the book's lack of perspective, and this led him to view *Ivan* as an experimental cul-de- sac, though one which provided a foundation for the appearance of later, more progressive socialist-realist novels (9). Though Lukács accepted that the perspectiveless 'form' of *Ivan* might be appropriate to its perspectiveless 'content' (prison camp life as static and changeless), he did not believe such form could provide a basis for progressive literary development.

Lukács's 1969 essay on Solzhenitsyn's novels is more multifaceted than the 1964 essay on *Ivan*, in part because the focus on the opposition between form and content in the latter is now mediated by the underlying episteme found in the *Aesthetic* (and later *Ontology*) and because such mediation leads Lukács, at least in part, to reconceptualise Solzhenitsyn's novels in terms of that episteme. For example, he argues that the 'new form' of novel created by Solzhenitsyn consists of a shifting nebulous mass of details which has a 'rich and varied dynamic' (46). In place of a 'unified plot', there is now a 'unified setting', and unified plots, with their high degree of structure, are not neces- sary (42–3). All this fits the underlying Lukácsian episteme. In addition to developing this model, however, Lukács, influenced by the controversies surrounding Solzhenitsyn in 1968–9, also had two pressing objectives for the 1969 essay. The first of these was to show that Solzhenitsyn's later novels were superior to the overly descriptive and perspectiveless *Ivan*, and the second was to demonstrate that the later novels were still nonetheless lacking in important respects (after all, Solzhenitsyn still remained suspect, in the eyes of the party). Lukács argued that the new 'dyanmism' found in Solzhenitsyn's *Cancer Ward* and *In the First Circle* (both 1968) marked a step forward from the 'stasis' of *Ivan*, and what he meant was that these novels show situations that change over time whereas, in *Ivan*, nothing changes. As Lukács put it in 1964, in *Ivan*, the future is 'heavily veiled in all directions' (15). Even though *In the First Circle* still covers the course of only a few days, 'the complex of human reactions needs only a few days in which to unfold. This short period is sufficient to develop these reactions to their logical conclusions.' (65) In addi- tion to this added temporal 'dynamism', which allows change to occur, Lukács also argued that, in these novels, 'dramatization' based around issues of moral choice and dilemma are 'shaded into individual details', and this additional dramatisation of ethical dilemma within 'individual details' also marks a step forward from *Ivan* (50). In *Ivan*, of course, no dilemmas of ethical choice are possible because the prisoners have no access to choice.

Following the tenor of the 1964 contribution, Lukács also concludes his 1969 essay by arguing that, as with *Ivan*, Solzhenitsyn has found a form appropriate to content in *Cancer Ward* and *In the First Circle*. All three novels still share a similar problem, however, in that, though form may be appropriate to content, form nevertheless remains problematic precisely because *content* is problematic. In *Ivan* the content is the 'stasis' of the Stalinist prison environment while, in *Cancer Ward* and *In the First Circle*, it is the 'transitional period' of the shift away from Stalinism and, while the indeterminate structures of the two later novels may reflect the intermedial and indefinite nature of transition, such figuration cannot show the way forward to a post-Stalinist socialist society (76). Like *Ivan*, a novel such as *In the First Circle* is set within a bounded period of time and, according to Lukács, 'if Solzhenitsyn does not develop in subsequent works it [the tendency to avoid providing models for the long term] will restrict his literary importance' (87). Over 1957–71 Lukács developed extensive accounts of the aesthetic and of social being based upon his underlying representational episteme. He did not really consider that episteme, however, when writing about the novels of Solzhenitsyn because he felt it necessary to toe the party line over the author and was unable to overcome the doctrinal position he insisted upon on the dichotomy of narration/content, description/form.

ONE DAY IN THE LIFE OF IVAN DENISOVICH (CASPAR WREDE, 1970)

This chapter is primarily concerned with Lukács and film, rather than Solzhenitsyn's novel, so only a few remarks will be made here concerning the novel (which will, as before, be abbreviated to *Ivan*) as a prelude to the analysis of its 1970 film adaptation (abbreviated to *Ivan Denisovich* in order to avoid confusion with the novel). There is no doubt that *Ivan* is a naturalist-like novel. Narrated in the third person, it goes into considerable detail in describing the minutiae of the routine of the prison camp during the course of a single day. The third-person narration here covers both the subjective thoughts of Ivan and descriptions of extrinsic situations, and, through this technique, everything that occurs is filtered through the mind and eyes of Ivan. Ivan, therefore, dominates the novel and, because he is an obtuse peasant farmer, that overlooking screen is characterised by a down-to-earth, shrewd and understated temper. As Ivan puts it, to survive in the prison camp, you have to be 'cagey and slow', rather than brave. The use of third-person narration to cover both Ivan's thoughts and objective descriptions of things also conflates the third-person narration with Solzhenitsyn's authorial voice, lending Ivan's understated observations and responses additional dramatic impact through association with the iconic author; and what emerges from this technique is a sense of Ivan as both peasant and stoic, reflective imperturbable survivor.

Because of the narrative model employed here, almost everything which is described in the novel also happens immediately before the eyes of Ivan. There are some passages in which limited extrinsic contextual information is provided, and others in which memory of pre-prison life is evoked. In addition to this, there is also some dramatic development, notably surrounding the building of a wall towards the end of the novel, Ivan's late return to the camp as a consequence of that, and the fate of one of the characters, 'the captain', who is given a possibly fatal sentence of ten days in the freezing cells for a show of defiance that the phlegmatic Ivan would never have contemplated. One would expect to find such limited departures from description in any naturalist novel, however, and their presence in *Ivan* does not invalidate the case for the novel to be considered as 'naturalist'. Additionally, for Lukács to say that, in *Ivan*, 'being', or 'Stalinism', lurks behind every detail is actually saying very little. In fact, if anything at all lurks behind 'every' detail, it is Solzhenitsyn's authorial presence as writer and actual prison-camp survivor; and this is a consequence of the narrative model employed, one in which authorial narration and third-person narration coincide. It is also not clear in what sense *Ivan* constitutes a 'totality' rather than a narrowly focused descriptive account. Though the novel has a clear and simple narrative structure, the amount of detail presented has a fragmenting effect, and this is also reinforced by Solzhenitsyn's characteristic use of short sentences.

Ivan Denisovich, the film adaptation of *Ivan*, suffered from three major difficulties from the outset. First, though a descriptive novel, *Ivan* also contains a considerable amount of narration and dialogue. The problem for the film then was how to set limits upon that so that the film did not become a work of filmed talking theatre. In the end, little third-person narration is used, though it does appear from time to time, and still feels inappropriate when it does. Considerable dialogue remains, however, making this a distinctly wordy film. The second major problem that this film faced is that it was a co-production and an unusual one at that in being between British and Norwegian film companies. This also means that the cast is a mix of British and Norwegian actors, and this unlikely amalgamation is rarely successful, as the accents range from broken Norwegian to crisply enunciated upper-class English. This is also a particular problem with the film's principal star, Tom Courteney, who plays the role of Ivan Denisovich. Courteney looks the part, with his shaven head and gaunt expression, but his rather high-pitched cultured and wearied diction does not quite evoke the obtuse peasant farmer that is Solzhenitsyn's Denisovich. The third difficulty faced by the film lay in the iconic status of *Ivan* and Solzhenitsyn in the West at the time. The overall tone of *Ivan* is matter of fact and muted as the convicts try to keep their spirits up in the face of relentlessly mundane adversity. The film plays this more solemnly and deferentially, however. In the end, the film is unable to surmount these difficulties, and this may explain why it remains little known.

The solemn deferential tone adopted by *Ivan Denisovich* does enable it to comply tangentially with Lukács's affirmation that, in *Ivan*, 'being' pulses beneath every descriptive passage. This is not necessarily to the benefit of the film, however, as that tone also affords stiffness to the acting, results in some of the sets appearing overstaged, and does not, anyway, conform to the true Lukácsian notion of being, or *Wesen*. What Lukács means by 'being' and what, in earlier works, he had referred to as 'soul', stand for the authentic and convincing portrayal of agonistic human substance, and this is not successfully attained in a film which relies more on easily understood stereotypical formulations of sombreness in order to reach a casual audience. And, if the issue of being does not take us far in relation to this film because the film does not approximate to the Lukácsian notion, neither, too, does the middle and late-period Lukácsian discrimination between 'form' and 'content' because that discrimination, though genuinely Lukácsian in this case, is not really worth considering within the terms that Lukács framed it. As has been argued, this segregation was largely the product of Lukács's stance on only accepting modernist technique if such technique was necessary to render content; a stance which is unfortunate in that it can hardly sustain much profitable discussion either per se or in relation to *Ivan Denisovich*. If this Lukácsian distinction is turned on its head, however, to assert that technique need not be subordinate to the needs of a content which is anyway pedestrian and also, in addition, always inextricably linked to language, and if such content can be used to express signification beyond such linguistic pedestrianism, then it can be argued that *Ivan Denisovich* succeeds, precisely, when the film prioritises evocative non-verbal form over its word-heavy content. It can also be argued that certain sections of the film which function in this way correspond more than others do to the Lukácsian prioritisation of the 'forms of appearance', that those sections also conform closely to the Lukácsian 'episteme', and that these are, ultimately, the most effective in the film.

With the above in mind it, can be argued that the most important contributions made in *Ivan Denisovich* are not made by Courteney or any of the other actors but by the film's Swedish cinematographer, Sven Nykvist, and Norwegian music composer, Arne Nordheim. Nykvist is best known for his work with the Swedish director Ingmar Bergman, and won the American

Academy Award for Best Cinematography in 1973 for his work on Bergman's *Cries and Whispers*. *Ivan Denisovich*, made three years earlier, is not usually considered one of Nykvist's major achievements, and is rarely mentioned in select filmographies of Nykvist's work even though there are moments of considerable photographic achievement in this film. Nordheim was a leading modernist composer of the day and his atonal electronic music score in *Ivan Denisovich* complements Nykvist's photography in evoking a sense of cold and desolate landscape. As will be argued, both interventions can also be related to authentic Lukácsian aesthetic categories.

Ivan Denisovich begins with a long, slow zoom shot of the prison camp. The impression here is that the shot is taken from a moving aeroplane as the camp, initially a small dot in the surrounding darkness, becomes progressively larger as the camera closes in. The intention here is to evoke the idea of the camp as an isolated settlement in the midst of dark wilderness. It is after this somewhat contrived shot, however, that Nykvist's and Nordheim's contributions become apparent. Once in the camp, the camera focuses on faces, often using extreme close-ups of eyes and mouths in order to indicate the amplified emotional feelings of the convicts as they prepare to face the rigours of the frozen morning. Much of this camerawork is reminiscent of Nykvist's work with Bergman where close-ups of faces are intended to portray heightened emotions. In the novel, Ivan's narration informs us that the lack of food available to the prisoners makes them concentrate fully on every morsel they eat, and Nykvist attempts to capture this through close-ups of Denisovich's mouth as he eats. After the prisoners eat breakfast they are lined up to go to the work site and this now presents the opportunity to show them in relation to the surrounding natural environment.

In the prison hut, the convicts appear as an amorphous mass of bodies. The camera moves among them, penetrating into their number, and showing an indeterminate shapeless mass of disorganised interactions taking place. The coloration here is dull grey to black – and the photography presents us with rounded shapes of parts of bodies, parts of shoulders, backs and so on – to the extent that the convicts are transformed into dehumanised objects rather than people. The convicts shuffle around uncertainly or reluctantly here and the shaky camera reinforces this sense of anxious uncertainty. There then follows a scene in which the convicts leave the prison camp for the work site some distance from the camp. In this scene, language is absent and the film relies entirely on image and sound to convey its meaning. As the sun rises, the colour scheme evolves into a faint blue-white. By this point, the convicts, initially disorganised, have been organised into a regimented column; a black rectangle gliding cautiously through the glowing snowfields in steady rhythm, one accentuated by the moving camera and editing (as all the shots have a similar duration). All this adds to the sense of transformation of the individual convicts into a collective human automaton. Colours now amend into a deeper, more ethereal purple. Now and again, extreme close-ups of frozen lips and icicle-encumbered noses punctuate the mid-shots of the marching column while Nykvist's camera and Nordheim's music evoke a sense of starkly beautiful solitary landscape, coldness and loss; and men robbed of their individual identities. After this, when the men reach the work site, language begins to be used again and the film becomes more conventional, and less effective.

This opening sequence can be described as Lukácsian in the terms set out by Lukács in both the *Aesthetic* and part of the 1969 essay on Solzhenitsyn. In this sequence the Lukácsian episteme emerges as an interactive complex of particularities which consolidates into structures and then disaggregates. In fact, this opening sequence emphasises gradual and increasing consolidation until, from the mess of confused movement in the convicts' hut, a human machine is established. Later, that structure will again begin to dissolve. There is an almost symphonic element to the build-up of this structure, and this again matches the Lukácsian episteme. While both image and music participate in this build-up, both also evoke the continuing background reality of the northern landscape, depicting that landscape as indifferent to the human mass moving through it, and bringing in a degree of impressionism and indeterminacy. None of this, however, can be related to the Lukácsian notion of *Geradesosein*, as none of objects or people shown, even in close up, retains a strong identity of their own as physical entity; and all signify something human instead. In the novel, this is also the case, both in the section covering the march from camp to work site, and elsewhere, and every detail relates to human predicament of some sort (in this sense Lukács is correct to say that 'being' lurks beneath every descriptive account in the novel, though that still remains a rather general thing to say). The more solemn tone adopted by the film, however, not just in this section but also throughout, further reduces the presence of *Geradesosein* even though the audiovisual nature of the medium should have provided the opportunity to manifest such a presence. In this sequence of the film, the complete absence of language does, however, remove the third-person narration that predominates in the novel and forces the convict Denisovich back into the convict collective. Being still exists here, with the sense of human brutalisation and suffering, but it is the forms of appearance which predominate, as the 'outside world' is brought out of its background status and foregrounded through Nyvkist's photography and Nordheim's music. This does not really occur in the rest of the film, however, where the absence of the third-person narration does not lead to a foregrounding of the forms of appearance but to a less effective and more conventional cinematic rendering of the plot of the novel. If the whole of *Ivan Denisovich* had been treated the way this opening sequence of the film was treated the results would have been very different and a major film would have emerged. But that was not to be.

CONCLUSIONS

To what extent do Lukács's positions prove expedient in understanding *Ivan Denisovich*? The key notions of Lukács discussed here are 'speciality' (*Besonderheit*), the 'forms of appearance' (*Erscheinung*), the 'just being so' of things (*Geradesosein*), the 'outside world' (*Aussenwelt*), and what I refer to as the underlying Lukacsian 'episteme'. All of these notions are intrinsically cinematic and also help identify the most and least successful aspects of *Ivan Denisovich*. To what extent these notions can be applied more generally to film analysis and to a variety of other films is something that cannot, in the end, be considered in this chapter owing to lack of space but they do, nonetheless, point to a type of vibrant, phenomenal film-making. Such film-making is anyway discussed widely in other chapters of this book which refer to films that are impressionistic and unsystematic in one way or another. What emerges here in particular, though, is, following Lukács, an emphasis on films in which interactive complexes of phenomenal particularities gradually consolidate into structures that foreground thingness and then disaggregate in an evolving process of becoming. It could be argued that the degree of temporal movement and fluidity involved here distinguishes this Lukácsian model from the Bazinian emphasis on the spatio-temporal unity of the shot and scene, and the Kracaurian focus on the more perfunctory recurrent intersection of human content with 'material reality'. In both these cases, there is more of a dialectic of being and becoming whereas, in Lukács, the greater stress is on becoming.

ACKNOWLEDGEMENT

I would like to acknowledge the financial support of Hong Kong Baptist University School of Communication.

REFERENCES

Aitken, Ian (2006) *Realist Film Theory and Cinema*, Manchester: Manchester University Press.
— (2012), *Lukácsian Film Theory and Cinema: A Study of Georg Lukács' Writings on Film, 1913–71*, Manchester: Manchester University Press.
Ericson, Edward E., Jr and Klimoff, Alexis (2008), *The Soul and Barbed Wire: An Introduction to Solzhenitsyn*, Wilmington, DE: ISI Books.
Lukács, Georg [1956] (1963), *The Meaning of Contemporary Realism*, London: Merlin Press.
— [1964] [1969] (1970), *Solzhenitsyn*, Cambridge, MA: The MIT Press.
— [1916] (1971), *The Theory of the Novel: A Historico-Philosophical Essay on the Forms of Great Epic Literature*, Cambridge, MA: The MIT Press.
— [1910] (1974), *Soul and Form*, London: Merlin Press.

— [1963] (1981), *The Specificity of the Aesthetic*, Berlin: Aufbau-Verlag.

— [1971–73] (1982), *The Ontology of Social Being*, Volume One: *Hegel*, London: Merlin Press.

Márkus, György (1983), 'Life and the Soul: The Young Lukács and the Problem of Culture', in Heller, Agnes (ed.), *Lukács Revalued*, Oxford: Basil Blackwell, pp. 1–26.

Meunier, Jean-Guy (1987), 'Form, Structure and Concept in the Young Lukács', in Joos, Ernest (ed.), *Georg Lukács and his World: A Reassessment*, New York and Paris: Peter Lang, pp. 165–80.

Pascal, Roy (1970), 'Georg Lukács: The Concept of Totality', in Parkinson, G. R. H. (ed.), *Georg Lukács: The Man, his Work and His Ideas*, New York: Random House, pp. 147–71.

Solzhenitsyn, Alexander, [1968] (1968), *In the First Circle*, New York: Harper & Row.

— [1962] (1973), *One Day in the Life of Ivan Denisovich*, New York: Bantam Books.

— [1968] (1983), *Cancer Ward*, New York: Modern Library.

Wrede, Caspar (1970, director), *One Day in the Life of Ivan Denisovich*.

CHAPTER 10

The Documentary Version of Film History

Henry K. Miller

Cavalcanti's *Film and Reality* (1942), a history of 'the realist film' in fifty-eight extracts, is largely remembered for the controversy it ignited within the British documentary film movement. On its release, a few weeks before Cavalcanti began shooting his first British feature, *Went the Day Well?* (1942), his erstwhile documentarist colleagues complained of his neglect of the movement's 'purposive', as opposed to 'aesthetic', aims. Basil Wright, in *Documentary News Letter*, wrote that Cavalcanti had missed 'the real meaning of the sociological approach [. . .] which under Grierson's inspiration and leadership has formed the permanent basis of all documentary production in this country for the past twelve years' (Wright 1942: 40), while Paul Rotha, in a letter to the *New Statesman*, accused Cavalcanti of ignoring the movement's 'real social purpose' (Rotha 1942: 162).

Writing in *Sight and Sound*, Forsyth Hardy, one of the documentarists' most important critical outriders, was more positive; yet it is Hardy who is most responsible for fixing *Film and Reality*'s reputation as a betrayal of documentarist first principles through his decision to include Grierson's response to the film in his collection *Grierson on Documentary*, first published in 1946. 'The Documentary Idea 1942' is the origin of Grierson's avowedly paradoxical statement that it had been 'with the first-rate aesthetic help of people like Flaherty and Cavalcanti that we mastered the techniques necessary for our quite unaesthetic purpose' (Grierson 1942: 83). Hardy's 'Introduction', which used similar Grierson quotations from elsewhere, claimed that 'Grierson's interest was aroused first in the cinema, not as an art form, but as a medium for reaching public opinion' (Hardy 1946: 12).

Though explicitly born of what Grierson considered to be the wartime duty to 'chill the mind to what, in the vacuum of daydreams, one might normally admire' (Grierson 1942: 83), the central propositions of 'The Documentary Idea 1942' have been backdated, contributing to the widely held notion of a fundamental division in the movement between Grierson and Cavalcanti in the mid-1930s. Thus, Andrew Higson, in his influential 1986 essay '"Britain's Outstanding Contribution to the Film": The Documentary-Realist Tradition', which he held to have 'produced a film culture which has been profoundly mistrustful of anything other than a particular de-dramatised naturalistic form' (Higson 1986: 76), argued that 'in order to "remember" Alberto Cavalcanti [. . .] it is necessary to remember *against the grain*, as it were, of dominant film cultural history' (75).

That the members of the documentary film movement did not always see eye to eye is unremarkable; that there was as deep a rift as has been suggested in the 1930s is untenable. The movement's leaders' inconsistent public pronouncements have to be read against the background of the movement's institutional history, and with their intended audience in mind, rather than as statements of disembodied principle; and their actions must be made to speak as loudly as their words. As Rachael Low justly observed, Grierson 'wrote and talked so much himself that one can find quotations for almost any view, and views on almost anything' (Low 1979: 161). More recently, Charles Drazin has devised the reasonable formulation that 'just as the aesthetic clearly mattered to Grierson, in spite of his occasional denials of its importance, so too the social mattered to Cavalcanti' (Drazin 2011: 46). In this spirit, it is time to remember *Film and Reality*, and its compiler, *with* the grain of the movement, and thereby reconsider the nature of the movement of which it was, despite the Griersonians' disavowals, an authentic expression.

To do so, it is first necessary to see *Film and Reality* which was a production of the National Film Library (NFL), a department of the British Film Institute (BFI), apart from the internecine squabbles of the British documentarists and within a larger frame. It is arguable that the most important word in the phrase 'documentary film movement' is the last one, and that its role in shaping the institutions and ethos of British film culture was as significant as the films it produced, if not more so. Characteristically, Grierson gave a number of conflicting views on the subject. In mid-1935, for example, in Geoffrey Grigson's symposium *The Arts To-Day*, he wrote dismissively of the film societies and their 'pleasant Sunday afternoons', championing instead the cause of 'civic education' (Grierson 1935a: 248); while in a digest of the same piece for the *Spectator*, he looked forward to 'an art of cinema which, free from the dithering compulsion of large-scale showmanship, is as adult in its power as the art of music and the art of poetry' (Grierson 1935b: 10).

Whatever Grierson might have said, he and his fellow documentarists, Cavalcanti included, regularly found themselves promoting the art of cinema: Grierson was an active member of the governing council of the original (London) Film Society, and was a regular guest at others – perhaps most notably the Edinburgh Film Guild, in which Hardy was a leading figure. Apart from that, he was invited to speak at the openings of two of the first art cinemas in Britain: the Cambridge Cosmo in 1933 and the Glasgow Cosmo (the similarity of name seems to have been a coincidence) in 1939.

On the other hand, Grierson's relationship with the BFI, which was to become the dominant force in British film culture, was extremely thorny. One of the Institute's first acts, on its foundation in 1933, was to attempt to appropriate the film library of the recently dissolved Empire Marketing Board (EMB), the body Grierson had worked for since 1927, and, while the library effectively went with Grierson to the General Post Office (GPO), Grierson saw this and other manoeuvres as an attack, and remained suspicious of the BFI's motives. Here, however, Grierson might himself be remembered against the grain of the movement he founded. Cavalcanti's collaboration with the NFL on *Film and Reality* was no aberration but the outcome of a dramatic reversal of fortunes in which the British documentary film movement came to co-operate extensively with the BFI, even while Grierson personally did not. Yet the film's lasting significance emerges only when it is seen in an international perspective, for it was in response to developments in international film culture, in which both the BFI and the documentary film movement were closely involved, that the film was conceived; and it is only in an international perspective that the novelty of Cavalcanti's argument becomes fully apparent.

Cavalcanti had stated the core thesis of *Film and Reality*, and even assembled a version of the film itself, before the documentary film movement had come into being. At the International Congress of Independent Cinema at La Sarraz, Switzerland, in September 1929, he gave a talk on the 'Evolution of Cinematography in France', accompanied by a 'composite reel made up of a résumé of cinematic work in France since 1893' (Cavalcanti 1930: 5). *Film and Reality*'s prologue consists of a reconstruction of E. J. Marey's experiments in motion photography, followed by a clip from the Lumières' *Arrival of a Train in a Country Station* (1896); Cavalcanti's talk, which appeared in the American little magazine *Experimental Cinema* in 1930, began with his memories of seeing the Lumières' film in childhood. The first section of *Film and Reality*, announced by a title reading 'The Invention of Cinematography Leads to a New Form of Dramatic Entertainment', starts with the Lumières' *L'Arroseur Arrosé* (1895); and, at La Sarraz, Cavalcanti had called this the film with which '[c]inematic art began' (5).

Cavalcanti went on to ask: 'Was the cinema aware of its possibilities? Was it going to interpret human emotion, the comic, life itself?' and answered that 'instead of catching its true voice in the beginning indicated so clearly in this film', the cinema had 'lost itself in encumbrances with theatrical tradition' (5–6). This became a central argument of *Film and Reality*, expressed in the title announcing its second section, 'Contact with Reality, Lost in Film Drama, is Maintained in Newsreels and Interest Films'. At La Sarraz, Cavalcanti had lamented that 'the intrusion of décor [. . .] shackled the growth of the cinema from the dramatic point of view', leaving 'life itself' to the actuality films (6); variations on the examples he gave of these in the 1929 talk – newsreel of race-track accidents, travelogues, and experiments in slow-motion – appear in the 1942 film. It was from the actualities and their 'cruder devices' (6), he argued, that the realist film had evolved. 'To have reverence for life, to guard its wild freedom, to interpret it in an act of true reconstruction –, this is something to look forward to in the cinema', said Cavalcanti in 1929, foreshadowing Grierson's famous phrase 'the creative treatment of actuality' well before they met (6).

In 1929 the films which Cavalcanti considered to have revered life included Cooper and Schoedsack's *Grass* (1925), Flaherty's *Moana* (1926), and Allégret's *Voyage au Congo* (1927) – all of which appear in the third section of *Film and Reality*, 'The Romantic Documentary of Far-off Lands'. Though Cavalcanti, like many others, regarded the coming of sound as a 'regressive phenomenon' because it led to 'filmed theatre', he hoped that the cinema would evolve along the lines these films suggested (6).

In Peter Wollen's seminal 1975 essay, La Sarraz is said to have witnessed the meeting of 'The Two Avant-Gardes', western and Soviet, but 'turned out to mark the end rather than the beginning of an epoch' (Wollen 1975: 172). From the point of view of Cavalcanti and his future colleagues, however, it can indeed be seen as a beginning, albeit not wholly in Wollen's terms. It was at La Sarraz that an extract from Len Lye's *Tusalava* (1929) was shown for the first time, and there is evidence to suggest that Grierson's *Drifters* (1929) was shown as well, two months before its Film Society debut.[1] The course described by the rest of *Film and Reality*, covering the 1930s, resembled the future Cavalcanti had imagined in 1929.

Grierson imagined much the same future. In his 1927 memorandum 'Notes for English Producers', commissioned by the EMB, he had written that 'in avoiding the natural world which it has at its command, cinema is depriving itself unnecessarily of much that lends itself to cinematic treatment', and proposed *Grass* and *Moana* as models for the production of the 'short glorified news reelers' that would become his stock-in-trade (Grierson 1927: 19). He was constrained in his choice of subjects at the EMB but less so, or differently so, in his column in the left-wing monthly *Clarion*. In the August 1929 issue, Grierson praised exactly the same films that Cavalcanti would mention a few weeks later in Switzerland, but wrote that in them, 'the cinema has, for the sake of an easy romance, gone primitive', advocating instead 'a wild expedition to the coal mines of Durham' (Grierson 1929: 9). This was more or less what Cavalcanti had done in his directorial debut *Rien que les Heures/The Book of*

Hours (1926), the idea behind which was, as he told Elizabeth Sussex many years later, 'that films were always about faraway places, about the sunsets over the Pacific etc., and nobody had an idea that life in the town in which you lived was interesting' (Sussex 1975: 207).

'I always think of documentary as having certain fundamental chapters,' Grierson told Sussex in what was billed as his last interview, around the same time. 'The first chapter is of course the travelogue, that is, the discovery that the camera can go about [. . .]. The second chapter is the discovery by Flaherty that you can make a film of people on the spot', he went on, with the qualification that 'of course he did that in respect of faraway peoples, and he was romantic in that sense. The third chapter is our chapter, which is the discovery of the working people, that is, the drama on the doorstep' (Sussex 1972: 29–30). It was the fourth part of *Film and Reality*, 'The Realistic Documentary of Life at Home', which provoked the most criticism, yet Cavalcanti could hardly be accused of neglecting the documentary's 'social purpose'. The section begins with an extract from *Rien que les Heures*, described in the commentary as 'an early attempt to draw attention to the miseries of unemployment'; when *Drifters* appears, its director is credited as having 'started a powerful movement to use film for civic education'; and Pare Lorentz's *The Plow that Broke the Plains* (1936), it is said, 'owes much to the example of the British school and is inspired by similar ideas of social purpose'.

In short, *Film and Reality*, until its fifth and final part, is a model of documentarist orthodoxy. By 1942, the basic progressions which it charts, 'from plain (or fancy) descriptions of natural material, to arrangements, rearrangements, and creative shapings of it', in Grierson's words (1932b: 69), and from the faraway to the doorstep, were commonplaces of the movement's literature. The same story had appeared, for example, in Rotha's 1936 book *Documentary Film*, whose central section, titled 'The Evolution of Documentary', begins with an account of the survival of interest and travel films despite 'the indifference of producing companies and renting concerns' (Rotha 1936: 72), and singles out for praise 'Percy Smith's *Secrets of Nature*', 'Jean Painlevé's beautiful fish films', and 'Canti's cancer film' (74), all of which appeared in *Film and Reality*'s second section, alongside Gaumont-British's newsreel of the assassination of King Alexander of Yugoslavia, also mentioned by Rotha. For Rotha, 'documentary may be said to have had its real beginnings with Flaherty's *Nanook*' (77); in *Film and Reality*, *Nanook of the North* is called 'the first documentary film in the modern sense'. Just as Cavalcanti would go on to say in his film, *Rien que les Heures* is described in Rotha's book as the first film to present 'the possibility of interpreting the reality about us, as opposed to the sentimental idyll in remote parts of the Flaherty method' (88).

One of the most striking forerunners of *Film and Reality* is Grierson's valedictory essay 'The Course of Realism', published simultaneously with his resignation from the GPO in June 1937. Its opening passages, in which Grierson recalls his first exposure to the Lumières' films in childhood, echo Cavalcanti's talk at La Sarraz, as does the essential problem it presents – the central problem also of *Film and Reality* – in its first sentences (Grierson 1937b: 137): 'Here is an art based on photographs, in which one factor is always, or nearly always, a thing observed. Yet a realist tradition in cinema has emerged only slowly.' With indecent haste, Grierson continued, the cinema's 'natural destiny of discovering mankind' was abandoned for the 'high false-hood of trickwork and artifice', and the 'near-realism of three-ply, plaster and painted glass' (138–9). In *Film and Reality* (as in the La Sarraz talk) the rot sets in with the Film d'Art production *L'Assassinat du Duc de Guise* (1908); likewise in Grierson's essay the trouble began with the 'grand people of the French and British theatres' who preceded Adolph Zukor in 'attaching famous players to famous plays' (139).

Like Rotha before him, and like Cavalcanti later, Grierson acknowledged the significance of interest films and newsreels, despite their 'lack of fibre' (142), and paid tribute to some of the very same science films by Canti and Smith. As Ian Aitken notes, the description of Painlévé's film in *Film and Reality* as a 'poetic treatment of reality' is a conscious echo of Grierson (Aitken 2000: 89). Grierson's chronicle of the documentary proper, from *Nanook* through 'the field of realism which Cavalcanti initiated with *Rien que les Heures*' to the British movement, 'less aesthetic and more social in its approach' (Grierson 1937b: 149–50), is equally familiar. It is true that Grierson went further by saying that 'our British documentary group began not so much in affection for film as in affection for national education' (153) – though, as we have seen, *Film and Reality* does not ignore this claim – but it is also true that Grierson, who was notoriously selective about credits, chose to give himself a producer credit, in what must have been one of his last acts as producer, on Len Lye's *Trade Tattoo* (1937), not a notably educative film, first shown in public a few months after his departure.

A year later Cavalcanti himself, having assumed some of Grierson's respon-sibilities as production supervisor, provided a restatement of what was by then a much-told tale. 'Documents on Celluloid', published in the September 1938 issue of the highbrow magazine *Life and Letters To-day*, begins with Lumière, laments that 'dramatic films very nearly killed the cinema', and argues that 'newsreel carried through these early years of films not only the documentary principle but Cinema itself' (Cavalcanti 1938: 89). Like Grierson in 'The Course of Realism', Cavalcanti identifies their weakness as a preoccupation 'with the unimportant activities of officials and society people' but mentions as a genuine 'historical record' the assassination film he would go on to include (90). So well trodden were these tracks that Cavalcanti felt he had to pre-empt the complaint himself: those who 'think that too much has been written about this documentary school', he joked, 'forget that the first duty of professional propagandists is to know how to advance their own propaganda' (91).

Film and Reality was in preparation within weeks of the appearance of Cavalcanti's article. The BFI's application to the Privy Council for its annual grant, submitted on 27 October 1938, mentions that the NFL, then in a period of 'rapid development', was 'starting work on a composite film of the art of Charles Chaplin and a history of the documentary film' (British Film Institute 1938: 5). According to the following year's annual report, the success of Marie Seton's *Drawings that Walk and Talk* (1938), a 'composite film of the development of the cartoon', first shown in May 1938, 'led the Committee to accept an offer from Mr Alberto Cavalcanti to compose a picture showing the development of actuality in the film' (British Film Institute 1939: 4). It was not Cavalcanti's first contact with the BFI, and no fuss was made at the time, but given the Institute's troubled relationship with the GPO Film Unit over the preceding five years – they were formed almost simultaneously – the occasion ought to be put into historical perspective.

Not without reason, Grierson had voiced his scepticism towards those agitating for a national film institute, 'the educationists and the uplifters', in a review of the BFI's founding document, *The Film in National Life*, on its publication in June 1932 (1932a: 650). The BFI which emerged in October 1933 was dominated by the film trade, rather than by educationists, and its attempt to seize the EMB's film library, which would have formed the nucleus of the 'National Film Library' as originally conceived, was conducted in parallel with a trade campaign to force Grierson's new film unit to limit its role to publicising the services of its parent body, the GPO. The Treasury officials who managed these arrangements did not think much of the BFI, and Grierson, with the support of his powerful superiors, weathered the storm. The institute's funding was strictly provisional and, when the formation of a National Film Library was announced in July 1935, it was as a charity case. Within a few months, the dubious commercial side ventures of some BFI governors had embroiled the young institute in scandal and, by early 1936, its closure seemed quite possible.

It was at that very moment, however, that Cavalcanti began to work with it. The educationists and the uplifters had encouraged like-minded people to set up branch societies across the country and, while most of these seem to have been ineffectual talking shops, the Merseyside Film Institute Society (MFIS), which actually came into being before the BFI proper, was by the end of 1933 one of the largest film societies outside London. The documentarists were regular guests: in October 1934, just months after the BFI's most damaging attack on the GPO Film Unit, Grierson introduced a screening of *Grass* in MFIS's new rooms in central Liverpool. In his biography, Forsyth Hardy quotes Grierson as calling MFIS's animating spirit Frank Heming Vaughan, a Unitarian minister in Toxteth, 'one of the goodest men I have ever known' (Hardy 1979: 212). His daughter Olwen, who had herself befriended the documentarists, moved to London in 1935, taking charge of the newly formed London Film Institute Society (LFIS), and then, in May, becoming secretary of the BFI.

It is really from this date that the BFI, which until then had had poor relations with the film society movement as well as with the documentary film movement, can be discussed as an institution of film culture. Under Vaughan's leadership, LFIS began operating along Liverpool lines. From early 1936, it put on Sunday screening programmes at the Forum cinema, underneath Charing Cross railway station, which would typically comprise a feature revival and new experimental or documentary films. In the same months Rotha, Wright, and Cavalcanti all contributed to an LFIS-sponsored lecture series, and Cavalcanti began to collaborate with the BFI's other most promising branch, the NFL, which held its first screening at the Regent Street Polytechnic, to mark the fortieth anniversary of the first Lumière screenings in London, that February. In March, Cavalcanti provided three pre-war films from his own collection (he discovered them on a Parisian market stall) for a joint LFIS–NFL show at Gaumont-British's private theatre in Wardour Street. One of these, the melodrama *Le Bouquet de Violettes* (1908), ended up in the first part of *Film and Reality*.

By the time Cavalcanti took over from Grierson at the GPO, the two bodies were regularly working together. The BFI, having narrowly survived its crisis, came under closer government inspection, gaining a new director, former Conservative party press officer Oliver Bell, who was more sympathetic than his predecessors to the kind of NFL which its young curator, Ernest Lindgren, was trying to build. In 1937 Bell won from the Privy Council a large budget increase for the NFL, and a £3,000 grant that made it a viable operation (Bell 1937). In the past, Grierson had understandably refused the NFL's requests for copies of his unit's films but, when Bell asked him to reconsider, he relented. On 4 June 1937, weeks before he left, Grierson explained to a colleague that the BFI 'is now working on a more solid basis than under the old regime and many of the negative points which I had in mind when considering their previous request, do not now arise' (Grierson 1937a).

Meanwhile, Cavalcanti had begun to forge links between the reformed BFI and its French equivalent, the Cinémathèque Française, to whose founders, Henri Langlois and Georges Franju, he had been introduced by his old friend Jean Renoir. In July 1937, the Cinémathèque included Len Lye's *Colour Flight* (1937), listed as 'Prod.: Cavalcanti–Grierson', in its first public show at the Cité Universitaire (Derain 1937: 10). Five months later, on 10 December, the Cercle du Cinéma, the Cinémathèque's screening arm, showed Cavalcanti's

GPO productions *Coal Face* (1935) and *We Live in Two Worlds* (1937) as part of a programme devoted to 'l'Avant garde anglaise', other highlights of which included *Trade Tattoo* and films by Grierson, Rotha, and Wright.[2] LFIS and the Cinémathèque began regular co-operation after the death of Georges Méliès in January 1938, again with Cavalcanti oiling the wheels. Langlois, raising funds for Méliès's widow, first addressed LFIS at the Forum on 30 January 1938, five days after the funeral; in May, Cavalcanti, the GPO, the NFL, and the Cinémathèque together mounted an exhibition devoted to Méliès in a Bond Street art gallery.

Langlois and Vaughan had by then made links with the Museum of Modern Art (MOMA) Film Library in New York, and, in June 1938 representatives of the three archives, together with the Reichsfilmarchiv in Berlin, met in Paris on the occasion of a major MOMA exhibition at the Musée du Jeu de Paume, 'Trois Siècles d'Art Etats-Unis', to discuss a more formal arrangement, the result being the establishment of FIAF (Dupin 2013: 47–50). The MoMA Film Library's contribution to the exhibition, arranged by its British curator, Iris Barry, and her husband, John Abbott, included three programmes of excerpts recounting the history of American film from Edison onwards. Three months later, at the Venice Film Festival, Langlois and Franju put on a similar show recounting the history of French cinema. In November, when Langlois and Franju restaged it in England, first for MFIS, then for its Manchester equivalent, then for LFIS, it began with Marey and Lumière and ended with Cavalcanti's *En Rade* (1927). Though Cavalcanti had anticipated both Langlois and Barry at La Sarraz, the Paris and Venice compilations may have provided an immediate model for his commissioners at the BFI. Unlike those of its FIAF partners MoMA and the Cinémathèque, however, the BFI's compilation would not be hemmed in by national borders.

While the documentarists were most critical of the fourth part of *Film and Reality*, none rose to the challenge of the fifth, of which Basil Wright professed himself 'entirely baffled' (Wright 1942: 41). Titled 'Realism in the Story Film', it is the most complex section of the film, and the most novel, though still concordant with documentary orthodoxy. It begins with extracts from three story films which had escaped the studio, and in which 'characters and action formed a whole with a natural background': Mauritz Stiller's *The Atonement of Gösta Berling* (1924), James Cruze's *The Covered Wagon* (1923), and the Tom Mix western *The Stage-coach Driver and the Girl* (1915). None of this was very baffling. 'To the Swedes', Rotha had written in *Documentary Film*, 'must go the credit of the first real imaginative use of the exterior in fiction films' (Rotha 1936: 79). *The Covered Wagon* was a long-standing feature of the Griersonian canon and, though Cavalcanti is unlikely to have known it, Grierson had once written of the Mix *oeuvre* that 'there is so plentiful a splashing of hills and horses and fresh air that one realizes on seeing it how cabined, confined, and claustrophobic our other films are' (Grierson 1933: 342).

It is the subsequent sequence that caused the most confusion. Made up of three comparisons, it first pairs *Battleship Potemkin* (1925), squarely in the documentary-realist tradition, with a scene from Zecca's *Revolution in Russia* (1905) depicting the same mutiny, 'by way of contrast', as the commentary puts it: the one shot on location, the other as if on stage. The point of the second pairing, Dieterle's *The Life of Emile Zola* (1937) and Méliès's *L'Affaire Dreyfus* (1899), again depicting the same events, is less obvious, since Méliès is described as 'one of the greatest film directors' and, while both the Zecca and Méliès extracts are static, single-shot scenes, the commentary does not draw attention to Eisenstein's montage nor to Dieterle's découpage. But one can infer Cavalcanti's intention from the documentarists' collective support for Dieterle's film, which Cavalcanti, not even its greatest admirer among them, had reviewed in *World Film News* on its release, singling out the scene he would later incorporate for its 'brilliance' (Cavalcanti 1937b: 16); Grierson, in the same issue, had even compared the film with *Potemkin* (Grierson 1937c: 18).

The third comparison, meanwhile, is meant to show 'no fundamental change' at all, pairing another Film d'Art, *La Dame aux Camélias* (1912) – one of Zukor's early successes – with a recent British film, *Love From a Stranger* (1937), both of them described as 'photographed plays'. Here, Cavalcanti returned to the argument of 'Documents on Celluloid', in which he had written that 'studio productions in London not only consistently avoid an English atmosphere; they bring to the screen stage-actors and stage-subjects, and record stage dialogue in the manner of the early dramatic films' (Cavalcanti 1938: 94).

The section's third and final sequence was meant to show the way ahead with 'three notable story films' of the 1930s, recalling Cavalcanti's hope at the conclusion of the same essay that, when the documentary 'is recognized by the commercial film companies, its influence may bring some flesh and blood into the English cinema as a whole' (94). Once again, while Cavalcanti's preference for narrative over journalism is held to be the source of the supposed split in the documentary film movement, there was actually nothing controversial in this. In a 1937 article, occasioned by Grierson's departure from the GPO, Wright had foreseen 'a step forward into the field of feature films, a new type of feature, in which the realist tradition will combine with the best production values of the theatrical movie' (Wright 1937: 15), and many critics saw just such a combination in films like Michael Powell's *The Edge of the World* (1937) and Carol Reed's *Bank Holiday* (1938). Even Grierson hoped for a producer who might 'wed studio and natural observation into a new and vital formula' (Grierson 1937b: 148), as he put it in 'The Course of Realism', and circumstances in which documentary directors might 'bring their realism to the range of full-scale drama' (160).

The first of the three films Cavalcanti chose to illustrate this tendency, Pabst's *Kameradschaft* (1931), was canonical – Rotha had said that it 'falls into the widest reading of documentary' (Rotha 1936: 179) – the third and last, the British film *Farewell Again* (1937), less so. It is mentioned in 'Documents on Celluloid' as one of the 'exceedingly rare' films like Powell's (Cavalcanti 1938: 94), but Cavalcanti might have done better to have included his own production *North Sea* (1938) here, rather than earlier, since it was central to the same discourse. In his review for *The Times*, for example, Rotha lauded it at the expense of 'the so-called journalistic style' (Rotha 1938b: 12) and, in a letter to Forsyth Hardy, who had praised it in the same terms in the *Scotsman*, Rotha wrote that 'there are some of us in documentary who are just ready to take the step into the semi-story semi-documentary film' (Rotha 1938a). *Farewell Again* lacked *North Sea*'s reputation and, in his review of *Film and Reality*, Hardy wrote that he 'would have preferred to see a conclusion which took into account the growing tendency in the British and French cinemas to make films of stories close to real life' (Hardy 1942: 4), naming both Powell and Reed's films, as well as Pagnol's *La Femme du Boulanger* (1938), as more worthy candidates.

What shines out from the sequence now, however, is Cavalcanti's second extract, from Renoir's *La Grande Illusion* (1937), implicitly queried by Hardy, and unremarked elsewhere. Renoir was a relatively little-known figure in Britain in the 1930s: *La Grande Illusion* was one of the handful of his films to be shown and, as Thorold Dickinson put it thirty years later, 'you can search the accepted opinion of the time and find no genuine assessment of his contribution' (Dickinson 1969). But it is Renoir's film that connects Cavalcanti's compilation to one of the main currents in post-war international film culture.

According to David Bordwell, in his book *On the History of Film Style*, the major film historians of the 1930s and 1940s promoted the 'Standard Version' of film history, in which 'film style could be understood as a development toward the revelation of cinema's inherent aesthetic capacities' (Bordwell 1997: 27), an evolutionary process in which the 'editing was the central and distinctive film technique' (33). Though the MoMA Film Library, through publications such as Lewis Jacobs's *Rise of the American Film*, took the lead in publicising this version of film history, in which D. W. Griffith was the seminal figure, the NFL was equally wedded to it. Lindgren, credited with 'assembling' *Film and Reality*, was one of its most eloquent exponents.

In Bordwell's scheme, the 'first full-blown alternative to the Standard Version' (46) arrived in the late 1940s with André Bazin, who proposed the contrary view 'that the medium's essence lies exactly in its recording capacity' (72). Contrasting 'directors who believed in the image and those who believed in reality', in his classic essay 'The Evolution of Film Language', first published in 1958 but composed of material published separately before then, Bazin constructed an alternative lineage epitomised in its mature phase by Renoir, Orson Welles and William Wyler, and the Italian neorealists (Bazin 1968: 26). *Film and Reality* does not touch on the central claim of Bazin's (later) essay, which is that in the work of these directors the sequence shot was not a rejection of editing but achieved its ends without 'fragmenting the world' (48); but the similarities are nonetheless worth exploring.

The sequence of *Film and Reality* in which *La Grande Illusion* appears begins with the assertion that 'the essence of cinematography lies in its power to represent reality' and 'to depict it in the most brilliant terms', and while it is not remarked upon in the commentary, the extract itself is a sequence shot in which the film's star, Jean Gabin, is not given special attention, arguably an instance of Bazinian 'ambiguity' *avant la lettre*. Literally so, since, for Bazin himself, the major 'linguistic evolution' (48) began later. The year in which *Film and Reality* was commissioned, 1938, figures in Bazin's essay as the year Hollywood cinema 'reached a degree of classical perfection' (33), the year in which 'the way shots were broken down in a shooting script was the same almost everywhere' (35). Seen in this light, *Film and Reality*, which in a sense ends where Bazin begins, is as prophetic of the Bazinian 1940s as Cavalcanti's talk at La Sarraz had been of the Griersonian 1930s.

For Bazin and Cavalcanti both, Hollywood classicism had led cinema 'away from its vocation for realism' (49), with only isolated figures bucking the main tendency: apart from Renoir, Bazin held Flaherty to be one such outsider for whom 'the images are important not for what they add to reality but for what they reveal in it' (31). For both of them, 'classical perfection' constituted only a minor advance on the mode of the Film d'Art, in which, as Bazin put, it the 'framing more or less takes up the position of the absent fourth wall of a theatre stage' (39). Bazin's argument that, if the classically constructed scenes of 1938 'were acted on stage and seen from a seat in the stalls, it would have exactly the same meaning', (35) is presaged in Cavalcanti's series of juxtapositions in the final section of *Film and Reality*.

Elsewhere in his writings Bazin compared the 'dramatic poetry of the landscape' in the western with that of 'the silent Swedish film', just as Cavalcanti had through his sequencing (Bazin 1971: 141), and he was, of course, aware of Cavalcanti's contribution to the realist tradition as well. In his review of *Bicycle Thieves* (1948), he attributed the 'recent cinematic rebirth' of British cinema, in which we might now substitute *Went the Day Well?* for Bazin's regretted example of Reed's *Brief Encounter* (1945), to 'the ten years of preparation by Grierson, Cavalcanti, or Rotha', seeing in it the combination of 'a highly refined aestheticism with the advances of a certain realism' (48–9) not unlike that which British critics, including Cavalcanti, had envisaged in the late 1930s.

Nor are these merely chance correspondences: Cavalcanti, who had been calling himself a neorealist since early 1937 at the latest, can be seen to have contributed to the background in which Bazin's ideas were formed.[3] Roger Leenhardt, the critic Bazin most admired, was an admirer of the documentary film movement, as of course was Langlois who continued to show its work in Paris after the war. Nor is Cavalcanti's self-identification as a 'neorealist' to be written off as a joke: his essay 'Le Mouvement néo-réaliste en Angleterre' appeared alongside contributions by Alberto Consiglio, later one of the writers of *Rome Open City* (1945), and Umberto Barbaro, co-founder of the Centro Sperimentale di Cinematografia, the state film school whose graduates included the neorealist directors Giuseppe De Santis and Pietro Germi. More tangentially, but nonetheless intriguingly, Bazin's future translator, Hugh Gray, served in the same capacity for Langlois during his British tour in 1938.

It should be evident by now that, with *Film and Reality*, Cavalcanti rendered in film form a clear precursor to one of the most influential theories in film history; and that, despite its reputation, it was in most respects faithful to the core doctrines of the British documentary film movement. If this connection has been underexplored, it is probably because Bazin concentrated on the fiction film – though hardly exclusively, as his treatment of Flaherty suggests. For the purposes of his book, Bordwell made a clean separation between fiction and documentary, writing that the 'stylistic history of documentary may differ considerably from that of the fiction film' (Bordwell 1997: 11), yet in the British case this was not really so. Rotha was, after all, both an exponent of 'Standard Version' history – Bordwell describes Rotha's *The Film Till Now* as 'the most ambitious and influential English-language film history of the era' (21) – *and* a leading documentarist. Cavalcanti went further, straddling the divide both in theory and in practice, and paid the penalty in condemnation and obscurity.

NOTES

1. British Film Institute Special Collections, Ivor Montagu Collection, Item 10: 'Film Society: Report upon little Cinema movement in England'. In this undated document, probably the basis for Montagu's presentation at the congress, *Drifters* is marked as among the films 'exhibited in Sarraz' in full or in part.

2. I am indebted to Celia Nicholls of the University of Warwick for this information.

3. *Edinburgh Film Guide*, March 1937, p. 2. I am indebted to Marc David Jacobs of the Edinburgh Film Guild for access to this document.

REFERENCES

Aitken, Ian (ed.) (1998), *The Documentary Film Movement: An Anthology*, Edinburgh: Edinburgh University Press.

— (2000), *Alberto Cavalcanti: Realism, Surrealism and National Cinemas*, Trowbridge: Flicks Books.

Bazin, André (1968), 'The Evolution of Film Language', in Graham, Peter (ed.), *The New Wave*, London: Secker & Warburg, pp. 25–51.

— (1971), *What is Cinema?* Volume II, Berkeley, CA: University of California Press.

Bell, Oliver (1937), Letter to Privy Council, 1 August 1937, National Archives, ED 121/277.

Bordwell, David (1997), *On the History of Film Style*, Cambridge, MA: Harvard University Press.

British Film Institute (1938), Application to Privy Council, 27 October 1938, National Archives, ED 121/277.

— (1939), 'Sixth Annual Report to 30 June 1939', British Film Institute Library.

Cavalcanti, Alberto (1930), 'Evolution of Cinematography in France', *Experimental Cinema*, June 1930, pp. 5–6. Reprinted in Aitken 1998, pp. 202–5.

— (1937a), 'Le Mouvement néo-réaliste en Angleterre', in *Le Rôle Intellectuel du Cinéma*, Paris: Institut International de Coopération Intellectuelle, pp. 235–41. Translated as 'The Neo-Realist Movement in England' in Abel, Richard (ed.), *French Film Theory and Criticism, 1907–1939*, Volume 2: *1929–1939*, Princeton, NJ: Princeton University Press, pp. 233–8.

— (1937b), 'Muni's Great Performance in *The Life of Emile Zola*', *World Film News*, November 1937, pp. 16–17.

— (1938), 'Documents on Celluloid', *Life and Letters To-day*, September 1938, pp. 88–94.

Derain, Lucie (1937), 'Le Gala de la "Cinémathèque française" à la Cité Universitaire', *La Cinématographie Française*, 2–9 July 1937, p. 10.

Dickinson, Thorold (1969), 'Inaugural Lecture', University College London Special Collections, Slade Film Department Archive, Box 13.

Drazin, Charles (2011), 'Alberto Cavalcanti: Lessons in Fusion at the GPO Film Unit', in Anthony, Scott and Mansell, James G. (eds), *The Projection of Britain: A History of the GPO Film Unit*, London: Palgrave Macmillan, pp. 45–52.

Dupin, Christophe (2013), 'First Tango in Paris: The Birth of FIAF, 1936–1938', *Journal of Film Preservation*, no. 88, April, pp. 42–57.

Grierson, John (1927), 'Notes for English Producers', National Archives, CO 760/37.

— (1929), 'From the Life', *Clarion*, August, p. 9.

— (1932a), 'The Melody of Life', *Everyman*, 16 June, p. 650.

— (1932b), 'Documentary (I)', *Cinema Quarterly*, Winter, pp. 67–72. Reprinted in Aitken 1998, pp. 81–93.

— (1933), 'Tom Mix, Man of Action', *New Britain*, 3 August 1933, pp. 334, 342.

— (1935a), 'One Hundred Per Cent. Cinema', *Spectator*, 23 August, pp. 9–10.

— (1935b), 'The Cinema To-day', in Grigson, Geoffrey (ed.), *The Arts To-day*, London: Bodley Head, pp. 219–50.

— (1937a), Letter to A. G. Highet, 4 June 1937, British Postal Museum and Archive, POST 33/4930, File No. 14.

— (1937b), 'The Course of Realism', in Davy, Charles (ed.), *Footnotes to the Film*, London: Lovat Dickson, pp. 137–61.

— (1937c), 'Five Films Reviewed', *World Film News*, November, pp. 18–19.

— (1942), 'The Documentary Idea 1942', *Documentary News Letter*, June, pp. 83–6. Reprinted in Aitken 1998, pp. 103–15.

Hardy, Forsyth (1942), 'Forsyth Hardy Reviews *Film and Reality*', *Sight and Sound*, Summer 1942, pp. 1–4.

— (1946), 'Introduction', in Hardy, Forsyth (ed.), *Grierson on Documentary*, London: Collins, pp. 11–25.

— (1979), *John Grierson: A Documentary Biography*, London: Faber and Faber.

Higson, Andrew (1986), '"Britain's Outstanding Contribution to the Film": The Documentary-Realist Tradition', in Barr, Charles (ed.), *All Our Yesterdays: 90 Years of British Cinema*, London: British Film Institute, pp. 72–97.

Low, Rachael (1979), *The History of British Film 1929–1939: Documentary and Educational Films of the 1930s*, London: Allen & Unwin.

Rotha, Paul (1936), *Documentary Film*, London: Faber and Faber.

— (1938a), Letter to Forsyth Hardy, 17 June 1938, University of Stirling Archives, Forsyth Hardy Collection, H.1.37.

— (1938b), 'Films of Fact', *The Times*, 28 June, p. 12.

— (1942), 'Correspondence', *New Statesman*, 7 March, p. 162.

Sussex, Elizabeth (1972), 'Grierson on Documentary: The Last Interview', *Film Quarterly*, Autumn, pp. 24–30.

— (1975), 'Cavalcanti in England', *Sight and Sound*, autumn, pp. 205–11.

Wollen, Peter (1975), 'The Two Avant-Gardes', *Studio International*, November–December, pp. 171–5.

Wright, Basil (1937), 'Ten Years of Documentary', *World Film News*, July, pp. 14–15.

— (1942), 'Film and Reality', *Documentary News Letter*, March 1942, pp. 40–2.

CHAPTER 11

The Grierson Testament, 1969–71

Gary Evans

This chapter covers the recorded and transcribed interviews that John Grierson gave in Ottawa from September 1969 until November 1971 to the newly minted CRTC, the Canadian Radio and Television Commission (Telecommunications was added in 1976). This regulatory agency, which licenses broadcasting, radio and television across Canada, delegated bureaucrats Rodrigue Chiasson and André Martin to conduct research regarding future policy directions. The founder of the documentary movement in Britain and the National Film Board of Canada offered critical advice to his hosts, aiming most of his attention at perceived weaknesses in contemporary media and the lack of ethical connection to Canadian audiences. He disdained what he called the media's contemporary 'show-biz' tendencies and lobbied for state-supported non-fiction film production that would bolster what he considered to be 'Canadian' values. All this was predicated upon reiterating his original definition of documentary as the creative treatment of actuality. To Grierson, actuality film was an iteration of a story about real social or educational purpose, delivered to a receptive audience that he considered a singular entity. In the end, though, his interviews did little to change CRTC policy direction.

In 1969, Grierson began his interviews with the CRTC while teaching at McGill University in Montreal. Their substance echoed his classroom rhetoric, where he demonstrated an entertaining ability to fly with ease from one esoteric theme to another, discussing art, classics, history and non-fiction film. He dismissed television as a device of domestic ease. He also railed against the dawning era of mass image-making with the inexpensive and (then) ubiquitous 8 millimetre camera, condemning the frantic need to make films by those with '8 millimetre minds'. Little could he imagine the technological cascade that would follow. Grierson believed that non-fiction film could play an important role in ensuring social improvement and stability. While many attribute the profound influence of Kant, Hegel and Bradley in formulating his thought (Aitken 2006; Babe 2000; Lovell 1972), one must not discount how childhood Presbyterianism played a role throughout his life. He saw himself as a vicar of moral truths who, it must be recalled, found his first post after university as a preacher. Over the decades the Grierson philosophy remained unchanged and unflinching in its sense of certainty. Some felt that this certainty amounted to a caricature of unflinching predestination, as when Grierson claimed to be a prophet with authority from Moses (Evans 1984).

Grierson enjoyed shocking people by proclaiming he was a propagandist for democracy, a totalitarian for the good. These heavily laden contradictory phrases triggered an association with the better-known propagandists of his era: Joseph Goebbels in Nazi Germany (who flaunted the word with his ministry's title) and Edward Bernays in the United States (who disguised it with the innocuous-sounding watchword 'public relations'). Goebbels sold the politics of revolutionary National Socialism through the psychology of mass suggestion; Bernays understood how to manipulate the mass unconscious, too, and, in working the clay of American economic dogma, moulded an ideology of mass consumerism. Grierson's propaganda objective combined both selling and persuading. He inspired idealistic acolytes, an elite of educators whose information tried to pull a supposedly uncomprehending working class away from the abyss of modern despair and mindless 'individualist' pursuits. His elites tried to win hearts and minds with carefully wrought non-fiction images that could teach the optimism and comprehension of a non-idyllic complex world. Critics who found the hoary Grierson a throwback to another era missed the point that the past was of no interest to him: he was always looking beyond the present to the future, searching for the next generation of idealists whose commitments to his definition of education would, he believed, serve the best interests of citizens and the state.

Typically, also, Grierson painted his world view with a very wide brush in the 1960s, perceiving an alienated public adrift and in need of a filmed reality that conveyed harmonies, hopes and a sense of totality. Grierson was a practitioner of what later was called 'effects' theory, a two-step flow of communication that assumes mass media can change people as a hypodermic syringe injects its contents into a patient (Lazarsfeld 1944). He was probably unaware of contemporary theorists who were beginning to identify audience constituents (Gerbner 2002) and asking what uses audiences made of media messages (Katz 1955). Before the CRTC, Grierson defined his conception of non-fiction film in biblical terms as a form of propaganda, arguing, in a way that must have mystified the CRTC, that its origins lay in the 1622 congregation of the Roman Catholic Curia (*Sacra Congregatio de Propaganda Fide*), the Sacred Congregation for the Propagation of the Faith, a body responsible for sending missionaries out to counter the spread of Protestantism (CRTC 27

February 1969: 13–14; 18 June 1969: 150–2). Grierson thus clothed himself with the vestments of a prophet, and considered democracy's citizens a congregation adrift and felt a moral obligation to instil faith in them: that is, faith in the inherent value of the existing institutions of the state, institutions that marked a stage along the path towards the Absolute. Grierson never identified with either the liberal/free-market public sphere of commercial cinema or unregulated capitalism. Had he read critics such as Siegfried Kracauer, he would have dismissed Kracauer's belief that fictional cinema's emphasis on the disorder of society could help an audience find its own reality and spark radical change (Hansen 2012: 53–4). Grierson preferred order to disorder, and did not read Kracauer whose *Theory of Film* appeared in 1960. Grierson's reading was all but done by the time he made *Drifters* in 1929.

As mentioned, Grierson wanted film to advance notions of order, though, at least in the inter-war period that was also related to progressive social reform. In the inter-war years, Grierson developed the documentary film movement as a vehicle to reach an undifferentiated classless mass which he articulated simply as citizens – basically, everyone apart from elites such as, but not limited to those who ran the documentary film movement and similar. He never analysed who the audience for the films and writings of the movement might be because he had absorbed the core notions of mass society theory when in America during the 1920s. The audience was a mass audience plus opinion leaders. At the CRTC, his repetitive sermons were based on hopes of seeing Canadian media policy reaffirm his 1930s' conception of progressive, politically centralist development, when, in response to the Depression, government-led state funding and corporate funding in the United States and elsewhere supported large-scale social improvement programmes – which included the use of the film – to both redistribute wealth and – important to Grierson – stop the radical drift to both Right and Left. He found individualism, which he took to be the opposite of such social action, to be a Romantic delusion. Such thinking, however, was contrary to a 1960s' era that was escaping from the authoritarian conservatism of the 1950s and endorsing notions of free individualism. As an idealist, who admitted that propaganda was his operative skill, Grierson's defence was that everything should be for the common good and nothing was for oneself. Propaganda was necessary when it was for the common good and because social need had to be elevated over an individual need that otherwise would triumph destructively and anarchically. There is something akin to a notion of sin here, of human beings existing in a fallen state and in need of stoic discipline. He started and ended with a hope for central planning, public unity, and social discipline connected to, and derived from, his own idealist conception of unselfish humanitarian virtue (Evans 1984: 38, 42). Recalling the history of the documentary film movement at the CRTC sessions, he emphasised his lifelong concern with the role of mass education in a democratic society. During these sessions, he acknowledged his United States experience of the influential journalist–writer Walter Lippmann. That public-opinion guru expressed ideas about inspiring intellectual elites whose duty was to reach the 'people', an amorphous entity that needed guidance far more than universal suffrage. During the 1920s, Grierson had robustly rejected the antidemocratic elitism in Lippmann's position, what he called the 'intellectuals' case against the people', though he also accepted paradoxically Lippmann's contention that mass communication had to be generalised to be effective because the mass audience was not sufficiently intellectual (Aitken 2013: 57). In the 1920s and 1930s, Grierson believed that democracy was essential to keep selfish and predatory (and non-idealistic) elites in check, and he demanded to know how positions, such as that adopted by Lippmann and others, differed 'from those of fascism' (Aitken 2013: 57). In the CRTC sessions, however, the strong criticism of the antidemocratic Lippmann has disappeared, and only the endorsement of directive, positive mass communication, aimed at the mass audience remains, as the following illustrates:

> If you dramatise the news, you found a means by which you could bring alive the nature of society. This was the key to the modern educational problem and its solution . . . The final task is to bring the world alive to people and to make it worth living in, to give people a sense of their country, a confidence in their country and a confidence in the future and to create a will toward the future. (CRTC 11 April 1969: 122–5)

Grierson's position on the documentary film, as restated in the CRTC tapes, has, of course, been widely criticised. For example, Brian Winston has argued that Grierson's overall stance did not lead to the production of films that engaged in serious and critical analysis (Winston 1995: 55–8). Yet, within the unpropitious context of the existing film industry, the strategy of state and industrial documentary film sponsorship was a valid one, and not without difficulty. The object was, as one early Grierson acolyte opined, 'to get away with what we could' (Evans interview with Stuart Legg, 1976). The 1930s' balancing act found Grierson benefiting from helpful civil servants, such as Stephen Tallents, Sir William Crawford and Frank Pick, yet also facing more sceptical civil servants who examined invoices of public monies being spent and were hostile to his sometimes questionable operational duplicities. (Swann 1989: 49–94).Working within state and corporate funding institutions clearly raises questions concerning the ability of films and film-makers to adopt a critical and independent stance. Yet, Grierson's view was that this pact had to be made because there was not much alternative and, anyway, he was by inclination a corporatist with a corporatist view of society: he wanted to work within a corporate situation, preferably close to the heart of the state. Yet another criticism of what is taken to be the standard Grierson position relates to the supposed subordination of aesthetics to social purpose. Grierson believed that the documentarian's role was to manipulate reality artistically to create an emotional condition for the receptive viewer to gain some sort of propitious understanding of social reality and her/his place within that reality. Art had to be harnessed to emotion as well as intellect if it was to lead to such understanding but also, from his corporatist outlook, to belief in the value of the existing system. There is some ambivalence here. Depending on need and circumstance, Grierson called the movement sometimes anti-aesthetic and sometimes aesthetic. He once chastised Alberto Cavalcanti for spending too long on aesthetic issues. The perturbed film-maker's response was palpable and clever. 'Yes Grierson,' he replied, 'And the opposite of aesthetic is ANAESTHETIC and I won't do that!' (Evans 2005: 40). Yet, as disciple Stuart Legg recalled, Grierson's single command was, 'Thou shalt not be dull!' This was the tightrope between social purpose and aesthetics, creativity and mission that the Griersonian documentary sought to negotiate, though it could be argued that, for Grierson, purpose and mission came first.

In the CRTC tapes this dialectic becomes one between idealism and the aesthetic rather than the aesthetic and distinct social purpose, partly because, in his final years, Grierson talks in very broad terms: terms inimical to distinct polity. Grierson acknowledged the importance of aesthetics in reference to the picturesque films of Robert Flaherty. The CRTC asked him to comment on Flaherty's use of staged footage in 1922 to recreate a walrus hunt where there was no walrus. *Nanook of the North* was an idyllic film, Grierson replied, about man against the sky and man against nature, a vision of Canada as infinite loneliness and a silent country. So, is distorting the truth allowed, asked one interviewer? Distortion is what film can do, Grierson maintained, but only for the right reasons. Yes, he admitted, the Nanook walrus hunt was fiction but the struggle for food was not (CRTC, n.d. November 1970: 42–4; *Grierson*: 1972). He is not averse here to the use of assorted visual techniques to manipulate, so long as what he considered to be fundamental verities are expressed: the struggle for food; the evocation of a timeless nature; even the spirit of the *Zeitgeist*. Grierson did not use this Hegelian term in the 1960s, but he had in the 1920s, and the broad character of its signification carried on into the CRTC interviews (CRTC 18 March 1969: 110–12).

Attending one session, the Canadian intellectual Northrop Frye asked Grierson if television and film would be the media of teaching in the future. Grierson's reply assumed his long-held belief that moving images were effective in reaching those who were young and less literate (and less educated). He answered with his usual roundabout axiom, declaring the need to prepare the imagination of the children through dramatic media and criticising the current operation of television. Television must reconsider its position in the matter of judgement, he stated. 'I think it must reaffirm its position as a creator of public opinion,' because of the importance of time needed to think, 'You are over-communicated in the sense that nobody is taking anything in . . . You are not giving yourself enough time for consideration,' he warned (CRTC 27 February 1969: 27; n.d. November 1970: 548). This was (and remains) the critical flaw in television where rapid image proliferation and surface information saturation leave no room for deep thought (Postman 1986; Potter 2012). Grierson surprised the interviewers by expressing contempt for film-making then being introduced as a university discipline. It was all a waste of academic time. The message was all important, he asserted, and could best emanate from traditional authoritative university disciplines of political science, social psychology and aesthetics, not new film departments. While championing the new media of film, he had little time for the emerging university discipline of film studies, perhaps seeing in it a potential challenge to his vision.

As to the present and future of film and television, he referred to the 'culture front', describing culture as a means of forwarding some national vision. Art was not just a means of communication, not only a means of mirroring society but also of moulding and integrating society (CRTC 18 March 1969: 85). The university should shape minds, he repeated, though he also thought the wrong people were doing just that in the wrong manner, if the excessive contemporary use of the term 'revolution', a word he dismissed as empty rhetoric, was taken as an example. He was probably objecting to the language of this voluble era and wondering why very few students seemed interested in understanding the conservative Hegelian foundation of his thought, a foundation based on abstract continuity rather than on concrete radical fracture. His student days had been filled with debates about idealist philosophy where the object was to explore the relationship between notions such as finite and infinite, particular and universal, and nature and freedom. He referred to the word 'neaniolatry', 'infatuation with the immature', to criticise the so-called '8mm revolution' (the abundance of cheap cameras and film stock) engulfing North American universities in the late 1960s (CRTC 25 March 1971: 374–7). Here, his paternalistic notions on the need to seek a general understanding of things were contrary to the contemporary liberal, pluralist tide. To him, dissent allowed easy chatterbox access to television when the times called for artists to help build loyalties, an involvement with peoples' feelings and sentiments. The artist's function was to give pattern, to give dramatic line and justification to hopes and dreams. 'Any political power worth its salt must be concerned with what these creative people are shaping up for tomorrow,' he opined, worried about what those 'creative people' were up to and suspicious of them. The artist and the political elite had a need and duty to propagate faith in the society as a whole. His idea of faith was non-religious and probably off-putting to his listeners but very much consonant with the idea of spiritual and ethical belonging to the larger community. His circumscribed idea of freedom was also far from what he took to be the exaggerated sense of release from rules that he may have heard, or thought he heard, in campus rhetoric.

Grierson thought that television posed a particular threat here. He thought it a very popular notion and an easy televisual technique to defy, disturb and dislocate and be disputatious with authority. Grierson condemned television's opinion leaders for allegedly abusing their power in this regard though it is not clear whether he was reacting to what he himself saw on television or to an a priori expectation of what television must inevitably be (CRTC 24 November 1971: 498–503). This conservative-sounding authoritarian oratory evoked his own idealist education in philosophy and respect for traditional verities. He would not have disagreed with Bill Nichols who has analysed documentary as argument in a discourse of sobriety. Reading Nichols is somewhat like hearing echoes of elements of Grierson: documentary tells a story by showing something that has happened. It can reflect an ethical argument where scenes are arranged differently from the single time and space practice of fiction. It can also use written dialogue to heighten the sense of authenticity. The key is that there must be an intellectual and emotional engagement in an expression that seeks some kind of social truth. Nichols found common ground with Grierson's dictum about what documentary intended: to mobilise viewers to act with a more fully elaborated conception of their social structure and historical process. Nichols went further by including audience reception and the active viewer in his analysis. The very act of representation denotes what is represented, yet that thing also has a symbolic layer of connotation and ideology open to reading (Nichols 1994: 1–4, 16–19, 47, 95). In short, social class, gender and other factors have everything to do with an audience understanding something. Grierson saw this more generally; it was enough that the thing itself was a universally understood verity by all observers, and it was this universality which he strove to portray.

Wearing his esoteric (if conservative) mortar board at the CRTC in the autumn of 1970, Grierson cited Plato in the *Crito*. Given the chance to escape the judgment of the court and death, Socrates refused. He rejected the idea of private persons nullifying and destroying legal judgments of the state: '[Socrates] goes on to speak of all the things the individual owes to society and comes to the inevitable conclusion that the only freedom possible is an ordered freedom . . . You either persuade us or you do what we say' (CRTC 24 November, 1970: 87). This arbitrary classical citation must have surprised his hosts. He had been using this oratory at McGill where he was trying to staunch the flow of radical campus rhetoric with a call for responsibility, not revolutionary bombast. Such responsibility, based on authority, should involve the use of television to articulate a clear and positive social message, and there was no need to disguise that message. On the contrary, it, and the 'attitudes' behind it, should be boldly spelled out:

You can't give information without having a relationship with attitudes. The only thing to do is to be totally brave and say I assure you my attitudes will be honest and will be positive and not negative. This, rather than the negative, is something that I believe to be an important thing to emphasize. (CRTC 10 July 1971: n.p.)

The mass media, he continued, were vital instruments in a complicated world that could no longer be totally apprehended, and there was a need for modern government to provide a propaganda design of hope and belief, a will to act and a will to order, using the medium of television. His phrasing was anomalous in the sense that few listening to him would support government televisual propaganda as such but he envisioned an information system that was less about problems and more about consonance and hope; and an almost religious sense of mission creeps in here. He expounded on this by referring to his role as presenter in the decade-long television programme, *This Wonderful World*, in Scotland. His programme had featured examples of internationally produced documentaries that evoked appreciations of excellence. As host, his secret bond was not to a vast audience but to a very small one, a virtual family he cosied up to and ensured he did not hurt. Grierson, having been married to the same woman for almost five decades, never had children. The idea of family thus resonated strongly. One should think of the audience not as a crowd, he illustrated, but five people, a boy, a girl, a man a woman, and somebody old (CRTC 27 February 1969: 10–14). This, of course, is a conception of 'family viewing' which does not sit easily with the notion of analytical current-affairs broadcasting. Given such a vulnerable 'family', in need of protection, his reluctance to encourage non-fiction film's developing tendency to pursue 'problems' is understandable, though also problematic. Grierson was not opposed to critical and analytical explorations in documentary film but he thought they needed to be both constructive and balanced by films that promoted an audience's common positive beliefs, or what he repeatedly called 'faith'. During the 1930s, Grierson's first commandment of documentary had been to provide the working class with hope, and this gave the films of the British documentary film movement a critical edge. As Ian Aitken has observed, however, in the 1960s, the working-class focus of the 1930s seemed to have been replaced by a sort of religious notion of unified community, a fusion of religious idealism, political conservatism and desire for social harmony that evacuates criticism and fits well with Grierson's underlying conservative Hegelian philosophy (Evans discussion with Aitken, June 2015).

If the challenge was to promote a common faith, Grierson stated that the difficulty was the commercial television medium itself, 'where the message is split up every three minutes with an appeal to something completely extraneous like soap or whatever' (CRTC 18 March 1969: n.p.). Grierson's miscalculation was to think that the CRTC might try to alter the North American trends linking commercial television to a consumerist ethos. Pierre Juneau, the chairman of the CRTC, sat in on this session and may or may not have been impressed with the familiar Grierson bromide of education and hope to sustain spiritual unity within extant national institutions. In the end, the chairman preferred the idea of concentrating more on the first nations and various ethnic cultural identities, which Grierson referred to as 'tribal memories', than on some abstract notion of 'Canadian' culture and society (CRTC 18 June 1969: 299, 306, 311).

Grierson appeared to articulate the same vision here that he had set out for decades. Canada's challenge, he believed, was to use non-fiction film to bring the nation and its horizons alive to itself at home and abroad by promoting themes such as health, indigenous issues, mines, metals and resources, the Arctic, food, and geopolitical strategy. These were dramatic subjects because they concerned hope, development and identity (CRTC 3 March 1969: 24). Given his negative attitude to films that pursued 'problems', it is not surprising that he also took issue with the practice of direct cinema portraying what he called, somewhat ungenerously, 'victimhood'. One such example was the National Film Board's (NFB) *The Things I Cannot Change*, a largely undirected observation of a poverty-stricken family *in extremis*. The family was bewildered by, and chastised for, their notoriety following the screening (Evans 1991: 158–9). It was not the technique itself Grierson opposed but, rather, what he perceived to be the exploitation of unsophisticated persons who were allowed or encouraged to reveal their private life incidentally. Grierson regarded this as immoral and an indictment of NFB and television producers:

> If a man wants to be fully known, best it be his own decision; but to do that fortuitously . . . giving false witness belongs to mediocre people and mediocre organizations . . . Television demands ministers representing the imagination of the nation . . . (CRTC 27 February 1969: n.p.; 10 March 1969: n.p.; 25 March 1971: 378–9; Saunders 2007; Mamber 1973)

Documentaries about 'victimhood' ultimately became so prevalent that the variety of public audiences became less responsive, if not unresponsive, to their overabundance. In 2002, Susan Sontag wrote about the excess of images of war, noting how horrific images were a species of rhetoric that reiterated, simplified, agitated and created an illusion of consensus: a temporary unity of response and emotion that was forgotten with the next outrage or injustice. Grierson would probably have agreed with her assertion if it applied to images of victimhood that might numb viewers to the point of indifference (Sontag 2002: 82–98).

Whether such a process of numbing and forgetting was the case or not, to Grierson, the obsession with 'problems' and 'victimhood' was simply too negative and led away from the mission that Canadian television should have, which was to articulate an affirmative national vision; and Grierson also linked this obsession with the general role played by vested commercial interests in Canadian television, affirming to the chairman of the CRTC (Juneau) that 'You've let the vested interests in for far too much and you'll have to push them back, have to throw them back'. This was an easily articulated elixir but Grierson did not have to overcome Ottawa's and Parliament's reservations as Juneau did, even if he agreed with Grierson, which he probably did not. Grierson recommended a communication strategy which would demand that the networks invoke a sense of loyalty, of underlining the importance of being 'Canadian'. The world had become more secular but the people still wanted to believe. Like religion, he repeated, the communication pattern needed to give faith and hope: 'When one deals with television on a network, you are shouting in the only crowded cinema you've got in the whole of Canada,' he said. Such rhetoric was a platitude and also strangely authoritarian enough to have emanated from a totalitarian regime rather than from liberal Canada. Faith and hope and top–down direction as policy in a post-war Western democracy were stillborn and inappropriate.

If the zealotry and rhetoric here were questionable, though, there was a point in his complaint about the impact of 'mediocre' television personalities, the opinion leaders who practised the national art of 'the interview' on television. These celebrities were a *national* problem, he continued: 'Take a mediocrity and watch the mediocrity at work . . . What does the mediocre do? Sensationalise, melodramatise and give false witness.' (CRTC 27 February 1969: 34; 18 June 1969: 212, 224, 232–4). The temptation of television is to fill in time with instant opinions, instant confrontations, with everybody speaking at the same time and many people totally unprepared, he complained. This led to an abuse of the medium and worse, creation of inadequate, second-rate opinions. Television is like a wildfire, he warned, and could spread the contagion of rumour, creating alarm and despondency. It was a terribly violent and dangerous force because, unlike the press, of which there were numerous media examples, television allowed no fact against which it could be balanced. He predicted (fairly accurately) that network television in the decades ahead would continue to lull the country with unchallenged banalities (CRTC 11 April, n.p.; 18 June 1969: n.p.). His assault seemed to echo the Frankfurt School's critique of the culture industry, where media 'advice' was seen as vacuous, banal or shamelessly conformist, providing satisfactions which did not exist while disseminating infantilised norms (Adorno 1991, 1997). Grierson was unaware of that critique, however, and, anyway, was a 'positive' Hegelian, disconnected from the Frankfurt School's overall negative critique of capitalist modernity. Grierson wanted positive, rather than critical, televisual 'advice'. Grierson surmised that television's weakness was to have been put in the hands of amateurs whose petit bourgeois standards of entertainment were insufficient. Television personnel should be constantly subjected to the higher standards of intellectual examination represented by 'academic types', he urged. The job was to 'imaginate,' he continued, a word derived from Quebec French that expressed the need to dramatise Canada's imaginative life realistically in film and television output (CRTC 3 March 1969: 71–2; 18 June 1969: 208).

Grierson also had opinions about the relationship between images, television and text, and one of the examples he chose to cite in relation to this is both revealing and disturbing. Referring to a distinction between television and photography, and to the 1968 Tet Offensive in Vietnam, in which North Vietnamese forces made major gains in the Vietnam War, he cited the well-known sequence, captured on television, showing the national police chief of South Vietnam shooting a captured un-uniformed Viet Cong suspect in the head at point-blank range. There was no reaction from the public, said Grierson, yet, when the iconic photograph of the event by Eddie Adams appeared in the Montreal press, the public could not stop talking about it. Why? Television had no time for deep thought nor did it provide context to explain this grisly event. The newspaper article, which accompanied the photograph, did, and later 'explained' that the captive's cold-blooded execution, in violation of international law, was for alleged guerrilla activity that included the accused perpetrator's murder of South Vietnamese police officials and their families. The key point here for Grierson was that television had no time for context and depth, only cursory imagery (CRTC 27 February 1969: n.p.; 18 March 1969: 85–6; 18 June 1969: 146). But that should not have been the key point. What is unfortunate here is that, in making his point about the context of revenge being part of an 'explanation', or even mitigation for the killing which caught the public mind, and one that television did not and the press did convey, Grierson made no attempt to criticise the violation of international law, the Geneva Convention and the United Nations Universal Declaration of Human Rights which had occurred. This was all secondary to him, or of no concern whatsoever, even though he was appearing before, and talking to, a government body, the CRTC, which presumably had an obligation to support lawfulness. This was the sort of crassness which had bemused and worried British officials in the 1930s. Human rights as a major international issue only really emerged after 1945 with the promulgation of the United Nations Charter. Grierson's stance positions him as a pre-1945 person, out of consonance with a 1960s world view.

Continuing his criticism of television, and on a more progressive note, Grierson set out a range of policies in the CRTC interviews. Beginning to understand the multiplicity of audiences being created by cable, he predicted that decentralisation of television would be the future. He wanted the CRTC to oblige local cable television to work with community league and local personalities so that communications might be more representative of participatory democracy. He believed that with image-making tools placed in local hands for local storytelling, cable might serve vital community interests (CRTC October n.d. 1969: 395–8, 407). Grierson was mistaken. Cable led to the creation of new conglomerates that would control multiple-themed channels with powers similar to the main broadcasters. Nevertheless, Grierson's pluralism here is curious, as it does not gel with the centralising and authoritarian tendencies implicit and explicit in many of his other comments given in the CRTC interviews. Grierson also suggested the establishment of a review body that would critique television itself, a variant on his theme of having television overruled by an intellectual elite (CRTC 24 November, 1971: 531–3). He recommended less dependence on advertising revenues. He suggested taking a whole year to make a programme so as to achieve deeper and more profound efforts. Those who produced television had a national duty to perform, a duty whose economic cost, he stated cavalierly, should be borne by the federal government (CRTC 27 February 1969: n.p.; 18 March 1969: n.p.). He urged Canadian film and television to avoid trying to imitate the United States commercial model, arguing that such a model was inappropriate to a country with a much smaller population, and was also over-influenced by commerce. Husband your resources preciously, he repeated: do not squander them on insignificant television output but, instead, look to the building of national imagination and intelligence at every level (CRTC 18 March 1969: n.p.). Such idealist rhetoric, though, was far removed from the concrete objectives and needs of policymakers. If the interviewee was enjoying his time at the microphone, the congregation was not impressed. The fact was that the Canadian Broadcasting Corporation and the National Film Board had neither the will nor the financial means to underwrite a Griersonian national, idealist mission for television which was so counter to the prevailing commercial model. Nevertheless, this does not detract from the fact that, here, Grierson is calling for television to be used in a serious rather than trivial manner, as an important constituent of reflective lived experience.

Though Grierson made, as mentioned, some reference to the need for Canadian television to be to localised and pluralist, the bulk of his comments in the CRTC interviews unquestionably focused on the need to develop 'national' forms of film-making and storytelling which would manifest a Hegelian idea of the nation as a matrix of continuing, evolving institutions, with the state at the centre. He assumed that there would be no resistance to such, without recognising that the paternalism and elitism inherent in the approach might generate resistance. Here, again, Grierson's reliance on a one-way stream of communication was problematic. Grierson also had little practical to say about the difficulty of representing the modern national event, seemingly taking it for granted that such representation should be understandable and accomplishable. Later, Nichols (1994) would identify the challenge of what he called the blurred boundaries of selection and arrangement of non-fiction imagery and the uncertainty of the whole non-fiction enterprise of representing national social 'reality'. Such a challenge was never Grierson's worry because, to his Hegelian mind, universal Good existed and was always waiting to be revealed.

The interviewers asked his opinion about feature films. Ottawa had created the Canadian Film Development Corporation (CFDC) to satisfy a cultural demand and create a technical infrastructure for such production (Fetherling 1988: 83–8). Grierson advised against Canadian feature-film production. It made little sense to set up new studios and the paraphernalia of feature-film production when United States production centres were so close by. The issue was to find production values that could compete internationally. Canadian features needed international stars and internationally good producers and directors so, it was best, he cautioned, to collude with the Americans and the international set at the feature film level. He suggested, in contrast, experimenting with hour-long featurettes that, if successful, could lead to international productions later. Grierson's views on this and other matters did not translate into practical policy. His error was both to have employed terminology which was decades old and to have believed the government would deliberately undertake the same sort of peacetime support of non-commercial films that it had in wartime. Whether he knew it or not, in 1970, the still fiery Grierson was heading towards his final act, as cancer was spreading through his body. Undeterred, he became part of a federal government/NFB mission to India to investigate how Canada could assist that nation's family-planning programme. Worsening health forced him to return to England where he entered hospital and shortly thereafter died. Loquacious to the end, he was found with a microphone in hand, a tape recorder reel spinning, its tape having run out.

CONCLUSIONS

Taken as a whole, the Grierson's CRTC interviews reveal a passionate patriarch recounting his former glories and sermons. If one ignores the cant and excessive language, there was also a point in calling for better non-fiction representations in the public service. And Grierson also emerges as a theorist of television. But times had changed, society was neither in crisis nor war, and his nostrums were too authoritarian for policymakers to take seriously. Perhaps he did not appreciate that a new era was more interested in promoting commercialism or libertarianism than state-oriented idealism. Grierson was obsessive and paternalistic about non-fiction imagery, perhaps for having no other offspring than his once-renowned documentary film movement and a classless audience he pictured as his cosy family. A psychologist might speculate about this contrarian personality who took pleasure in verbal jousting while challenging contemporary truisms that celebrated individual freedom without responsibility, or seemed to take an immature or uninterested approach to revelations about defects in the social system. He had started professional life as a sermoniser and continued this work until his death. After all, a sermoniser must provide faith and positive ideals to his congregation, and this Grierson assumed was his self-appointed lifelong task. He elided over the issue of what should constitute non-fiction content by calling for the same social idealism (propagandising) that had once motivated him and his acolytes. His criticisms of broadcast television were (and still are) valid but the CRTC thought that, besides favouring Canadian content and multiculturalism, it was best to leave the public and private broadcasters and media celebrities largely alone. Grierson had shifted his focus from concern for the working man in the crisis-laden 1930s and 1940s to urge again public funding to harness and create some sort of human good. He called it faith, expecting his use of the radical phrase totalitarian would receive a positive resonance. But repeating such homilies probably annulled the impact he intended to have. Recalling the lesson of Lippmann, his objective was to inspire a new congregation of faithful, gifted elites to push civilisation forward technically, artistically, and spiritually. Grierson, the Hegelian moral philosopher, erroneously believed that an educated elite might reach a single audience with inspiring positive non-fiction imagery. But multiple and sophisticated audiences now demanded and consumed media texts like a smorgasbord of desserts, from sports to varied entertainments to fictions, and – lastly – non-fiction genres. Grierson's authoritarian testament stated that a propagandist must never bear false witness, nor articulate a state-supported Big Lie. Today, he would probably denounce a media-saturated society that applauds personal celebrity, self-congratulation and perhaps even the vicarious stimulation of viewing worldwide violence. In spite of the abundance of competing media texts that constitute audience composition and reception, he would probably repeat everything he articulated above. His single-minded paternalism aside, one can appreciate his mission: to waken uninformed audiences of all stripes to understand they have a purpose and useful place in an incomprehensible present, and that non-fiction images and words may replace neglect or nonchalance with hope. A few days before his death, he told his wife that the most dangerous pitfall is the loss of faith in the human spirit. To the end, he never lost that ideal, and the influence upon him of the idealist tradition also grew stronger in his final years.

REFERENCES

Adorno, T. W. (1991), *The Culture Industry*, London: Routledge.

Adorno, T. W. and Horkheimer M. (1997), *Dialectic of Enlightenment*, trans. J. Cummins, London: Verso.

Aitken, Ian (1990), *Film and Reform: John Grierson and the Documentary Film Movement*, London: Routledge.

— (2006), *Realist Film Theory and Cinema*, Manchester: Manchester University Press.

— (2012), *Documentary Film: Critical Concepts in Media and Cultural Studies*, London: Routledge.

Babe, Robert (2000), *Canadian Communication Thought: Ten Foundational Writers*, Toronto: University of Toronto Press.

Bazin, André (1997), *Bazin at Work: Major Essays and Reviews from the Forties and Fifties*, trans. Alain Piette and Bert Cadullo, New York and London: Routledge.

Blais, Roger (1972), *Grierson*, Montreal: National Film Board of Canada.

Ellis, Jack C. (2000), *John Grierson: Life, Contributions, Influence*, Carbondale, IL: Southern Illinois University Press.

Evans, Gary (1984), *John Grierson and the National Film Board: The Politics of Wartime Propaganda*, Toronto: University of Toronto Press.

— (1991), *In the National Interest: A Chronicle of the National Film Board of Canada, 1949 to 1989*, Toronto: University of Toronto Press.

— (2005), *John Grierson: Trailblazer of Documentary Film*, Montreal: XYZ Publishing.

Fetherling, Douglas (1988) (ed.), *Documents in Canadian Film*, Peterborough, ON: Broadview Press.

Gerbner, George (2002), *Against the Mainstream : The Selected Works of George Gerbner*, Morgan, Michael (ed.), New York: Peter Lang.

Grierson, John (1979), *Transcripts of André Martin and Rodrigue Chiasson's interviews with John Grierson, 1969–1971*, Ottawa: Canadian Radio-television and Telecommunications Commission (CRTC). There are four bound volumes and three additional binders that contain fragments of interviews, with and without dates.

Hansen, Miriam (2012), *Cinema and Experience*, Berkeley, CA: University of California Press.

Hardy, Forsyth (1979), *John Grierson, a Documentary Biography*, London: Faber.

Katz, Elihu and Lazarsfeld, Paul F. (1955), *Personal Influence: The Part Played by People in the Flow of Mass Communications*, Glencoe, IL: Free Press.

LeMahieu, D. L. (1988), *A Culture for Democracy: Mass Communication and the Cultivated Mind in Britain Between the Wars*, New York: Clarendon Press.

Lovell, Alan and Hillier, Jim (1972), *Studies in Documentary*, London: Secker and Warburg.

Mamber, Stephen (1974), *Cinéma Vérité in America: Studies in Uncontrolled Documentary*, Cambridge, MA: The MIT Press.

Nichols, Bill (1994), *Blurred Boundaries: Questions of Meaning in Contemporary Culture*, Bloomington, IN: Indiana University Press.

Postman, Neil (1986), *Amusing Ourselves to Death : Public Discourse in the Age of Show Business*, New York: Penguin.

Potter, W. James (2012), *Media Effects*, Thousand Oaks, CA: Sage.

Plantinga, Carl (1997), *Rhetoric and Representation in Nonfiction Film*, New York: Cambridge University Press.

Saunders, Dave (2007), *Direct Cinema: Observational Documentary and the Politics of the Sixties*, New York: Wallflower Press.

Sontag, Susan (2002, 9 December), 'Looking at War', *The New Yorker*, pp. 82–98. Retrieved from: www.college.colombia.edu/core/files/pages/Sontag-essay.pdf

Swann, Paul (1989), *The British Documentary Film Movement 1926–1946*, Cambridge: Cambridge University Press.

Tudor, Andrew (1974), *Theories of Film*, London: Secker and Warburg.

Winston, Brian (1995), *Claiming the Real: The Griersonian Documentary and its Legitimations*, London: British Film Institute.

CHAPTER 12

John Grierson: From the Poster Movement to the Informational State

Scott Anthony

This chapter has its genesis in the 'Re-thinking the British Official Film' presentation I gave at *The Documentary Film in South and South-East Asia* conference held at Hong Kong Baptist University in August 2013. In addition to benefiting from conversations there I would particularly like to thank, along with Ian Aitken, Line Hjorth Christensen, Henry K. Miller, James Purdon and John Wyver for helping me to further develop my thoughts. Thanks also to Eve Colpus, Peter Mandler, Lisa Onaga, Patrick Russell and Martin Stollery who helped improve an earlier draft of the essay. This research was made possible by the generous support of Nanyang Technological University, Singapore.

The work and writings of John Grierson hold a foundational place in film history. Grierson's essay *First Principles of Documentary* has become a staple of serious anthologies of film.[1] The ubiquity of Grierson's writing – along with that of his acolytes, such as Paul Rotha and Forsyth Hardy – is both a testament to its forcefulness and clarity and also to a degree of temporal good fortune. Grierson is afforded a generous – if not kind – place in early film history because he lurks behind the writing of much of it.[2] Punchy, well-informed and enjoyably partisan books such as Rotha's *The Film Till Now: A Survey of the Cinema* (1930) were pioneers in their field when published, and the generous space they afforded Grierson helped ensure that he remained a much-discussed figure as film became an object of serious study in post-war universities.

To date Grierson's influence has been evaluated against the relationship between changing representations of reality and social and political change. Grierson's efforts to mould 'documentary cinema' – first in Britain, then across the British Empire, and later across the world – have become grist to a series of sizeable critical mills (Druick and Williams 2014). At the same time,

Grierson's reputation appears to have become steadily more precarious. His work on documentary has, for a while, attracted a degree of ill-humoured ideological denouncement (Winston 1995). Now, massive digitisation programmes – in the United Kingdom very much driven by the British Film Institute – have brought to wider appreciation both the existence of an enormous amount of documentary cinema that pre-exists his 'documentary movement', as well as a large number of 'documentaries' that were produced at the same time as those of Grierson's 'movement' but which are excluded from discussion with them despite their formal similarities. As scholars such as Charles Musser have pointed out, the adjective 'documentary' was in common use in English-speaking contexts by the late nineteenth century as a description of certain types of photography, and was applied to certain types of film-making in France in the early 1920s (Musser 2013: 123). 'Documentary' as a term and as a practice is thus undergoing a period of reformulation, and one consequence of this is that our understanding of John Grierson's contribution to the field is also changing.

Yet we should be cautious. The enormous film digitisation programmes of the early twenty-first century have clear interpretative limits. In particular, they risk overlooking formative non-filmic influences. As film scholarship took root in universities and as universities became centres for the mass production of film criticism, huge amounts of intellectual effort were expended on understanding 'film as film'. The danger is that mass film digitisation compounds this tendency of further bracketing out significant non-filmic influences. We need to recognise that Grierson was not just a theorist of documentary realism in the 1930s, he spent his entire career developing theories of visual communication and media technology as well as building the administrative apparatus to put them into practice. Without diminishing the profundity of Grierson's engagement with film and film history, it is worth stressing that the practices he encouraged were at least as informed by non-filmic currents of thought and practice. As a lecturer, Grierson would praise the new generation of 'direct carvers' in modern sculpture, praising the work of artists such as John Skeaping (whom he would later employ as a set designer on his 1929 film *Drifters*) for their truth to materials in critical terms very similar to those that he would use when encouraging documentarians to record everyday life on celluloid (Grierson 1930; Skeaping 1977). Similar analogies could also be drawn between the British documentary movement and the emerging critical vocabularies of British modernist architecture and ballet developed by such figures as John Summerson and Arnold Haskell. Such borrowings were necessary. As a theorist of an emerging medium and a pioneering film producer, how could it have been otherwise? There is no longer much mystery about the immediate filmic context that Grierson operated in. What is at present still missing from the debate is an appreciation of Grierson's intellectual reach – an understanding of the resources he drew upon, and engaged with, outside the cinema.

The contribution of this chapter to recent debates about Grierson's role in film theory is to step outside the normal parameters of film scholarship and revisit Grierson's employment at the Empire Marketing Board (EMB) in order to tell the story of his involvement with a wider modernist 'poster movement' and his engagement with the political, artistic and social operation of that movement. By doing this we can reconnect Grierson's writings on film with broader currents of cultural activism, as well as the post-war emergence of media theory. For the last thirty years film scholars have acknowledged that a full appreciation of Sergei Eisenstein's theories on cinema demands an appreciation of far wider artistic, intellectual and cultural terrain. Now seems a good time to pay John Grierson's work similar respect.

THE EMPIRE MARKETING BOARD, THE 'POSTER MOVEMENT' AND JOHN GRIERSON

The relationship between the EMB and the birth of documentary cinema in Britain has long been established. Set up as a political pacifier to tariff reformers under the direction of Stephen Tallents, the board served as something of a cultural (as well as a scientific) laboratory sponsoring interesting and idiosyncratic work in a variety of applied arts, ostensibly to encourage 'Empire-mindedness' but implicitly to combat a coterie of protectionists pressurising the then government of Prime Minister Stanley Baldwin to introduce economic protection measures for imperial trade. Grierson was recruited by Tallents on the recommendation of the poet Robert Nichols, and eventually persuaded his superior to underwrite experiments in non-fiction film. Grierson's *Drifters*, a documentary about the fishing industry produced in a style that referred to experimental Soviet cinema, was a beneficiary of EMB patronage. The film's *succès d'estime* afforded Grierson the opportunity (which he hungrily grasped) to build an ad hoc non-fiction film school and propagate theories about the past, present and future of documentary cinema. The stage was set for documentary to become – in that now notorious phrase – Britain's 'outstanding contribution' to film (*The Factual Film* 1947: 11).[3] While the EMB has long been recognised as an important financial sponsor of documentary cinema, however, it has been afforded little significance in actually shaping conceptions of documentary film. Those sympathetic to Grierson and 'the Griersonian project' have tended to emphasise his entrepreneurship: during an economic slump Grierson found a way to channel Civil Service money into an experimental venture (Rotha 1973). By contrast, a larger group of more sceptical or ideologically strident critics have argued that British documentary's roots in an imperial or governmental project (though the nature of the 'imperialism' that the board promoted is seldom examined) hardwired a series of fundamental political and aesthetic limitations into the form (Pronay 1989: 227–46). One of the melancholy consequences of this impasse has been to obscure the importance of the Empire Marketing Board in understanding the genesis of Grierson's conception of 'the documentary movement'. Unpicking Grierson's involvement with 'the poster movement' at the EMB is essential to improving further our understandings of the 'Griersonian' documentary.

The term 'poster movement' was coined in the 1920s by Martin Hardie, Keeper of the Department of Engraving, Illustration and Design at the Victoria and Albert Museum, to describe the network of patrons, critics and artists orbiting around Frank Pick (Christensen 2015: 146). Posthumously labelled a 'modern Maecenas' by the art historian Nicholas Pevsner, Pick used his position as chief executive officer on the London Underground to instigate major programmes of artistic and educational patronage that self-consciously aspired to echo those of the Renaissance (Pevsner 1942: 31–48). Driven by ideas appropriated from John Ruskin, Henry Maine and religious Non-conformism, Pick sought both to spiritually re-animate and modernise what he saw as the hierarchical conventions of high art and formal education. For example, just as Pick's fellow Non-conformists rejected High Anglican forms of worship, he sought to encourage a broad-based intervention in the arts that was participatory; and cross-class cohesion and moral growth were the looked-for consequences of such social and cultural communion. Not only were posters and the reconfiguration of public buildings and spaces central to Pick's project of social and moral renewal, as President of the Design Industries Association (DIA) he also pursued the idea of design-led social transformation on a grander scale.

The 'poster movement' gathered pace through the interwar period. According to Line Hjorth Christensen, its broad (and in European terms radical) significance was that it prompted galleries, museums and prestige publishers to take note of public taste and involvement in areas of cultural activity usually understood as being the province of cultural–social elites (Christensen 2015: 143). Institutions which responded in this manner ranged from the Royal Academy, to the Mansard Gallery based in the retailer Heals, and the charitable Arts League of Service; and the significant public appetite for high-quality modern (and often modernist) art had these institutions and a whole stratum of post-World War I civil society scrabbling to keep pace with demand from provincial schools, clubs and voluntary associations. Along with the EMB, the key patrons of this poster movement included the London Underground, the Shell Oil Company, and the General Post Office, along with national and regional aviation, rail and shipping companies. Their employment of leading fine and commercial artists ultimately pushed poster art beyond narrow instrumental functionalism, and the geographical spread of these companies' economic interests also led them – with varying degrees of enthusiasm – to underwrite the larger social projects of the poster movement. Pick's commitment was to raise popular aesthetic standards and, with them, he and his acolytes believed, moral qualities. The ethical and political dimensions of this project – which both rejected and drew upon aspects of the Arts and Crafts movement – were further strengthened through its holistic operation. The British poster movement was not simply concerned with the production of high-quality posters, it concerned itself with democratising practices of curation, criticism and education. The significance of the movement thus rests not just on the formal and technological innovations developed by a talented group of artists, including Edward McKnight Kauffer, Ashley Havinden and Abram Games, but the ways in which this work provided a forum for the worlds of business, politics and the arts to reconfigure their relationship with a wider populace. Thanks to their efforts, popular and poster art was to become an object of cultural care and discussions about public spaces central to larger debates about the nature of democracy.

What should be obvious, even from the brief written portrait of the British poster movement above, are its many points of overlap with the goals of Grierson's British documentary movement. What is more, the 'documentary movement' shared many of its patrons, personnel and creative infrastructure, not to mention ethos, with the poster movement: the 'footnote men' of British modernism, such as Stephen Tallents, Jack Beddington and Frank Pick, have, until recently, been even more overlooked influences on the development of British film culture (Artmonsky 2006; Anthony 2012; Green 2013).[4] In terms of the development of Grierson's thinking about documentary cinema, his contribution to the Exhibition of British and Foreign Posters at the Victoria and Albert Museum (V&A) in 1931, curated by Martin Hardie, is also worth outlining in greater detail.

The Significance of the V&A Poster Exhibition of 1931

The staging of the Exhibition of British and Foreign Posters at the Victoria and Albert Museum in 1931 represented an apogee for the poster movement. This important exhibition represented a major break with the V&A's norms of display. Previously criticised by both a Royal Commission and the Federation of British Industries for its bias towards collectors and connoisseurs, Hardie's exhibition saw the V&A eschew formal presentation to turn the gallery into something approaching the equivalent of a 'typical' urban street scene, in the process breaking up the standard chronological logic of the museum's displays

(Christensen 2015: 150). The exhibition was large in scale, with more than six hundred posters displayed. It was the first time the Museum had dedicated a show to popular poster images, and the appeal was directed squarely towards the general public. The staging of the exhibition emphasised a variety of dynamic viewing positions – the show was not of posters simply being hung as if they were in a conventional art gallery. The exhibition also mixed work from the nineteenth century with contemporary examples, thereby establishing an historical continuity and also a link between popular experience and the museum. Hardie's ambition was to bring the V&A to life, just as the EMB and General Post Office (GPO) Film Units sought 'to bring alive' the operation of the Empire and the General Post Office (Tallents 1934; Constantine 1986a).

Grierson was himself actively involved with aspects of the poster movement. Part of his own collection (he was a Toulouse-Lautrec enthusiast) was loaned to the V&A for the 1931 exhibition. The posters and frames of the Empire Marketing Board were at the heart of the show and the recipients of considerable critical acclaim.[5] Here it is worth drawing out the significance of the Board's custom-made poster frames. By the end of 1928, EMB frames occupied nearly a thousand sites around the country (Constantine 1986b). Made up of five panels – three large pictorial panels and two smaller panels dominated by text – these large wooden frames formed the bedrock of a new kind of information infrastructure. This distinctive arrangement was born of several factors. Perhaps most importantly the formal separation between image and text betrayed the board's Civil Service roots. For reasons of official propriety, statistics about production (or consumption) in the Empire had to be presented separately from the artistic impressions of production (or consumption) (Grant 1994; L'Etang, J. 2008; Anthony 2012). The EMB was attempting to forge an idiom of public information, and part of that effort was self-consciously to present its messages in ways that both avoided accusations of illicit persuasion and that straightforwardly harnessed both 'objective' facts about the Empire and aesthetically sophisticated imaginings of it.

It is also striking that the separation between image and text here echoed the form of silent cinema. We tend to think of Grierson purely in terms of his writings about documentary film but there is very little recognition of Grierson's experiments with artistic form. Just as Grierson oversaw the production of poster displays which mirrored forms of silent cinema, so the EMB Film Unit also commissioned 'poster films' which were formally innovative. Paul Rotha's *Australian Wine* (1931) was projected on to public spaces (such as the concourses of railway stations) or toured in specially converted vans that served as mobile community cinemas. Working with H. D. Waley, the EMB patented a small daylight projector designed to work as an 'automatic cinema' at the V&A.[6] The EMB also appear to have experimented with 'visual jukeboxes' in the mould of the Mills Panoram.[7] At the least, then, understanding Grierson's position in terms of his participation in the poster movement helps us recover the material reasons for his enthusiasm for the non-theatrical display of film, and encourages us to revisit the ways in which he conceptualised audiences.

It could also be argued that the norms established by the poster movement were integrated into the production and exhibition of *Drifters*. The film's release was accompanied by the production of a series of poster displays (whose images were apparently based on stills from the film) in support of the 'Eat More Fish!' campaign. Underwritten by the British Trawler Federation, this multimedia campaign, co-ordinated by the EMB, was credited with leading to a surge in fish and chip sales (Walton 1994). Perhaps because of this, Andrew Buchanan, a film producer and historian, described *Drifters* as an epic that 'places the advertisement film on an entirely new level' (Buchanan 1932: 202). Buchanan's observation was a shrewd one. The 'process film', which shows how raw materials are transformed into packaged products, distributed, delivered and consumed, has a long prehistory in non-fiction film (Sargeant 2012: 38–56). Films such as Cricks and Sharp's *Peak Freans* (1906), Charles Urban's *A Day in the Life of a Coalminer* (1910) and Lever Brothers' *Port Sunlight* (1919) are illustrative of the ways in which such process films had long been embedded in advertising practice. Even a cursory flick through Pitman's 1939 manual *The Technique and Practice of Advertising* illustrates the extent to which techniques and idioms refined at the EMB were practised elsewhere. Consulting the trade literature of the time illustrates that the EMB often utilised standard forms. In *Drifters*, this legacy can be glimpsed in the series of overlapping dissolves that brings the film to a close and which serves to underline the social interconnectedness of different aspects of the work and life of the herring fishermen.

Nevertheless, while *Drifters* appropriated part of its structure from the process film, it imbued those borrowings with a symbolic purposefulness. The cycle of production, distribution and consumption was configured in terms that were social as much as economic. The 'process film' was a form that could be used as a metaphor on which to hang a political vision of an interconnected society. The central narrative thread of *Drifters* is connection; the trawler's log-line, the row of women gutting herring, the roads and railway lines. The film emphasises the bravery of the fishermen but celebrates their integration into the modern world rather than their exceptionalism. *Drifters* illustrates how, from its inception, Grierson's documentary movement participated in a potent visual idiom that made mutually beneficial relationships between Britain's extractive, manufacturing and consumer industries into the dominant political, economic and moral truth of the mid-century United Kingdom. From Britain's departure from the gold standard in 1931 until the end of the Bretton Woods monetary agreement in the early 1970s, the national socio-economic imaginary was also rebalanced away from consumption towards production. The documentary movement nurtured, and was nurtured by, this shift in political economy and these newly imagined relationships. The idiom in which it participated, however, was one whose patrons and imaginative potency would be steadily undermined by the resurgence of economic and social liberal individualism towards the end of the twentieth century as the so-called post-war consensus (which had its roots in the 1930s) was replaced by a different conception of political economy propagated by the Thatcher governments but also supported by wider shifts in global trade.

Additionally, while these connections within which the documentary movement was embedded – together with the revelation that advertising techniques were as least as important to the Griersonian project as those of Soviet modernism – have often been used as a critical stick with which to beat the publicly declared aims of the movement, in its particular socio-economic and artistic context we can perhaps see how fulfilling an objective instrumental purpose was understood as an appropriate path to much grander social and artistic ambitions and not an abnegation of them as critics of the documentary movement in the later twentieth-century have tended to assume. Sir William Crawford, the dominant figure in the UK's advertising industry, believed himself on a mission to 'civilise' as well as modernise his profession – and was a conspicuous sponsor of both scientific research and high-quality applied art (Saxon-Mills 1954; Anthony 2008). No one would argue that Games's work for commercial and government clients diminished its importance, or that William Morris's political commitments were invalidated because money from the Anglo-Persian Oil Company paid for his work at Stanmore Hall; so it is far from apparent why the Griersonian project should be summarily dismissed simply because of its origins and relations with corporate industry (Anthony and Russell 2014: 252–61).

REINTERPRETING 'THE GRIERSONIAN TRADITION'

Looking back on the early history of the British documentary movement from more than twenty-five years ago, Paul Swann wrote that it was increasingly difficult to claim that Grierson's interventions had any kind of lasting influence (Swann 1989). He argued that Grierson's efforts – though much publicised at the time – had proved fruitless. The economic and organisational advantages possessed by Griersonian rivals in Hollywood and on television, in addition to their greater imaginative appeal, had ensured that the efforts of British documentary cinema to build a distinct film-making culture were doomed to failure. Not only did Grierson wage an unwinnable war but he was inhibited by an 'elitist' middle-class mindset that sought only to 'collect, collate, and represent those aspects of political and social life they felt the public ought to know' (Swann 1989: 178). If John Grierson had a legacy, it was that he had encouraged the state to play an active role in the arts: the cultural industries being among the few remaining parts of Britain's economy where something approaching an industrial policy exists.

One can sympathise with much of what Swann wrote. In 1989 the Griersonian documentary had become synonymous with the sponsored film but that source of work dried up with the privatisation of key industries and utilities. Privatisation was underpinned by new theories of management, ways of accounting inimical to the idea that social and economic interrelations were deep rooted, let alone that these had a moral as well as economic basis. The idea of the process film had become redundant as industrial production was no longer foundational to the national imaginary. In the 1930s, Britain had imported food and energy and exported manufactured goods but by the 1980s the position had reversed, and the export of energy and agriculture paid for the import of manufactured goods. Where the Grierson tradition survived it appeared to have mutated into the considerably less ambitious corporate training video. It is easy to see why Swann judged that Grierson's theories about film had operated primarily as 'a bridge between the communications and public relations philosophies that emerged in the United States and a Britain that was learning to operate on the basis of consensus' (Swann 1989: 178). Other academics, such as the Marxist former *World in Action* film-maker, Brian Winston, have pointed to the total irrelevance of 'the Grierson tradition' to television documentary practices in Britain (Winston 2014: 101–15).

In the early twenty-first century the world looks a very different place from the one described by Swann. If much of his research remains impressive, the contingent nature of his interpretation has become more obviously problematic. It certainly appears to be the case that, at least until the advent of Channel 4 on British television in 1982, the Griersonian tradition had little influence on formal practices of documentary on television in the United Kingdom (although this is hardly surprising – the BBC had been the formative influence on British television and its television documentary formats developed out of techniques first honed in radio broadcasting). At its inception, Channel 4 perhaps returned a documentary form rooted in modernist rather than journalistic traditions to public prominence, a form that had otherwise migrated on to the more specialised pastures of the education, scientific and official film. What has been of more significance to the upsurge of interest in 'the Griersonian tradition' has been the growing plurality of the national media industry (of which Channel 4 was an early example) and the technological changes that have framed (and also perhaps contained) this plurality.

In an age where the moving image has escaped from both the cinema and the television set, Grierson's interest in non-traditional forms of film distribution now appears prescient. In an age of digital connectivity, 'films' come in many forms: they can be shared and discussed in multiple forums and have become sites for all manner of social and political activism. The poster film has become ubiquitous. Previously, marginal work, such as *The Peace Film* (1936), *We Live in Two Worlds* (1937), and *Advance Democracy!* (1938), suddenly appear as precursors to campaigning productions as different as *Luke's World* (2012) by the Private Equity Foundation and Russell Brand's *The Trews* (2014–15). Grierson and Waley's efforts to project images inside and outside museums segue into the recent popularity of 'live exhibitions' projected into cinemas by the Royal Academy, the National Ballet and the V&A. Equally, now that a large national audience cannot be simply taken for granted by British television producers and is, instead, imagined by them as a series of separate constituencies that need to be knitted together, his insistence in working through a variety of voluntary and civic associations appears increasingly contemporary.

The assertion that 'the documentary movement' was limited by its middle-class mindset is also open to challenge. Part of the issue is that Swann's work was written under the influence of cultural studies and therefore, to some extent, reproduces Marxist assumptions that significant social change must be led either by the working classes or by an assortment of avant-garde shock troops. Malte Hagner recently tried to invert the usual story of the 'heroic failure' of the interwar cinematic avant-garde by instead focusing on the lasting legacy of innovative institutions, creative networks and educational practices that figures like Grierson helped to build (Hagener 2007). For historians of interwar Britain, the broad cultural sweep that Hagener identifies as significant is not news. It's been long argued – by everyone from Michael Frayn to Arthur Marwick – that middle-class commitment was the bedrock of Britain's dawning 'social-democratic moment' (Frayn 1963; Marwick 1964). The fact, however, that the post-war consensus associated with Clement Attlee's Labour administration was not 'revolutionary' was one of the things that led the new Left, as well as the new Right, to condemn it in the 1970s.

It is worth looking at the evidence that underpins Swann's argument that the EMB's 'middle-class' attitudes (where 'middle-class' is understood to be synonymous with tepid and ineffective) ensured that the EMB's posters as well as its films were of limited value, utility and interest: parliamentary interventions from three minor Conservative MPs and a quote from a trade body in direct competition with the EMB (Swann 1989: 24, 49). The recent work of scholars such as Christensen suggests the opposite: that the astonishing popularity of initiatives such as 'the poster movement' was one of the factors that made British modernism unique, drawing together a wide cross section of enthusiasm for artistic forms that were elsewhere colonised entirely by elites. The transference of energies from various avant-garde groupings into large institutions identified by Hagener became possible because it was partly driven by public enthusiasm.

Drawing on recent research by Henry K. Miller, we can also make a connection back to our understanding of interwar film culture (Miller 2014: 412–28). Miller has argued that the self-conscious efforts of film scholarship in the 1970s to 'rehabilitate' popular forms of British cinema entailed an equally self-conscious project dedicated to propagating a version of 'high' British film culture that overstated the latter's antagonistic relationship with 'popular' British film culture. Through a painstaking process of critical recovery Miller has illustrated that the polarised and polarising critical dichotomies of the 1970s are questionable – during the interwar period, Britain developed a film culture where there were both popular enthusiasm for 'high art' film and 'high art' critics freely praising popular films. Here, our understanding of British modernism, like British film culture and British politics (let alone the inter-relations between them) has arguably suffered because of the bulge in the numbers of film and cultural academics who came of age post 1968, and whose default position is all too frequently to characterise the norms of post-war Britain as fundamentally comprised and compromising.

This is not just a matter of historiography for notions of democracy are also at issue here. The accusation in Swann's canonical text is that the documentary movement sought only to 'collect, collate, and represent those aspects of political and social life they felt the public ought to know'. My own research into the early history of public relations in Britain makes me wary of such a pointed generalisation – figures, such as Tallents and Grierson, spent their careers pursuing lengthy and personally risky battles continually to open to scrutiny government and commercial practices (Anthony 2012). They also went to equally great lengths to extend and improve government research about the public; in their view, one of the major problems with democratic governance in Britain was that too many presumptions about 'the public' were being made. They rejected both what they saw as the overly officious presumptions of government and what they saw as the demeaning crassness of commercial popularism. Nevertheless, the popularity of notions of 'direct democracy' in our own age have seen the more republican vision espoused by Grierson fall dramatically from intellectual fashion. In Grierson's case, this fall has been exacerbated because the extent to which the poster movement was driven from below, as well as the ways in which the EMB's initiatives evolved in relation to self-generated initiatives in municipal cinema, have been all but forgotten (Lebas 2011).

Elite attitudes to posters in interwar Britain can shed further light on Grierson's particular conception of democracy and the attitudes he battled against. Writing in the wake of the 1910 British General Election, Graham Wallas was critical of the impact of posters and cartoons on the political process (Thompson 2014).[8] In his influential book, *Human Nature in Politics*, Wallas argued that the place of intellect in a democracy was being subverted by emotions, that reason was making way for a new politics of symbolic association. Wallas's work as an educational reformer (in particular, his insistence on universal education for everyone and resistance to 'streaming'), his ideals (drawn heavily from the Greek *polis*) and his emphasis on the importance of psychology and emotions to social transformation are important to understanding the intellectual foundation of both Tallents's and Grierson's approach. The poster movement was a hopeful response to this deep strain of cultural pessimism.

At a more philosophical level, as Ian Aitken has explained, the British documentary movement and the media innovations they were created alongside share a debt to idealist philosophy (Aitken 1990: 184–95). Or, to be more accurate, Grierson reinterpreted philosophical ideas to support his approach to media activism. Grierson's approach to film was informed by the belief that the modern world had obscured the existence of a foundational social connectedness, and that these connections could be made visible if modern media technologies were utilised imaginatively. Poster films, along with the EMB's other experiments in film form and distribution, were at the aesthetic and political heart of Grierson's conception of film. This vision was itself developed out of the poster movement which sought to redesign public spaces to amplify and emphasise shared experiences along with social and economic unity. Understood like this, it is far from surprising that the post office (letters, posters, telecommunications, transport, meeting places) stimulated the Griersonian documentary movement to the extent it did, that the conditions of 'total war' would raise it to a creative zenith, and that the age of social media should see a reassessment of its reputation.

CONCLUSION: TOWARDS AN 'INFORMATIONAL STATE'

Even as film scholars and documentary practitioners became progressively more sceptical about both the nature and importance of Grierson's work, there remained small pockets of enthusiasts. This enthusiasm would culminate in the founding of The Grierson Trust in 1972. Revealingly, the driving force behind the formation of the trust was not a prominent film academic or a practitioner but John Chittock, media correspondent at *The Financial Times* and founder of *Screen Digest*. Throughout the 1960s Chittock had bemoaned the decline of British-sponsored film – even as output had increased – which he saw as evidence of a drift away from Grierson's imaginative approach. The trust's establishment of the Grierson Awards were supposed to help resurrect some of the animating spirit of 'the documentary movement' but, in other respects, Chittock was more optimistic about Grierson's legacy which he saw as bound up with the idea of media as a social tool. The work of the documentary movement was valued not just for its 'realist' representation of everyday Britain but also for the idea that media technologies had a role to play in increasing the capacity for participation in national life.[9] For Chittock, this observation was bound up with his interest in developments such as Ceefax and the promise of a future dominated by 'direct' media. For Grierson, Chittock imagined, it had been bound up with his involvement with the poster movement, his multifaceted work at the Post Office, and the attempts he had made to propagate ideas about the use of media technologies to stimulate global democracy while Director of Mass Communications and Public Information at the United Nations Educational Scientific, and Cultural Organization (UNESCO).[10]

Towards the end of the 1940s, Grierson attempted to write both a history of the development of 'public information' and a theory about its role in social progress over the *longue durée*.[11] It was a history of social relations being successively ruptured and then rendered anew by technological change from Ancient Greece to the present day. As Grierson had it, two world wars, economic depression and then a nuclear stand-off between the United States and the Soviet Union, in addition to the global impact of accelerating industrial change, had undermined the idea that individual self-interest was a solid basis for citizenship. Indeed, a key component of the argument was that the definition of self as an isolated individual was itself historically contingent. The task of the modern 'public information' professional was thus twofold: it had both to 'remould the image of democracy' and 'increase the representative factor in society' to build an 'informational state'.[12] It's worth saying here that Grierson took considerable pains to separate his conception of the state (made up of independent units and associations) from centralised government (which he was wary of). James Purdon has recently argued that Grierson's concept that 'representation is information' can be understood as a precursor to post-war conceptions of cybernetics (Purdon 2015) that focus on how people manage and organise information within their immediate and general environment. This is, for example, prefigured in Grierson's continuing insistence that public information was primarily about 'a pattern of thought and feeling which will enable [the everyman] to approach a flood of material in some useful fashion'. Purdon is probably on to something but, even if he is overstating the continuities, the evidence certainly points to rethinking Grierson's work in the context of later developments in media theory as well as realist cinema. What this chapter has sought to do is to show that there existed awareness, even in modernist pre-war thought, that there was a growing gap between information and embodied experience which interwar democrats were anxious to address. Grierson's efforts to close this gap, to aestheticise scientific, economic and social information into living knowledge, rested on more than is usually understood in discussions of 'Griersonian documentary': it depended on dynamic and active relationships between people, public spaces and the moving image.

NOTES

1. Reprints include Hardy, F. (1946; 1966; 1979) ed. *Grierson on Documentary*, London: Faber; Dyer MacCann, R. (1966) ed., *Film: A Montage of Theories*, New York: E. P. Dutton; Barsam, R. (1976) ed., *Nonfiction Film Theory and Criticism*, New York: E. P. Dutton; Macdonald, K. and Cousins, M. (1996) eds, *Imagining Reality: The Faber Book of Documentary*, London: Faber; Aitken, I. (1998) ed., *The Documentary Film Movement: An Anthology*, Edinburgh: Edinburgh University Press.

2. A theme explored in some depth in an excellent and soon to be submitted article by Martin Stollery. Stollery, M. (TBC) 'Grierson's "First principles" as beginning and origin: The documentary tradition in the field of non-fiction film'.

3. For a canonical 'critical' response see Higson, A. (1986), '"Britain's outstanding contribution to the film": The Documentary-Realist Tradition' in Barr, C. (ed.), *All our Yesterdays: 90 Years of British Cinema*, London: BFI, pp. 72–7.

4. See also Saler, M. (1999), *The Avant-Garde in Interwar England, Medieval Modernism and the London Underground*, Oxford; Oxford University Press.

5. V&A Archive, Blythe House, London, MA/1/E679, Empire Marketing Board file.

6. V&A Archive, Blythe House, London, MA/1/E679, Empire Marketing Board file.

7. As alluded to in a recent keynote speech by Haidee Wasson. Wasson, H. (2015), 'The expansionist apparatus: histories of film projection and the American military', Keynote presentation at *What is Cinema History?* HoMER conference, 22–24 June, Glasgow.

8. See also Burgess, C. (2014), *From the Political Pipe to Devil Eyes: A History of the British Election Poster from 1910–1997*, unpublished doctoral thesis, University of Nottingham.

9. See for illustrative example, Chittock, J. (1974), 'Industrial Films Change Course', *Financial Times*, 19 March, p. 28.

10. See, for example, Chittock, J. (1980), 'The home video revolution is well underway', *Financial Times*, 23 August, p. 19; Chittock, J. (1981), 'Video: Financial Times Survey: The Mutation of Media and Technology', *Financial Times*, 14 September, p. II; and Chittock, J. (1982), 'Technological developments make the future indefinite', *Financial Times*, 20 January, p. 18.

11. Grierson Archive, University of Stirling, G5/8/10, J. Grierson, *The Voice of the State: The interchange of public information between government and people from Pericles to Elmer Davis*.

12. Grierson Archive, University of Stirling, G5/8/10, J. Grierson, *The Voice of the State: The interchange of public information between government and people from Pericles to Elmer Davis*, p. 93.

REFERENCES

Aitken, I. [1990] (2013), *Film and Reform: John Grierson and the Documentary Film Movement*, London and New York: Routledge.

— (1998) (ed.), *The Documentary Film Movement: An Anthology*, Edinburgh: Edinburgh University Press.

Anthony, S. (2008), 'Crawford, Sir William Smith (1878–1950)', *Oxford Dictionary of National Biography*, Oxford: Oxford University Press.

— (2012), *Public Relations and the making of modern Britain: Stephen Tallents and the birth of a progressive media profession*, Manchester: Manchester University Press.

Anthony, S. and Russell, P. (2014), 'Post-war documentary: A new way forward', *Journal of British Film and Television*, 11: 2, pp. 252–61.

Artmonsky, R. (2006) *Jack Beddington: The Footnote Man*, London: Artmonsky Arts.

Barsam, R. (1976) (ed.), *Nonfiction Film Theory and Criticism*, New York: E. P. Dutton.

Buchanan, A. (1932), *Films: The Way of the Cinema*, London; Isaac Pitman.

Burgess, C. (2014), *From the Political Pipe to Devil Eyes: A History of the British Election Poster from 1910–1997*, unpublished doctoral thesis, University of Nottingham.

Christensen, Line Hjorth (2015), 'Tracking the Poster Movement: An Inquiry into British Modernism by Way of the 'British and Foreign Posters' Exhibition, Victoria and Albert Museum, 1931', *Journal of Design History*, 28: 2, pp.142–60.

Constantine, S. (1986a), 'Bringing the Empire Alive: The Empire Marketing Board and Imperial Propaganda', in MacKenzie, J. M. (ed.), *Imperialism and Popular Culture*, Manchester: Manchester University Press, p.192–231.

— (1986b), *Buy & Build. The Advertising Posters of the Empire Marketing Board*, London: Public Records Office.

Druick, Z. and Williams, D. (2014) (eds), *The Grierson Effect: Tracing Documentary's International Movement*, London: BFI Palgrave.

Dyer MacCann, R. (1966) (ed.), *Film: A Montage of Theories*, New York: E. P. Dutton.

Frayn, M. (1963), 'Festival' in Sissons, M. and French, P. (eds). *The Age of Austerity 1945–1951*, London: Penguin, pp. 317–38.

Green, O. (2013), *Frank Pick's London: Art, Design and the Modern City*, London: Victoria and Albert Museum.

Grant, M. (1994), *Propaganda and the Role of the State in Inter-War Britain*, Oxford: Clarendon Press.

Grierson, J. (1930), 'The New Generation in Sculpture', *Apollo*, 12, July–Dec, pp. 347–51.

Hagener, M. (2007), *Moving Forward, Looking Back: The European Avant-Garde and the Invention of Film Culture 1919–1939*, Amsterdam: Amsterdam University Press.

Hardy, F. (1946; 1966; 1979) (ed.), *Grierson on Documentary*, London: Faber.

Higson, A. (1986), '"Britain's outstanding contribution to the film": The Documentary–Realist Tradition' in Barr, C. (ed.), *All our Yesterdays: 90 Years of British cinema*, London: BFI, pp. 72–97.

L'Etang, J. (2008), *Public Relations: concepts, practice and critique*, London: Sage.

Lebas, E. (2011), *Forgotten Futures: British Municipal Cinema 1920–1980*, London: Black Dog.

Macdonald, K. and Cousins, M (1996) (eds), *Imagining Reality: The Faber Book of Documentary*, London: Faber.

Marwick A. (1964), 'Middle Opinion in the Thirties: Planning, Progress and Political "Agreement"', *The English Historical Review*, LXXIX (CCCXI), pp. 285–98.

Miller, H. K. (2014), 'Return to the lost continent', *New Review of Film and Television Studies*, 12: 4, pp. 412–28.

Musser, C. (2013), 'Problems in Historiography: The Documentary Tradition Before *Nanook of the North*', in Winston, B. (ed.), *The Documentary Film Book*, London: BFI Palgrave, pp. 119–28.

Pronay, N. (1989) 'John Grierson and the Documentary – 60 years on', *Historical Journal of Film, Radio and Television* 9: 3, pp. 227–46.

Pevsner, N. (1942), 'Patient Progress: the life work of Frank Pick', *The Architectural Review*, Vol. XCII, pp. 31–48.

Political and Economic Planning (1947), *The Factual Film: A Survey Sponsored by the Dartington Hall Trustees*, Oxford, Oxford University Press.

Purdon, J. (2015), *Modernist Informatics: British Literature and the Government of Information, 1900–1950*, Oxford: Oxford University Press.

Rotha, P. (1973), *Documentary Diary: An Informal History of the British Documentary Film, 1928–1939*, New York: Hill and Wang.

Saler, M. (1999), *The Avant-Garde in Interwar England, Medieval Modernism and the London Underground*, Oxford: Oxford University Press.

Sargeant, A. (2012), 'GPO Films: American and European models of Advertising in the Projection of Nation', *Twentieth-Century British History*, 23: 1, pp. 38–56.

Saxon-Mills, G. H. (1954), *There is a Tide*, London: Heinemann.

Skeaping, J. (1977), *Drawn from Life: An Autobiography*, London: Collins.

Swann, P. (1989), *The British Documentary Film Movement, 1926–1946*, Cambridge: Cambridge University Press.

Tallents, S. (1934), *Post Office Publicity*, London: GPO, 1934.

Thompson, J. (2014), *British Political Culture and the Idea of 'Public Opinion', 1867–1914*, Cambridge: Cambridge University Press.

Walton, J. K. (1994), *Fish and Chips, and the British Working Class, 1870–1940*, Leicester: Leicester University Press.

Winston, B. (1995), *Claiming the Real: The Griersonian Documentary and its Legitimations*, London: British Film Institute.

— (2014) 'Current Debates: The Griersonian Tradition Post-War – Decline or Transition?', *Journal of British Cinema and Television*, 11: 1, pp. 101–15.

Contributors

Ian Aitken is Professor of Film Studies at the School of Communication, Hong Kong Baptist University. Among other book publications, he is the author of *Hong Kong Documentary Film* (Edinburgh University Press, 2014), *Lukácsian Film Theory and Cinema: An Analysis of Georg Lukács' Writings on Film 1913–1971* (2012), *Realist Film Theory and Cinema: The Nineteenth-Century Lukácsian and Intuitionist Realist Traditions* (2006), *Encyclopedia of the Documentary Film* (ed.) (2006, 2012), *Alberto Cavalcanti: Realism, Surrealism and National Cinemas* (2001), *European Film Theory and Cinema* (Edinburgh University Press, 2001), *The Documentary Film Movement: An Anthology* (ed.) (Edinburgh University Press, 1998), and *Film and Reform: John Grierson and the Documentary Film Movement* (1990, 1992, 2013).

Scott Anthony is an Assistant Professor at Nanyang Technological University, Singapore, and By-Fellow of Churchill College. He is the author of *Night Mail* (2007) and *The Projection of Britain: A History of the GPO Film Unit* (ed.) (2011).

Gary Evans is an Adjunct Professor at the Department of Communication, Faculty of Arts, University of Ottawa. His published books include *In the National Interest: A Chronicle of the National Film Board of Canada 1949–1989* (1991), *John Grierson and the NFB: The Politics of War-time Propaganda* (1984), and *John Grierson, Trailblazer of Documentary Film* (2005).

Tara Forrest is a Senior Lecturer in the Faculty of Arts and Social Sciences, University of Technology, Sydney. She is the author of *Alexander Kluge: Raw Materials for the Imagination* (2012) and *The Politics of Imagination: Benjamin, Kracauer, Kluge* (2007).

Ramona Fotiade is a Senior Lecturer in the Department of French, School of Modern Languages and Culture, University of Glasgow. Her published books include *André Breton: The Power of Language* (1999), *À Bout de Souffle* (2013), and *Pictures of the Mind: Surrealist Photography and Film* (2015).

Angelos Koutsourakis is a Post-Doctoral Research Fellow at the University of Queensland. He is the author of *Politics as Form in Lars von Trier: A Post-Brechtian Analysis* (2013).

Henry K. Miller teaches at Cambridge University and is a regular contributor to *Sight and Sound* and other film journals. His PhD dissertation, at Birkbeck College, University of London, supervised by Professor Ian Christie, is entitled 'Where We Came In: Minority Film Culture in Britain 1917–1940'. He is also the editor of *The Essential Raymond Durgnat* (2014).

Seung-hoon Jeong is an Assistant Professor of Cinema Studies at New York University, Abu Dhabi. He is the author of *Cinematic Interfaces: Film Theory after New Media* (2013).

Pierre Sorlin is a Professor at the Sorbonne University, Paris. His many published books include *Sociology of the Cinema* (1977), *The Film in History* (1980), *European Cinemas, European Societies 1939–90* (1991) and *Ombre passeggere, Cinema e storia* (2014).

Temenuga Trifonova is an Associate Professor in the Department of Cinema and Media Arts in the School of Arts, Media, Performance and Design at York University, Toronto. Her published books include *The Image in French Philosophy* (2007), *European Film Theory* (ed.) (2008) and *Warped Minds: Cinema and Psychopathology* (2014).

Tyson Wils is currently working in the School of Media and Communication at RMIT University, Melbourne, Australia. His recent publications include a series of entries on the films of Werner Herzog in *Directory of World Cinema: Germany* (Books I, 2012 and II, 2013) and 'Dialectical Modes of Nature in Terrence Malick's The Thin Red Line', *European Journal of Media Studies*, 2013. His forthcoming publications include 'Film Festivals and Activism: The Ethico-Political Spectator' (co-edited with Dr Sonia Tascon) (2016), and 'Klaus Kinski in the films of Jess Franco and Harry Alan Towers', in *The Wrath of God: The Cinema of Klaus Kinski* (2015). His PhD dissertation, which was externally examined by Ian Aitken, is entitled 'The Aesthetic Alienation of Nature in Werner Herzog's Cinema and the Realist Phenomenology of Siegfried Kracauer'.

Apple Xu Yaping is a Lecturer at China University of Political Science and Law, and a PhD graduate from the School of Communication, Hong Kong Baptist University, where she was supervised by Ian Aitken. The title of her dissertation is 'The Oral Testimony and the Embodied Witness: Orality, Intersubjectivity and Chinese Oral History Documentary Film' (2013).

Index